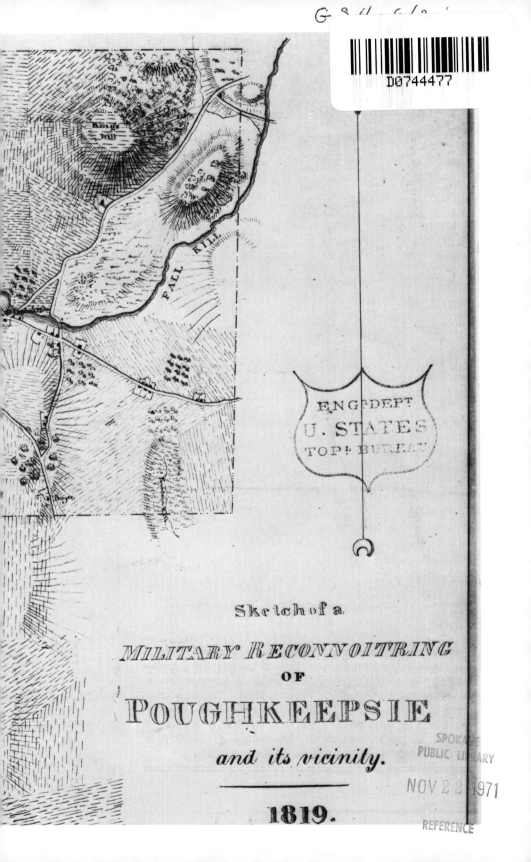

King's Hill

FALL KILL

ENG. DEPT
U. STATES
TOP. BUREAU

Sketch of a

MILITARY RECONNOITRING

OF

POUGHKEEPSIE

and its vicinity.

1819.

Guide to Cartographic Records

in the National Archives

RICHARD NIXON
President of the United States

ROBERT L. KUNZIG
Administrator of General Services

JAMES B. RHOADS
Archivist of the United States

Guide to Cartographic Records
in the
National Archives

The National Archives
National Archives and Records Service
General Services Administration

Washington: 1971

National Archives Publication No. 71-16

Library of Congress Catalog Card No. 76-611061

FOREWORD

The General Services Administration, through the National Archives and Records Service, is responsible for administering the permanent noncurrent records of the Federal Government. These archival holdings, now amounting to about 900,000 cubic feet, date from the days of the Continental Congresses and include the basic records of the legislative, judicial, and executive branches of our Government. The Presidential libraries—the Herbert Hoover Library, the Franklin D. Roosevelt Library, the Harry S. Truman Library, the Dwight D. Eisenhower Library, the John F. Kennedy Library, and the Lyndon Baines Johnson Library—contain the papers of those Presidents and many of their associates in office. Among our holdings are many hallowed documents relating to great events of our Nation's history, preserved and venerated as symbols to stimulate a worthy patriotism in all of us. But most of the records are less dramatic, kept because of their continuing practical utility for the ordinary processes of government, for the protection of private rights, and for the research use of students and scholars.

To facilitate the use of the records and to describe their nature and content, our archivists prepare various kinds of finding aids. The present work is one such publication. We believe that it will prove valuable to anyone who wishes to use the records it describes.

ROBERT L. KUNZIG
Administrator of General Services

PREFACE

From time to time the National Archives publishes special guides to significant Federal records which have research value to a broad spectrum of scholars. In this category are the previously published *Federal Records of World War II* (2 vols., 1951), *Guide to Materials on Latin America in the National Archives* (Vol. 1, 1961), *Civil War Maps in the National Archives* (1964), *Guide to Federal Records Relating to the Civil War* (1962), and its companion volume *Guide to the Archives of the Government of the Confederate States of America* (1968). In this informal series of publications we now include the *Guide to Cartographic Records in the National Archives.*

It is hoped that the publication of this guide will focus the attention of researchers on the vast potential of the cartographic archives in the National Archives, and that it will aid prospective researchers in the use of this material. If it serves either or both of these purposes we will consider the effort that went into the preparation of the guide well spent.

JAMES B. RHOADS
Archivist of the United States

CONTENTS

Page

INTRODUCTION

Among the holdings of the National Archives are more than 1,600,000 maps and about 2,250,000 aerial photographs, comprising one of the world's largest accumulations of such documents. This guide describes those that are maintained in the Cartographic Branch, but there are many maps filed with closely related textual documents in other records divisions of the National Archives. The holdings of the Audiovisual Branch include many aerial photographs unrelated to the major Federal aerial survey programs.

The United States Government has, from its beginning, recognized exploration, surveying, and mapping as activities vital to the development of the Nation and to its defense in times of danger. In 1777 Robert Erskine was appointed geographer and surveyor on General Washington's staff, with particular responsibility for making sketches and maps relating to the operations of the Continental Army. Erskine died in 1780 and was succeeded by Simeon De Witt and Thomas Hutchins, each of whom received the official title "Geographer of the United States of America."

After the Army's demobilization Hutchins retained his title and, under the provisions of the Ordinance of 1785, directed the surveys of the Seven Ranges of Ohio during the period 1785-87. This was the first tract of public land to be surveyed under the rectangular land survey system, a system that was to be of immense importance in shaping the cultural geography of the United States. In 1812 the system was institutionalized with the establishment of the General Land Office and by 1900 the rectangular surveys had been extended all the way to the Pacific coast.

Running well in advance of the public land surveys were the reconnaissances and explorations necessary for the delineation of the major geographical features of the new territories. The Lewis and Clark Expedition of 1803-6, authorized by Thomas Jefferson, was the earliest and in many ways the most significant of the Government-sponsored expeditions, but there were many others, each of which made its contribution to filling in the map of the West. Most of these expeditions were conducted by the Army, particularly by the Corps of Topographical Engineers (1838-63), before the establishment of the Geological Survey in 1879 as the Government's chief mapping agency.

The operations of commercial and naval vessels on the high seas and along the coastal areas and internal waterways of the United States necessitated the early development of nautical charting and surveying programs by the Federal Government. The early and middle decades of the 19th century saw the establishment of the Coast Survey, the Navy Hydrographic Office, and the Lake Survey of the Army's Corps of Engineers.

As the conservation, public service, and regulatory responsibilities of the Federal Government increased during the 20th century many additional agencies began producing maps, some for specific cartographic programs, and others for use as working tools or for the dissemination of information. The wide range of Federal activities is reflected in the variety of subjects shown on these maps. These include topography; geology and hydrography; weather and climate; soil classification and conservation; irrigation and drainage; agriculture and other types of rural land use; demography and ethnography; housing and city planning; and road and railroad surveys.

In the United States, as in virtually every other modern nation, much of the Government mapping has been closely associated with military operations. During the course of the Civil War, the two World Wars, and the numerous lesser conflicts in which the United States has been involved, mapping agencies and tactical forces in the field have compiled hundreds of thousands of maps, some relating specifically to the various campaigns and engagements and others showing the topography of the areas in which military operations were conducted.

A significant part of the holdings of the Cartographic Branch consists of a body of aerial photographs covering collectively about 90 percent of the land area of the United States, excluding Hawaii and Alaska. Most of these photographs were compiled during the period 1935-41 by agencies in the Department of Agriculture, particularly the Soil Conservation Service and the Agricultural Adjustment Administration. They provide a unique record of the physical and cultural landscape of prewar America and are especially valuable when compared with later aerial photographs that are held by other Federal agencies.

The basic unit of records maintenance in the National Archives is the record group. A typical record group consists of the records of a bureau or of an independent agency of comparable importance. When the records of such an agency are first transferred to the National Archives a record group is established and given a number and a title. Other records received later from the same agency are assigned to the same record group. There are more than 400 record groups in the National Archives and the Federal Records Centers, 134 of which contain separately maintained cartographic records.

This guide was planned as a central source of information about the cartographic holdings of the National Archives; the maps and aerial photographs described are those that were in the Cartographic Branch on July 1, 1966. The record group descriptions are arranged according to the order in which agencies are listed in the *United States Government Organization Manual*. The record group that contains the general records of an agency comes first and is followed in alphabetical order by the record groups of subordinate organizations within the agency. The record groups of independent agencies follow those of the Departments. Terminated agencies are listed separately from existing independent agencies. Brief statements about the mapping activities of the various agencies generally precede the descriptive listing of their cartographic records.

Inquiries about maps may be made either in the Research Room of the Cartographic Branch or through correspondence. The National Archives staff does not normally perform substantive research in response to individual inquiries, but it does describe pertinent documents and quote reproduction costs. A wide variety of photoreproductions is available, but the photostatic process usually is the most suitable for maps.

Finding aids to the maps and aerial photographs include card catalogs, descriptive lists, index maps, and aerial photo indexes. The staff of the Cartographic Branch prepares additional finding aids as the need arises. Many of these finding aids have been prepared for use in the Research Room of the Cartographic Branch, where the maps and aerial photographs may be examined in accordance with regulations issued by the Administrator of General Services.

A number of cartographic records inventories and special lists, compiled by record group, are available from the National Archives in published or processed form. Among these are *List of Cartographic Records of the Bureau of Indian Affairs,* Special List No. 13 (Washington, 1954), *List of Cartographic Records of the General Land Office,* Special List No. 19 (Washington, 1964), *Cartographic Records of the American Expeditionary Forces, 1917-21,* Preliminary Inventory No. 165 (Washington, 1966), and *Cartographic Records of the Forest Service,* Preliminary Inventory No. 167 (Washington, 1967). Maps from a number of different record groups are described in *Civil War Maps in the National Archives* (Washington, 1964), which is available for $0.75 from the U.S. Government Printing Office, Washington, D.C. 20402.

This guide was prepared by Charlotte M. Ashby, Laura E. Kelsay, and other staff members of the Cartographic Branch and former members of its predecessor units, including Franklin W. Burch, Thomas A. Devan, James B. Rhoads, and Charles E. Taylor. It was compiled initially under the direction of Herman R. Friis and was revised and updated by Patrick D. McLaughlin under the supervision of A. Philip Muntz.

GENERAL

UNITED STATES GOVERNMENT DOCUMENTS HAVING GENERAL LEGAL EFFECT. RG 11

This record group consists of papers of the Continental Congress, papers relating to the Constitution and to various laws and treaties, documents having the force of law, and similar or related materials.

1. THE CONTINENTAL CONGRESS. 1781. 1 item.

A manuscript map by Lt. Col. Jean-Baptiste Gouvion of the plan of attack on Yorktown, Va., during the Revolutionary War, showing the locations of the British defensive works and the siege works of the Americans and the French. Reproductions of this map, accompanied by historical notes, are available for purchase at the National Archives.

2. TREATIES OF THE UNITED STATES. 1819-48. 2 items.

A copy of the 1818 edition of the Melish map of the United States referred to in the treaty of 1819 with Spain and a copy of the 1847 edition of the Disturnell map of the United States of Mexico with attached certificate verifying it as the map used by the United States-Mexican Boundary Commission in preparing the treaty of 1848.

LEGISLATIVE BRANCH

RECORDS OF THE UNITED STATES SENATE. RG 46

Most of the manuscript and annotated maps in this record group were prepared by executive agencies, primarily the Coast and Geodetic Survey, the General Land Office, and the Office of the Chief of Engineers, for use as exhibits or as appendixes to accompany reports to Congress. Some of the manuscript maps were used in the compilation of maps ordered published by Congress. Most of the maps in sets were published by private concerns under contract with the Government. See Martin P. Claussen and Herman R. Friis, *Descriptive Catalog of Maps Published by Congress, 1817-1843* (Washington, 1941) for detailed descriptions of those maps published through 1843.

3. OFFICE OF THE SECRETARY. 1800-1955. 1,469 items.

Manuscript and annotated maps forwarded to the Senate, usually from executive agencies. Many of these maps were submitted to the Senate in connection with progress reports. Others were specifically requested by Congress.

Among the manuscript maps, arranged by number of the Congress, are a map entitled "Ancient possessions of the upper Prairie" north of Vincennes, Ind.; maps from surveys of contested State boundaries; maps relating to Indian land cessions, including a map of the United States annotated by J. Goldsborough Bruff to show Indian cessions to 1839; maps from river and harbor surveys showing proposed improvements; maps from road surveys; maps relating to surveys of international boundaries; maps by David Dale Owen showing the geology of the North Central States, including a detailed map of southeastern Wisconsin Territory, ca. 1838, showing mineral diggings and the names of early settlers; maps relating to private land claims; a series of annotated maps presented to the Senate Military Committee in February 1865 by Gen. Richard Delafield, Chief Engineer, U.S. Army, showing the limits of the loyal States in 1861, the area controlled by Union forces in November 1864, and military divisions and departments, campaigns, and battlefields of the Civil War; railroad right-of-way maps; maps relating to litigation over the Grantsville Townsite, Utah, 1879-81; maps of Washington, D.C., showing proposed roads and approved subdivisions, and plans of the District Building and its proposed site; a map of the United States showing the progress of surveys conducted by the Coast and Geodetic Survey and the limits of published and proposed charts,

1885-87; plats of reservoir sites in Colorado, New Mexico, California, Utah, Nevada, and Montana, 1891-93; maps of Alaska and parts of Alaska showing fish traps and salmon canneries, 1895-97; maps of the Western States and parts of Alaska showing coal deposits, 1905-7; and maps relating to the San Francisco River and Gila River flood-control projects, 1917-19.

Included in the manuscript maps without a Congress number are a series of approximately 150 maps and profiles of projects for the improvement of rivers and the construction of roads, canals, and railroads, about 1825-40; a map of the Cherokee country (Indian Territory) and the Cherokee Outlet showing lands claimed by the Cherokees and the reservation assigned to the Arapahoes and Cheyennes in 1867; and a series of undated maps of the United States annotated to show railroad switching and terminal companies.

An incomplete set of maps published for inclusion in Senate documents is arranged by number of the Congress, thereunder by session number, and thereunder by document number. Included in the set are maps made by Army Engineers and Topographical Engineers consisting of plans for river and harbor improvements; maps from road and railroad surveys; maps from surveys made by exploring expeditions, some showing the routes of those expeditions; maps showing troop movements and battles during the Indian wars; maps of Mexican War battlefields; plans of foreign fortifications and a map of the theater of war in the Crimea prepared to accompany General Delafield's report on the art of war in Europe, 1860; plans, profiles, and maps made in connection with surveys for an interoceanic canal, 1861; a map of the Red River Raft, 1856; progress maps for the surveys of the Great Lakes, 1861; maps of Civil War battlefields; and maps from surveys of State boundaries.

General Land Office maps showing the United States with boundaries according to the treaties of 1783, 1795, 1803, 1819, and 1842; the land districts and land offices in the United States, and the progress of the public land surveys, 1867; the progress of the public land surveys in the States and territories for various dates during the period 1838-65 and for 1867, the latter with railroad land-grant limits; land claims in parts of Alabama and Louisiana; railroad rights-of-way; and patented lands in Yosemite National Park, Calif., 1905.

A map of the St. Lawrence River Basin compiled for I. C. Andrews' report to the Secretary of the Treasury, 1853.

Maps compiled from surveys by Lt. W. L. Herndon, USN, in the Amazon River Basin, 1854.

Maps accompanying Dr. E. K. Kane's report on thé discoveries of the First and Second American Arctic Expeditions, 1856.

Maps of the Platte River and Running Water River Wagon Road; the El Paso and Fort Yuma Wagon Road; the Fort Kearney, South Pass, and Honey Lake Wagon Road; and the Fort Ridgely and South Pass Wagon Road. Compiled in the Pacific Wagon Roads Office, Department of the Interior, 1859.

Maps showing improvements to the navigation of the Potomac River at Washington, D.C., prepared by special boards authorized by Congress, 1858-73.

A Coast and Geodetic Survey atlas of the Philippine Islands, and maps showing anchorages in Alaska.

Maps of Alaska, 1885-1905, including a map showing missions and reindeer stations, accompanying the annual reports of Sheldon Jackson, U.S. General Agent of Education to Alaska; and a map of Alaska showing the mineral belt, accompanying the annual report of the Governor. Maps of Alaska showing areas explored by the U.S. Geological Survey and by the U.S. Army in 1898 and a copy of the 1899 edition of the Fortymile Quadrangle.

Three volumes of maps from the Alaskan Boundary Tribunal; one volume contains 47 maps accompanying the case and the countercase of the United States, the second contains 37 maps accompanying the case of Great Britain, and the third contains 25 sheets showing the boundary as fixed by the Tribunal.

Maps, profiles, cross sections, and plans of locks and dams from surveys for an interoceanic canal across Nicaragua, compiled by the U.S. Nicaragua Ship Canal Commission, 1886.

Maps of countries in Latin America accompanying handbooks issued by the Bureau of American Republics, 1892-94. An atlas accompanying the report of the Venezuela Boundary Commission on the Venezuela-British Guiana boundary, consisting of maps showing the geography and the historical development of the area, 1898.

Plans for lighting and buoying the Panama Canal, prepared by the Isthmian Canal Commission, 1913.

A profile of the Pacific Ocean from Salinas, Calif., to Honolulu, Hawaii, compiled by the Navy Hydrographic Office, 1892.

Maps of the New England-New York region prepared by the New England-New York Interagency Committee, 1951, showing fisheries and game resources, recreation facilities, forest and park areas, flood-endangered areas and flood-control projects, extent of soil erosion, percentage of area in croplands, decline in farmlands, water transportation facilities, and the distribution of population.

Maps and plans of unidentified origin, including plans of the District of Columbia jail, the United States Hospital for the Insane, and buildings at the U.S. Naval Academy; maps of Liberia, 1853; maps relating to a study of artesian water in the Missouri River Basin, 1892; a map of the United States showing post offices, customs districts, offices of the Quartermaster Department, Indian schools, and routes of examiners, 1893; maps of the southern Appalachian region relating to the proposed National Appalachian Park, 1902; maps of Puerto Rico showing roads, railroads, and telegraph and telephone lines, 1908; and a map of Latin America showing Pan American Railway transportation routes by railroad, river, and sea, 1911.

Included in the records of the 27th Congress is a bound volume containing many of the maps published by both Houses of Congress up to 1843. Most of these are Army Engineer maps pertaining to river and harbor improvements.

Unnumbered maps published by order of Congress are arranged chronologically by date of publication. These include a map of the coast of North Carolina,

1806; 89 published copies of the internal improvements maps, about 1825-40, found in the manuscript series; the 1842 and 1843 editions of Nicollet's map of the hydrographical basin of the upper Mississippi River (three manuscript versions of this map are in the Headquarters Map File of Record Group 77, Records of the Office of the Chief of Engineers); a map of Texas and the Southwest prepared in the Bureau of Topographical Engineers for the State Department, 1844; Fremont's map of Upper California and Oregon, 1848; a seven-sheet map of the Oregon Trail compiled by Charles Preuss, cartographer with Fremont's expedition, 1846; a map of the U.S. territory west of the Mississippi River, compiled in the Bureau of Topographical Engineers, 1850; a map of the Straits of Florida and the Gulf of Mexico accompanying a report of the Secretary of the Treasury, 1852; Sheets 4 and 10-12 of the Bachelder map of the Gettysburg battlefield showing the operations of Gregg's and Stuart's cavalries; and a statistical atlas of the United States compiled from information obtained in the Ninth Census, 1870.

A map of the United States showing mail routes to the Pacific, prepared in the General Land Office to accompany Senator Gwin's bill, 1852.

A volume entitled "Third Report on Meteorology, with Directions for Mariners, Etc:," by Prof. James P. Espy, 1851, containing 111 charts illustrating weather in the United States for selected days, 1843-45.

4. SENATE COMMITTEES. 1856-66. 3 items.

A map of Central America showing boundaries and proposed interoceanic canal routes, compiled by the Coast Survey from information furnished by the Senate Committee on Foreign Relations.

Two versions, differing only in colors, of a topographical sketch of the environs of Washington, D.C., made by the Corps of Engineers for the Senate Public Buildings and Grounds Committee in compliance with a Senate resolution of July 18, 1866, to survey for the location of a public park and the site for a Presidential mansion.

RECORDS OF THE UNITED STATES HOUSE OF REPRESENTATIVES
RG 233

Most of the cartographic records of the House of Representatives in Record Group 233 were prepared by executive agencies to accompany reports or to fulfill special requests of the House. From time to time, however, the House has commissioned persons outside the executive branch to prepare maps for special purposes. See Martin P. Claussen and Herman R. Friis, *Descriptive Catalog of Maps Published by Congress, 1817-1843* (Washington, 1941) for detailed descriptions of those maps published through 1843.

5. GENERAL RECORDS. 1828-1930. 378 items.

A map of the United States, Mexico, and Central America annotated to show the lines of march of U.S. troops during the year ended June 30, 1858. Compiled by the War Department's Office of Explorations and Surveys.

An incomplete set of maps published by order of the House of Representatives, principally to accompany House documents; arranged by number of the Congress and thereunder by session number. Most of the maps were published by executive agencies. They include a bound report and accompanying maps prepared by the Commissioners assigned to determine the northern and northwestern boundaries of the United States under the terms of the Treaty of Ghent, 1828; a map showing various routes surveyed for a national road from Zanesville to Florence, Ohio; a map of the United States showing the national boundaries according to various treaties from 1783 to 1848; maps from surveys of rivers and harbors (many of which show proposed navigation or flood-control improvements), prepared by Army Engineers; maps showing Mexican War troop movements and battles; maps of various State boundaries prepared by the General Land Office and by Army Engineers; maps showing the progress of public land surveys in several of the public land States, 1862-66, prepared by the General Land Office; a report on irrigation in the San Joaquin, Tulare, and Sacramento Valleys, Calif., prepared by a special board and illustrated with a map of the valleys, maps of the United States showing summer and winter rainfall in 1870, and maps illustrating irrigation in parts of India, 1874; maps of the United States showing Indian reservations, prepared by the Office of Indian Affairs, 1866-1906; atlases relating to the geology of quicksilver deposits on the Pacific slope of the United States and to the Marquette iron district, Mich., prepared by the Geological Survey, 1890-96; a statistical atlas of the United States for 1890 prepared by the Census Bureau; a series of maps of forts and Indian battlefields in Ohio showing their condition in 1888; underground water and alkali maps of parts of New Mexico and Utah prepared by the Agriculture Department's Division of Soils, 1899; an atlas of the battlefields and campaigns of Chickamauga and Chattanooga prepared by the Chickamauga and Chattanooga National Park Commissions, 1901; a map accompanying the report of the Naval Station Board on the establishment of a naval base at San Juan, Puerto Rico, 1902; feeder diagrams and station plans for waterpower facilities at Great Falls, Md., prepared by the Corps of Engineers, 1903; an atlas illustrating the report of the Board on the Examination and Survey of the Mississippi River, 1908; a series of maps and profiles of railroad routes in Alaska prepared by the Alaska Railroad Commission, 1912; a 41-sheet map of the District of Columbia showing Federal properties in 1915 prepared by the Commission To Investigate the Title of United States Lands in the District of Columbia; a series of maps illustrating activities of the American Expeditionary Forces in France during World War I; and an atlas containing plans of damsites on the Mississippi River between the Missouri River and Minneapolis prepared by the Corps of Engineers in 1930.

Among the records of the 27th Congress is a bound volume of 66 maps published by order of both the Senate and the House. The volume, with records in Record Group 46, Records of the United States Senate, is described on the title page as being incomplete, containing only the maps found when it was bound in 1843.

6. HOUSE COMMITTEES. 1880-1900. 17 items.

Records of the Committee on Rivers and Harbors, consisting of manuscript and photoprocessed maps and charts of rivers and harbors in Georgia, Indiana, Michigan, Oregon, and Texas prepared by the Corps of Engineers; photo-processed maps of Niagara Falls, N.Y., prepared by the Cataract Construction Co., showing the level of the Niagara Falls Power Co., lands belonging to the Niagara Falls Power Co. and the Cataract Construction Co., and plans of tunnels under the Niagara River; and Coast and Geodetic Survey charts of New York Harbor (annotated to show the lengths and widths of dredged channels) and of Cape Cod Bay.

RECORDS OF MINOR CONGRESSIONAL COMMISSIONS. RG 148

From time to time Congress establishes temporary commissions that include other Government officials or private persons in addition to Senators and Representatives. The Commissions are established for such purposes as planning and conducting anniversary celebrations, supervising the design and construction of memorials, and representing the United States in connection with international fairs and expositions. Record Group 148 includes the records of those commissions whose records do not form parts of other record groups.

7. GEORGE WASHINGTON BICENTENNIAL COMMISSION. 1932. 1 item.

A published atlas containing 85 maps, of which 28 are reproductions of maps made by George Washington, seven are maps used or annotated by him, eight are maps made for him or under his direction, and 42 are maps compiled for the atlas under the direction of the Commission. The maps used or annotated by Washington or made for him pertain to activities during the Revolutionary War. Those compiled under the direction of the Commission include maps showing Washington's travels, routes of his campaigns during the Revolutionary War, places he visited, places named for him, and properties he owned.

8. UNITED STATES SESQUICENTENNIAL COMMISSION. 1937-40. 22 items.

Two published maps of the United States and maps of each of the Thirteen Original States and Maine, Tennessee, and Kentucky reproduced from maps compiled in the 1780's. One of the maps of the United States is a copy of the "Franklin red-line" map located in Spain and identified by the Library of Congress; it shows the boundaries of the United States in 1782. The other map of the United States shows State boundaries at the time of the ratification of the Constitution and includes a series of inset maps showing, by periods, claims and cessions of the original colonies relating to lands west of their present boundaries. There is also a plan of New York City at the time of Washington's first inauguration, with insets showing his and Adams' routes to the city.

Three brochures containing maps and other illustrations relating to various States or groups of States, compiled for the use of local newspapers in publicizing the sesquicentennial celebration. The maps generally are simplified versions of those in the atlas.

RECORDS OF THE UNITED STATES GENERAL ACCOUNTING OFFICE.
RG 217

The General Accounting Office, established in 1921, operates independently of the executive departments and provides a uniform settlement of all claims and accounts with which the United States is concerned, either as debtor or creditor.

9. OFFICE OF ADMINISTRATIVE PLANNING. 1952. 2 items.

A published map of the United States, with an inset of Alaska, showing regional audit-office boundaries and headquarters for the General Accounting Office and locations of records depositories controlled by the General Services Administration and audit areas served by the respective depositories; and a copy of the same map annotated to show changes in the Alaska office.

10. CLAIMS DIVISION. 1922-37. 25 items.

Records of the Indian Tribal Section consisting of maps of the area embracing Iowa, Kansas, Minnesota, Missouri, Montana, Nebraska, North Dakota, Oklahoma, South Dakota, Wisconsin, and Wyoming annotated to show unidentified numbered areas; and maps of each of these States annotated to show military establishments and trading posts prior to Indian title. There are two sets of the annotated State maps. In one set each map is labeled "Exhibit A in re: Sioux Petition No. C-531." The maps in the other set are unidentified.

JUDICIAL BRANCH

RECORDS OF THE UNITED STATES COURT OF CLAIMS. RG 123

The United States Court of Claims, established in 1855, decides suits filed with it against the United States and determines claims referred by Congress and the executive departments. Cases are classified according to the type of jurisdiction: general jurisdiction cases are those brought directly by claimants under general provisions of law; congressional and departmental cases are those referred by Congress or the executive departments. The segregated cartographic records of the court that are in the National Archives are related to general jurisdiction cases.

11. GENERAL JURISDICTION CASES. 1940-47. 194 items.

Cartographic records from the United States Court of Claims Case No. 45585, *Confederated Bands of the Ute Indians* v. *the United States*. The records were prepared and submitted as exhibits by the plaintiff and by the defendant. They are arranged in two separate series; within the series they are arranged by exhibit number.

The records of the plaintiff consist of large-scale aerial mosaics, enlarged topographic quadrangles, and other maps of Ute tribal lands in western Colorado annotated to show types of rangelands and forest lands, cultivated lands and croplands, and sales of land identified as "comparable sale with county number," "comparable sale proven by witness," and "independent sale confirmed witness"; aerial mosaics of Ute tribal lands, some with unidentified annotations, possibly denoting boundaries of land classified either by use or by condition; and other maps. The latter include reference maps of Colorado and of Ute tribal lands in parts of Colorado published by private agencies and by other Government agencies, including the Forest Service, the Bureau of Reclamation, the General Land Office, and the Geological Survey; and maps compiled expressly for use as exhibits in the case. Among the latter are manuscript and annotated maps of Colorado showing rates of streamflow and water consumption, topography, precipitation, and public landownership; and maps of the area within the general bounds of the Ute tribal area showing lands owned by the Utes, land use or ownership of non-Ute lands, undisposed withdrawals of public lands, undisposed withdrawals of non-coal-bearing lands, undisposed land pending entries, sales of lands from 1910 to 1934, lands in controversy, and an index map showing the numbers of the inspection reports for specific tracts. There is also a map of New Mexico annotated to show comparable sales of lands.

13

Many of these maps are noted as compiled or used by Bowes and Hart, valuation consultants.

The cartographic records of the defendant, the United States, consist of binders containing maps and related textual reports on grazing units within the Ute tribal lands in Colorado. Included are base maps of the grazing units annotated, probably by the Grazing Service, to show vegetation, abandoned farmlands, and cultivated lands. The maps are accompanied by photoprocessed copies of "Range Survey Computation Summaries" and "Range Survey Write-up Sheets" compiled by the Grazing Service. The range survey computation summaries give for each township within the grazing unit the total acreage and number of "AUM" in specified kinds of ground cover. The range survey field writeup sheets give specific information, usually for several sections within a township, about plant species, numbers and kinds of grazing animals the land can support, optimum grazing seasons, the quality of current land-use practices, and related information.

EXECUTIVE BRANCH

AGENCIES

RECORDS OF THE BUREAU OF THE BUDGET. RG 51

The cartographic records in this record group are those of the former Federal Board of Surveys and Maps, which was established in 1919 as the Board of Surveys and Maps of the Federal Government. In 1942 the Bureau of the Budget was given the Board's functions, which were the coordination and improvement of the Government's surveying and mapping activities.

Federal Board of Surveys and Maps

12. GENERAL RECORDS. 1920-42. 2,000 items.

The records of this agency and its predecessor, the Board of Surveys and Maps of the Federal Government, primarily textual in nature, relate to mapping programs of the Federal Government. These records, chronologically arranged, include the minutes of the general meetings held by the Board, which was composed of representatives from Government mapmaking agencies. The meetings concerned the establishment of standards for mapping and mapmaking to be used by Government agencies. Among the topics covered are map scales and symbols, mapping techniques, map projections, nomenclature, terminology, and instruments for use in surveying and in compiling maps. Reports on mapping activities in special fields often appear in these minutes.

The general correspondence files of the Secretary of the Board have been reduced to a minimum of correspondence regarding the operating policies of the Board and answers to questions on Government mapping policies. The files of the committees, arranged by committee, are more voluminous. Included are reports on studies of mapping and mapmaking undertaken by Government agencies, studies made as a result of proposals for improvements in surveying and mapping techniques, studies of map terminology, and studies of mapping needs.

Other records include a few published maps of the United States showing, by counties, the status of aerial photography and topographic mapping for various years during the period 1934-38; a published chart showing standard mapping symbols; and mimeographed reports on mapping and mapmaking compiled by members of the Board.

RECORDS OF THE NATIONAL RESOURCES PLANNING BOARD. RG 187

Four successive agencies were established in the Federal Government during the period 1933-43 to study the Nation's natural resources, to formulate and correlate plans for their most effective use, and to advise administrative agencies responsible for their development. These agencies were the National Planning Board (July 20, 1933-June 30, 1934), the National Resources Board (June 30, 1934-June 7, 1935), the National Resources Committee (June 7, 1935-July 1, 1939), and the National Resources Planning Board (July 1, 1939-August 31, 1943). The National Planning Board was established in the Public Works Administration. Its three successors were independent agencies.

The National Resources Board (NRB) absorbed, on its establishment, two existing committees: the Mississippi Valley Committee, which became its water-investigating unit, and the Committee on National Land Problems. It continued its predecessor's programs, with particular emphasis on research affecting the Federal Government's land and water policies. It also broadened its scope to include research on human and technological resources in addition to natural resources.

The National Resources Committee (NRC) had virtually the same functions as its predecessor, but during the 4 years of its existence it greatly amplified its research and planning activities. Existing studies concerning water, land, minerals, public works, and industrial policies were expanded and new programs were developed in the fields of education, science and technology, population, health, housing, urbanization, transportation, and energy.

The National Resources Planning Board (NRPB), which succeeded the National Resources Committee, also assumed the functions of the Federal Employment Stabilization Office. Under the defense and war programs the Board became increasingly concerned with emergency planning and simultaneously developed programs for postwar planning. The Board was terminated in 1943.

Each of the successive planning agencies had a regional or field organization in which many of its activities were centered. The boundaries of the regions varied with different agencies.

The Board and its predecessors had no central organization for their mapmaking activities. Some of the activities were handled by the central office and some by the regional offices. Maps were prepared as operational tools; maps made by other Federal agencies often were used as bases for plotting information assembled in the various planning studies.

The cartographic records of the Board and its predecessors are described under the headings of the agencies in which they originated. Those that could not be assigned to one agency are described first, under the heading "General Records." The central office records of each agency are described separately from the regional or field office records, although many of the records in the central office files probably originated in the regional offices.

General Records

13. CENTRAL OFFICE. ca. 1933-43. 64 items.

These maps are similar to many of those described in entries 14 through 32. They bear neither date nor authority, however, and hence cannot be correctly assigned to one of the agencies. Among them are maps of the United States showing drainage basins, water problem areas, project areas, population characteristics, the status of topographic mapping, Federal lands, and regional activities of the agencies. One series consists of Coast and Geodetic Survey published charts of the Atlantic and Pacific coasts of the United States annotated to show "areas where surveys are required to modernize charts." There is also a manuscript map showing land use in Italy.

14. REGIONAL OFFICES. ca. 1933-43. 224 items.

Maps compiled by the regional offices of the NRPB or its predecessors. These maps, arranged by region, bear neither date nor authority and hence cannot be correctly assigned to one of the agencies. Included are base maps and maps of States and regions showing polluted streams and measures taken to combat pollution, population characteristics, transportation routes, drainage basins, water resources, and activities of Federal land agencies. There are special maps of local areas and project areas, including maps of drainage basins showing projects.

National Planning Board of the Federal Emergency Administration of Public Works (Public Works Administration)

15. CENTRAL OFFICE. 1933-34. 14 items.

Maps of the United States including base maps and maps showing the administrative regions of the Board, information about cities undertaking planning activities, highways, drainage basins, the extent of topographic mapping, and precipitation averages. Also included is a series of maps annotated to show the proposed flood-protection system for Kansas City, Mo.

16. REGIONAL OFFICES. 1933-34. 14 items.

Records of Region 1, comprising the New England States, including a manuscript map of the region showing principal drainage areas and existing and potential waterpower developments, and a series of photoprocessed maps of the region showing information about population distributions. Other records consist of a series of maps compiled and submitted by the State Consultant in Connecticut. Among them is a composite map of the State showing transportation facilities and public and semipublic lands, a map of Tolland County showing the results of a rural electrical survey, and an aerial photograph of part of the Connecticut River Valley.

National Resources Board

17. CENTRAL OFFICE. 1934-35. 97 items.

Published maps of the United States showing principal mineral resources, population regions, the status of State planning board legislation, boundaries of administrative regions of other official agencies, and the status of topographic mapping; a base map of the United States annotated to show Federal Emergency Relief Administration districts for determining rates of pay; and a series of published maps of 38 of the States annotated to show existing and proposed uses of land by Federal and State agencies.

Other records relate to characteristics of local areas. Included are maps of Nevada, prepared by the NRB with the assistance of the Nevada Emergency Relief Administration, showing resource problem areas, the extent of soil erosion, and irrigated areas; a preliminary map report on the Paint Creek Reservoir submitted by the Water Conservation Board of Ohio; maps of the Great Lakes-Red River area showing stream pollution and annual precipitation and runoff; and a series of maps of counties in New York showing land classification, public lands, submarginal lands, eroded areas, and metropolitan areas.

Also included are maps compiled by the land planning consultants to the State planning boards, including maps of Arizona, Arkansas, Texas, and Washington showing problem areas; maps of Arkansas and Washington showing resettlement areas, State-owned lands, and the percentage of farmlands used for nonagricultural purposes; a map of Illinois showing proposed Federal and State purchase units; a map of Michigan showing areas in which 20 percent or more of the farms are on "poorest land"; a map of Utah showing recreational areas; and a bound volume of maps of parts of Louisiana showing land in State ownership because of nonpayment of taxes.

18. MISSISSIPPI VALLEY COMMITTEE. ca. 1930-35. 200 items.

Base maps of the United States annotated with information about the entire Mississippi Valley or about the major drainage basins within the region. Included are maps showing information about population characteristics and changes, farm economics, climate, precipitation and runoff, recreational facilities, and transportation facilities; a series of maps of States within the region showing electric transmission lines and waterpower plants; a folio of maps and charts used in a preview of the Missouri Valley study, including maps showing physical regions, agricultural lands, crops harvested, transportation facilities, population characteristics and changes, waterpower, irrigated lands, flood-control projects, soil erosion, and recreational facilities.

Also included are maps showing projects along the various rivers in the region and drawings of the Muscatine Hydroelectric and Flood Control Development, submitted to the Committee by the Muscatine (Iowa) Chamber of Commerce.

19. WATER RESOURCES SECTION. 1934-35. 92 items.

Published maps of the United States showing drainage projects, principal waterways, stream-gaging stations, the extent of surface-water pollution, average hardness of surface and ground waters, iron content in ground water, areas of coastal erosion, interstate and international water problems, shortages of public water supplies, main electrical transmission lines, and runoff characteristics.

Maps of the North Atlantic States showing ground-water use, precipitation and runoff, isofluvials, and mean monthly precipitation. Maps of drainage basins in Region 2, the Middle Atlantic States, showing mean annual precipitation and runoff, isohyets, and boundaries of physiographic regions. Maps of the Great Lakes States showing capacity requirements for all rail shipments of iron ore, from ranges to consuming centers, and locations of bituminous coalfields in relation to lake ports. A series of maps compiled from a water-resources inventory of the South Pacific and Great Basin District showing electric powerplants and transmission lines, stream-gaging stations, precipitation and evaporation measurement stations, agricultural areas, isohyets, and mean annual runoff.

Maps and profiles of the Colorado River Basin including maps showing underground-water areas, stream-gaging stations, Weather Bureau stations, average annual temperatures, and mean annual runoff. Also included is an isofluvial and isohyetal map of the North Pacific region.

20. LAND USE SECTION. 1934-35. 7 items.

Manuscript and published maps of the United States showing the extent of irrigation, the relationships between centers of urban population and locations of recreational areas, existing and proposed national parks, public lands under organized public use, and preliminary land-use problem areas of the United States. A map of the western United States showing the seasonal use and carrying capacity of western rangelands.

21. TRANSPORTATION SECTION. 1934-35. 8 items.

Base maps of the United States annotated to show the volume of intercity passenger traffic of railroads originating in Washington, D.C., the volume of interregional passenger traffic on railroads, and the amount of interregional highway passenger revenue. Maps of the Eastern United States consisting of a base map and a map showing the volume of railroad traffic originating in Washington, D.C., and the points of termination. Maps of the Middle Atlantic States consisting of a base map and a map showing the amount of rail passenger revenue originating and terminating in Washington, D.C., and in Buffalo, N.Y.

22. REGIONAL OFFICES. 1934-35. 148 items.

Maps compiled in District 1, the New England States, including base maps and maps showing transportation facilities, existing and suggested uses of the soil, land use, physiographic regions, and population characteristics. There is also a map showing the names of U.S. Geological Survey quadrangles covering the New England States.

A map of north-central Montana, compiled in District 5, showing resources.

Maps compiled in District 11, the Northwest States, including maps showing the status of aerial photography and topographic mapping; maps of physiographic regions, transportation facilities, recreational areas, major drainage basins, existing and proposed irrigation, Agricultural Adjustment Agency marginal purchase and resettlement areas, average annual precipitation, soil types, population characteristics, and major national forest projects; a series of maps compiled for the Columbia Basin Study including base maps and maps of the basin showing electric powerplants and transmission lines, areas served by public utilities, and the circulation of daily newspapers; and a physiographic diagram of the Columbia Gorge area.

National Resources Committee

23. CENTRAL OFFICE. 1935-39. 76 items.

A publication giving suggested symbols for maps and charts prepared by the Committee as a progress report to the Federal Board of Surveys and Maps.

Manuscript maps of the United States including base maps and maps showing cities, villages, and farm sections to be covered in the family consumption survey, county and metropolitan planning agencies, city planning boards, and State and regional planning areas and suggested planning regions. Other maps of the United States show gasoline pipelines and flood-control projects. A diagrammatic map of the United States represents the area of each State as proportional to its population.

A series of maps of the United States showing information about industries including maps showing industrialized counties, locations of coalfields and oilfields, petroliferous and nonpetroliferous regions, the value of coal produced. by State, and the distribution of iron-ore deposits.

Records pertaining to local areas include a map of New York and New England showing metropolitan areas, areas of serious erosion, and resettlement or intersettlement areas; a series of maps of the northern Great Lakes States showing industrial centers; a map showing the natural regions of Texas; land maps of the Rio Grande Valley prepared during the Rio Grande Joint Investigation; a map of Washington, D.C., and vicinity annotated to show the route of a trip taken by planning technicians, September 25, 1938; several maps of special project areas; and a series of maps showing information about population in South Carolina for the period 1890-1930.

24. RESEARCH COMMITTEE ON URBANIZATION. ca. 1935-39. 29 items.

Manuscript and photoprocessed maps of the United States showing information about the westward development of urban areas and transportation routes during the period 1800-1930, post roads, urban population in relation to water transportation, and urban population in relation to coal and oil resources.

25. WATER RESOURCES COMMITTEE AND WATER RESOURCES SECTION. 1935-39. 259 items.

General records of the Water Resources Committee, including manuscript maps of the United States showing, by agency of control, stations for the study of various kinds of precipitation and of evaporation, water quality, and stream gaging. Maps of the United States showing water planning districts, interstate drainage basins, costs of investigating and constructing projects (by State), drainage basin subdivisions, water facilities, reports on areas surveyed for underground water, and the percentages (by State) of farms having insufficient water for livestock. Maps of the northeastern United States including a base map and maps showing areas flooded in 1936 and projects authorized in the flood-control act of 1936. A series of maps showing water use in the Yellowstone-Missouri River Basin compiled by the Corps of Engineers for the National Resources Committee. A base map of the Trinity River Basin in Texas.

Maps compiled for the Drainage Basin Study of the Water Resources Committee. Included are maps of the United States showing regions for the drainage basin studies and personnel assigned to each region; maps of the United States showing projects relating to irrigation, navigation, flood control, wildlife conservation, recreation, and coastal erosion; and a Corps of Engineers atlas of parts of the United States showing potential waterpower sites and existing drainage basin districts.

Maps of the United States compiled by the Division of Land Planning of the U.S. Forest Service for the Drainage Basin Study showing, in relation to watersheds, the areal extent of Forest Service programs, natural vegetation, the influence of forests, forest lands and submarginal farming areas, soil erosion, flood areas and principal waterways, and population density.

Other records relating to the Drainage Basin Study, including manuscript base maps of the major drainage basins and their tributary basins. A series of maps of subordinate drainage basins within the Ohio Basin, showing information about stream pollution and flood-control activities.

Records of the Water Resources Section, consisting of a base map prepared for the Neosho River studies and map studies of the Pensacola Hydroelectric Project showing the service areas of electric utility companies, the percentage of farms using electricity, and major types of farming areas.

26. TRANSPORTATION SECTION. 1935-39. 4 items.

Manuscript maps illustrating studies relating to trade areas proposed for a study of traffic and commodity movements in Delaware and adjacent parts of Maryland, Virginia, New Jersey, and Pennsylvania.

27. DISTRICT OFFICES. 1935-39. 294 items.

Maps of District 1, the New England States, including base maps and maps showing water resources, average annual temperatures and precipitation, water supplies, sewage and pollution problem areas, recommended projects, watersheds, gaging stations, soil erosion, transportation facilities, economic activities, population characteristics and urban areas, recreation facilities, electric transmission lines and generating plants, and regional planning activities. A map of Rhode Island annotated to show selected sites, a map of Green Mountain National Forest, a map of White Mountain National Forest annotated to show purchase units, a map showing proposed improvements in the Blackstone Valley of Rhode Island, and base maps of several of the drainage basins.

A series of maps of District 3, the Southeastern States, prepared from the results of the Forest Resources Survey. Included are base maps of the region and maps showing the extent of forests, expenditures for fire protection in the District, income received from forests and forest products, major timber regions, State health departments, and population characteristics. Also included are maps showing land use in the Coosa River Basin of Georgia and Alabama; maps of the Cumberland Drainage Basin prepared for the National Resources Committee by the Tennessee State Planning Commission showing recreation projects, physiographic regions, forest densities, airways, traffic areas, and plans for the development of the basin; a map of Georgia showing stream gages; and a map of Tupelo, Miss., showing the path of the tornado of March 23, 1936.

"Situation" maps of District 4, the Great Lakes States, including base maps and maps showing Soil Conservation Service and land-utilization projects, types of zoning ordinances in counties, the population-fertility ratio, water conservation districts, the status of aerial photographic surveys and a record of prints received, types of farming areas, public forest areas, numbers of tenant farms, physiographic regions, coal deposits, population densities, principal streams, and the status of flood-control projects. Maps of the Ohio Valley, prepared by the Ohio Valley Regional Planning Commission, including base maps and maps showing land use, numbers of industrial wage jobs by type of industry, and information about income, taxes, values of land sales, population distribution and changes, and the extent of illiteracy. Other records of District 4 include maps of drainage basins showing soils, major streams, waterpower sites, dams and reservoirs, and the status of waterpower and flood-control projects; a map of Illinois annotated to show sewerage and sewage-treatment plants; and a map showing symbols and colors suggested for use in preparing public land inventory maps.

Records of District 5, the South Central States, including base maps of drainage basins, a series of maps of parts of the region summarizing critical water problems, and maps of Arkansas annotated with information about water supply and electric-power facilities.

Records of District 11, the Northwestern States, including base maps and maps showing city and county planning commissions, geology, potential settlement areas and types of development needed, population density by counties, forest regions, dominant ownership of forests and numbers of persons employed in forest industries, and transportation facilities and plans for their improvement. Maps compiled from a drainage-basin study of the Pacific Northwest showing drainage basins, gaging stations, Federal reservations, navigational improvements, problem areas, topography, the volume of discharge from rivers, climatic characteristics, and the coverage of topographic quadrangles issued by the Geological Survey. A map compiled from a study of urban areas of the region showing highway distances between cities. Statistical maps of Oregon and Washington showing agricultural production. Maps prepared from the Columbia Basin Study, including a plan for the development of the basin and maps showing fishery and mineral resources, boundaries of the Northwest Regional Planning Commission, and the flow of telephone messages between toll points. Maps from the Columbia Gorge Conservancy Program, including a location map of the Columbia Gorge and maps showing transportation systems, topography, recreation facilities, boundaries of the Columbia Gorge Park and Game Refuge, and the progress of the detailed mapping of the area.

National Resources Planning Board

28. GENERAL RECORDS. 1939-43. 181 items.

Maps of the United States including base maps and maps showing regional boundaries and field offices of the NRPB, work programs, the status of public works projects, locations of land-utilization and hydroelectric projects, Soil Conservation Service demonstration areas, Civilian Conservation Corps camps, and areas reported by the area analysis method. Maps of the United States showing information about defense housing locations, war industries, and the total values of defense contracts, by States and regions; strategic highway routes studied, the military significance of major highways, and a tentative interregional highway system; and information about population distribution and changes, the ability of States to finance schools, dominant types of employment, gasoline pipelines, trade centers and markets, and livelihood areas.

Maps compiled for use in a study of industrial locations and natural resources in the United States including maps showing metropolitan areas, locations of natural resources and resource-consumption areas, the values of resources including farm resources and employed workers, and the locations of activities of selected industrial companies. Maps illustrating the natural features of Pennsylvania.

Maps of cities and urban areas annotated with information about housing facilities near industrial locations. A series of maps annotated with information about proposed sites for aluminum plants in New York and Pennsylvania. Maps relating to suggested sites for bomber fields in Wisconsin and Michigan. Maps of the South Platte Basin showing average precipitation, types of farming, extent of erosion, and population trends. Maps of the northern Sierra Nevada showing physiographic divisions and the distribution of population. Maps of the Eastern United States showing principal highway routes and rail routes for tank cars in the eastern petroleum service. Maps of the Massachusetts-Rhode Island-Connecticut area showing average daily passenger travel and commodity tonnage, by all means of transportation.

29. INDUSTRIAL LOCATION SECTION. 1941. 2 items.

Maps of the United States showing the expansion of manufacturing facilities for defense and existing and proposed production of alumina, aluminum, and magnesium.

30. WATER RESOURCES COMMITTEE. 1939-43. 50 items.

Maps of the United States showing drainage basins and the administrative regions and offices of the Committee. A map showing the extent of stream pollution in the Des Moines-Skunk Basin of Iowa. A plan of the first-stage basin in the upper Rio Grande.

The records of the Gila River Subcommittee including maps showing drainage areas, soil vegetation, land utilization, stock tanks, water-spreading areas, gaging stations, and precipitation and runoff statistics; and graphs showing the storage capacity of the San Carlos Reservoir.

31. PROJECT REVIEW COMMITTEE. 1943. 1 item.

A map of the United States annotated to show the locations, status, and agencies of control of projects operated by the Federal Government.

32. REGIONAL OFFICES. 1939-43. 784 items.

Maps of Region 1, the New England States, showing highways in New Hampshire, activities and facilities of the regional plan, a plan for airport development in New England, natural forest types in New England, the distribution of workers in New England by major type of industry, and industrial production and distribution centers and communications routes; a diagrammatic map showing values of production in the chief industrial centers and volumes of freight traffic on the main rail routes; a diagrammatic map showing the relative pollution loads carried by New England streams; a contour map of New England; an outline map of the region; and a map showing the chief urban centers.

Maps of Region 2, the Middle Atlantic States, showing recreation facilities, locations of coal deposits, population characteristics, metropolitan areas, industrial regions, subregions, problem areas, planning organizations, and suggested areas for the application of "Colby techniques." Maps from the Baltimore, Md., and northern New Jersey defense area surveys.

Maps of Region 3, the Southeastern States, including base maps and maps showing the status of county land-use programs, Federally owned land, and the progress of the Federal land inventory. Maps showing drainage basins and project areas. Maps showing information about land use, types of farms, climate, physiographic regions, forest regions, crop yields, and numbers of cows milked. Maps showing mineral resources, manufacturing areas, public health activities, recreational areas, public housing areas, defense activities, and the circulation of newspapers and magazines. A series of maps relating to studies of employment, distribution and population density, and the distribution of deaths from specified causes. Bureau of Public Roads county maps annotated in the Federal land inventory to show all lands in each county owned or administered by Federal agencies. A series of maps prepared for the regional development of the Alabama-Coosa River area, including base maps and maps showing population distribution, manufacturing and business establishments, roads, agriculture, water and mineral resources, and an overall plan for the development of the region. A map of Alabama showing the Federal aid system of highways. A series of maps of metropolitan areas showing information about the locations of defense establishments, housing, roads, and other facilities.

Maps of Region 4, the Great Lakes States, including a base map and a map showing boundaries of Federal Reserve districts. Maps of the individual States in Region 4 showing locations of defense industries and their value and the locations of military establishments. Maps of individual drainage basins including development plans and maps showing land characteristics, projects, activities of the Corps of Engineers, and the extent of erosion. A map of the United States showing the mean February evaporation from shallow lakes and reservoirs, compiled by the Minnesota Resources Commission of the NRPB.

Maps and related records of Region 5, the South Central States, including base maps and maps showing land subregions; war production areas; locations of deposits of strategic minerals; the status of the Federal land inventory; changes in population; transportation facilities, including international highway routes through the region; major water-control projects; and the status of flood-control projects and watershed reports. Maps of drainage basins relating to elements of a comprehensive water plan showing existing and proposed reservoirs, pollution sources, and irrigation activities. Defense-related maps of Region 5 and of individual States in the region showing industrial expansion, improvements to installations, locations of housing authorities, and the numbers of units and costs of defense housing. A plan of the proposed Rio Grande Delta Bird Refuge submitted to the NRPB by the Bureau of Biological Survey; a Soil Conservation Survey map showing the status of land use in Oklahoma, Arkansas, and Louisiana; maps of the Arkansas River Valley showing the locations of hospitals and of mineral deposits; a plan for the lower Rio Grande; plans of Corpus Christi, Tex.; a map of the Houston-Galveston water-supply problem area; maps showing the suggested Dallas-Fort Worth and Houston-Beaumont planning areas; and a map showing the status of Bureau of Reclamation projects in the southwest part of the Mississippi River Basin.

Records of Region 6, the North Central States, including base maps and maps showing boundaries of regional offices of various Federal agencies, boundaries of economic regions and subregions, flood-control investigations of the Soil Conservation Service, special problem areas, transportation routes, water projects, proposed recreational areas and historical sites, public land development projects, mineral resources, and changes in population. Defense-related maps including a map of the region showing defense expenditures in specific localities and maps of urban areas showing industrial and housing sites and transportation and sanitary facilities. A map showing agricultural potentials in Nebraska and a land survey of certain sections in T. 14 N., R. 13 E. (6th P.M.), Nebraska.

Records of Region 7, the Intermountain States, including base maps and maps showing national forests and Indian lands, deposits of strategic minerals, drainage basins, and major water developments. Maps and other records relating to the Joint Investigation of the Pecos River, including a published set of detailed sheets of the basin showing the water table and water-consuming areas, general maps of the basin including index maps and maps showing drainage basins, wells and springs, land grants, gaging stations, and the extent of aerial surveys; manuscript field maps showing vegetation, landownership, flood problem areas, and crops; detailed maps of local areas in the basin; river mileage sketch maps; graphs showing streamflow and channel losses; maps showing precipitation distribution; maps showing ground-water availability; and maps showing routes of inspection trips. Maps relating to the possibilities of a joint investigation of the Platte River, prepared in cooperation with Region 6, including base maps and maps showing the boundaries of the Platte Project, irrigation activities, mapping requirements, precipitation, evaporation, stream-flow-measurement stations, and "Weiss's and Conklin's zones." A map of the upper Arkansas River Basin showing the occurrence of minerals. Maps relating to the Denver Defense Area showing the locations of defense industries, schools, and transportation facilities.

Records of Region 9, the Pacific Northwest States, including a topographic map and maps showing main transportation lines, generalized farming areas, water-storage facilities, and deposits of metallic and nonmetallic minerals. Maps of the States within the region showing estimated population as of May 1, 1942. Maps of the various subregions showing existing and suggested areas of artificial drainage and irrigated and potentially irrigable areas. A series of maps prepared for a study of postwar planning in the Puget Sound region, including base maps and maps showing trade and manufacturing centers, population characteristics, climate, farm areas, flood-control activities, water supply, hydroelectric power, transportation and navigation facilities, Federal lands, and educational, health, and recreational facilities. A map of Linn County, Oreg., showing forest lands and irrigated and irrigable areas; a map showing area analysis in the Willamette Valley; a land-use map of Fairview, Oreg., and vicinity; and a map showing characteristics of a hypothetical sustained-yield unit in the Douglas-fir region.

Records of Region 10, Alaska, including maps showing the population distribution in 1941, forest types, existing and proposed railroads, and Federal lands.

Records of Region 11, Puerto Rico and the Virgin Islands, including a base map of the Carribbean; maps of the Virgin Islands including maps showing public landownership, current land use and suggested land use, and rainfall; and maps of Puerto Rico showing industries, the distribution of crops, public landownership, population characteristics, hospital districts and fire department zones, sanitary facilities and water supply, climatic characteristics, soils, farm types, irrigation districts, the principal drainage divide, hydrologic stations, and the electrical network.

RECORDS OF PRESIDENTIAL COMMITTEES, COMMISSIONS, AND BOARDS. RG 220

The Presidents of the United States have from time to time appointed committees, commissions, or boards responsible immediately to them to perform duties of a temporary nature not readily assignable to an established agency. Record Group 220 was established for the records of those bodies. There are, however, separate record groups for the records of some agencies of similar origin, such as Record Group 187, Records of the National Resources Planning Board.

33. COMMITTEE ON THE CONSERVATION AND ADMINISTRATION OF THE PUBLIC DOMAIN. 1926-31. 35 items.

This Committee, commonly known as the Public Lands Commission, was provided for in 1930 by an act that authorized the President to study and report on the conservation and administration of the public domain. The maps for this Committee were prepared by several of the Federal agencies interested in the administration or use of public lands. Included are several maps of the Western United States annotated to show areas proposed by the Forest Service as additions to national forests or as new forests; areas in which all remaining unappropriated public lands should be reserved for future forest lands; and areas in which the best economic and social service could be accomplished only under some form of public control but where designation as a national forest was not proposed. A series of maps of individual Western States annotated to show proposed additions to national forests and potential values of the lands for timber, watershed, or grazing purposes. A series of maps of individual public land States published by the General Land Office from 1918 through 1930 and annotated to show unsurveyed areas in each State as of the publication dates of the respective maps and areas surveyed after those dates. A map of the Western United States annotated by the Conservation Branch of the Geological Survey to show outstanding mineral withdrawals and classifications west of the 100th meridian as of June 1930. Maps of Arizona and New Mexico showing forest lands, Indian reservations, and land grants; these maps also show by township the acreage of vacant public domain and the area of State lands. A series of maps of Nevada showing the locations of water appropriations by kind, range claims, land tenure and use, and forage types. A map of Alaska compiled by the Alaska Railroad, Department of the Interior, showing routes of the Alaska Railroad and River Service, steamship routes, commercial river lines, the line of the Copper River and North Western Railroad, the White Pass Route, and the Richardson Highway, 1926.

DEPARTMENTS

DEPARTMENT OF STATE

GENERAL RECORDS OF THE DEPARTMENT OF STATE. RG 59

The Geographer of the Department of State advises and represents the Department in matters pertaining to political geography and cartography. The Office of the Geographer is responsible for compiling information on international boundaries. During World War II and until 1947 the predecessors of this Office were responsible for the preparation of specialized maps of strategic foreign countries showing current statistics and other information pertaining to population, natural resources, industry, agriculture, transportation, and commerce.

In the performance of their duties of reporting on economic and geographic developments in foreign countries, consular representatives and geographic attachés have submitted numerous maps to the Department, most of them compiled by commercial firms or official agencies in those countries.

34. GENERAL RECORDS. 1844-1951. 20 items.

Published maps compiled or reproduced for the Department of State, including a map of Texas, 1844; a map of the Virgin Islands, 1855; a map of Alaska showing Russian and Eskimo settlements, 1867; a series of maps of parts of the world showing the diplomatic and consular posts of the U.S. Government, 1871; and a map of the world showing the width of the zone of coastal waters over which sovereignty was claimed by the adjacent nations, 1951.

Published maps from the Department of State map series consisting of a map of the world showing the trade agreement program for 1938 and a photoprocessed copy of a map of Europe and the Near East which had been marked with pins to show representation of foreign interests by diplomatic and consular establishments of the United States, 1941.

A published base map of Liberia, 1922. An untitled, undated manuscript map of the world apparently emphasizing island groups. A chart of the Atlantic Ocean annotated to show the track of the German ship *Werra* from England to New York, 1887; and a published chart of the Marianas, about 1890, with an attached report recommending their acquisition by the United States.

35. BUREAU OF AMERICAN REPUBLICS. 1900. 1 item.

A published map of Mexico showing political boundaries, topography, railroads, telegraph lines and submarine cables, lighthouses, mining districts, and mineral resources.

36. COUNCIL OF FOREIGN MINISTERS. 1947. 21 items.

Maps published as a supplement to Annex I, "Statements of the Allied Governments on the German Problem," which was presented to the London Conference of the Deputies of the Foreign Ministers of France, the United Kingdom, the United States, and the Soviet Union in January 1947. Among these are maps of Belgium showing segments of the national boundary; maps of Czechoslovakia showing the boundary with Germany; maps of Luxembourg showing territorial claims and coal mines under concession in the Aachen area; and maps of the Netherlands showing frontier adjustments, the population of frontier areas, canals, watersheds of streams crossing the frontier, and flooding in frontier areas.

37. FOREIGN SERVICE INSPECTION CORPS. 1906-39. 259 items.

Published and photoprocessed maps of cities in foreign countries annotated by U.S. consular representatives abroad to show American embassies, consulates, and consular residences, American properties, customhouses, commercial and industrial districts, harbor facilities, and petroleum reserves and refineries. Some of the maps also show embassies and consulates of other nations and the locations of other significant buildings. A few general maps show information relating to transportation and communication facilities, particularly in China. Included are a card catalog and list.

Arranged by continent, thereunder by country, and thereunder alphabetically by city when applicable.

38. DIVISION OF POLITICAL AND ECONOMIC INFORMATION. 1923. 1 item.

A published map of Central America showing demarcated and undemarcated international boundaries, provincial boundaries, and railways.

39. CONSULAR TRADE REPORTS. 1943-49. 220 items.

Enclosures removed from trade reports of U.S. consuls. Most of the items are cartographic, but several graphs and tables and a few map-illustrated textual publications are included. Among these records are maps of the world and of Europe, Africa, and the Atlantic Ocean showing air routes; maps of foreign countries showing geology and topography, mineral deposits and mining areas, irrigated areas, electric-power production and distribution systems, and transportation and communications networks.

40. OFFICE OF THE GEOGRAPHER. 1921-64. 101 items.

Records of the Geographer including published maps of the world showing foreign posts and the jurisdictional areas of the various offices and agencies of the Department of State, United States visa-issuing offices, and immigration quota areas. Published maps of the Near East, the Federal Republic of Germany, Southeast Asia, Africa, France, Mexico, Brazil, Japan, the United Kingdom, Canada, the Netherlands, Belgium, and Luxembourg showing U.S. consular districts. Map-illustrated serial publications concerning various aspects of political geography, including the Geographic Reports, 1961-62; the International Boundary Studies, 1961-64; and Geographic Bulletins 1 and 2 (1963) entitled, respectively, "Profiles of Newly Independent States" and "Status of the World's Nations."

Files of Geographers Lawrence Martin, 1921-24, and S. W. Boggs, 1924-54, including 32 boxes of textual records consisting of correspondence, diaries, and work reports. Much of this material pertains to special mapping projects, many undertaken during World War II. Among these are research reports compiled by employees of the Work Projects Administration under the supervision of the State Department. These projects were known as the "Central Pacific Islands Study" and the "Annotated Bibliography of the Polar Regions" and were terminated in 1942 and 1943, respectively. Transparencies of special maps, many prepared under the direction of Boggs, and two globes and a transparent plastic hemisphere designed by Boggs for the measurement of distance and areas on globes.

Records of the Office of the Geographer, 1932-43, including published outline maps of the world on various projections, a generalized contour map of the continents, a map showing U.S. Foreign Service posts and passport and dispatch agencies, and a map showing immigration quota areas; a map of Palestine showing annual rainfall; and a map of Liberia with insets showing tribal distributions, physiography, and Liberian boundary history, including an index to geographic names. An outline map of the Near East giving population and area statistics for specific countries. Maps of China and Manchuria showing railway, caravan, and motor routes.

41. DIVISION OF GEOGRAPHY AND CARTOGRAPHY. 1943-44.
890 items.

Five bound volumes of published maps and related graphs entitled "Map Studies made in 'G.E.' (Division of Geography and Cartography), Department of State, during World War II, chiefly for use of the committee headed by Dr. Leo Pasvolsky, in preparation for a peace conference after the War." The maps cover areas throughout the world and include information about topographic relief, rainfall, population distribution, the distribution of religions and ethnic groups, boundaries and territorial changes and claims, navigable waterways, industrial and agricultural development, transportation facilities, and mineral resources. Arranged in volumes by area.

A bound volume of graphs, charts, and a few maps identified as "Miscellaneous." Included are charts showing the organization and activities of inter-Allied agencies during and after World War II and of United Nations agencies; charts and graphs showing the organization, activities, and appropriations of the Department of State; and charts, graphs, and maps relating to the supply and demand of rubber.

A bound volume entitled "A Selection of Maps and Charts Prepared by Division of Geography and Cartography, Department of State." The maps and graphs included are similar in content to those compiled by Dr. Pasvolsky's committee; some are duplicates of those maps. Arranged in a numerical system based on geographic regions.

42. DIVISION OF MAP INTELLIGENCE AND CARTOGRAPHY. 1946-47. 56 items.

Published maps including an atlas of Japan showing administrative subdivisions, a map of India showing the distribution of Moslems and the largest cities in 1941, a map of Bengal and Assam showing the largest cities in 1941, a map of the Venezia Giulia area on the Italo-Yugoslav border, maps showing the Allied occupation zones in Germany and Austria, a map of the Rhineland showing the Ruhr and the Saar, and azimuthal equidistant projections of the "Pacific Ocean Hemisphere" and the "Land Hemisphere."

43. OFFICE OF INTELLIGENCE RESEARCH. 1946-47. 10 items.

Mimeographed reports with maps and descriptive texts evaluating the map coverage of Turkey and Spain, maps pertaining to reconstruction in Greece, the map coverage of Germany with an evaluation of German town plans, and the coverage of political and administrative maps of Germany; an analysis of the borderlands of Hungary and Czechoslovakia; and an intelligence report on the boundaries and territories of the states in the Arabian Peninsula. A mimeographed report describing German cartographic and map-collecting agencies, the laws and regulatory statutes governing those agencies, and the geodetic bases of German cartography. Many of the maps illustrating these reports were prepared by the Division of Map Intelligence and Cartography.

RECORDS OF BOUNDARY AND CLAIMS COMMISSIONS AND ARBITRATIONS. RG 76

The records pertaining to boundary and claims commissions, arbitrations, and awards were preserved by the Department of State and later deposited in the National Archives. The boundaries of the United States have been defined and described by treaties and conventions with Great Britain, France, Russia, Spain, Mexico, and Texas; cartographic records relating to these treaties and conventions are in Record Group 76. Also in this record group are maps submitted as evidence in support of private claims of U.S. citizens against foreign governments and claims of foreign citizens or subjects against the United States; and the cartographic records of arbitrations by the President and other officials in disputes between foreign governments, most of which concerned boundaries of Latin American countries.

44. UNITED STATES BOUNDARIES AND CESSIONS. 1794-1952.
4,448 items.

Published and photoprocessed maps and atlases, some annotated, used in negotiating boundary settlements and cessions to the United States. Manuscript, published, and photoprocessed maps (some bound in volumes) of border areas prepared as a result of agreements delineating U.S. boundaries and cessions to the United States. These maps contain a variety of incidental information about topography, Indian tribal locations, transportation routes, waterways, settlements, fortifications, and exploration routes.

For the northeastern boundary of the United States, maps prepared in connection with the treaties of 1794, 1814, 1842, 1908, 1910, and 1925; the conventions of 1827 and 1892; and the act of 1840. Among the records of the treaties of 1794 and 1814 and the convention of 1827 are many published maps of North America and its parts, including several versions of John Mitchell's map of the British colonies in North America that was originally published in 1755. Included are single- and multiple-sheet copies. An atlas of North America and other parts of the world compiled by Herman Moll and two incomplete editions of an atlas of the Americas assembled by Thomas Jefferys containing maps of individual American colonies, some with insets of city plans, compiled by various explorers and surveyors. Manuscript and published maps resulting from surveys and resurveys of the boundary line in compliance with the act of 1840; the treaties of 1908, 1910, and 1925; and the convention of 1892. Also among the records are some watercolor sketches of areas along the boundary line.

For the northern boundary of the United States, extending from the Great Lakes to the Rocky Mountains, maps prepared in connection with the treaties of 1814 and 1909; the conventions of 1818, 1908, and 1925; and the act of 1902. Manuscript and published maps, and field sketches, of the line surveyed in accordance with the treaty of 1814 and the convention of 1818 (the survey prescribed by the convention was not actually completed until 1876). The maps relating to the act of 1902 and the convention of 1908 were prepared under the direction of the International Waterways Commission. Those for the act of 1902 are manuscript and annotated maps from studies of proposed and existing diversions of international waters along the boundary and plans for waterpower projects. Those for the convention of 1908 include manuscript compilations and field maps, and published maps relating to the international boundary through the St. Lawrence River and the Great Lakes. The maps relating to the treaty of 1909 are manuscript and published maps resulting from a study of the levels of the Lake of the Woods. Those for the convention of 1925 are manuscript and published maps resulting from a study on the improvement of the St. Lawrence River from Montreal to Lake Ontario.

For the northwestern boundary of the United States, records of surveys made during the 1860's in compliance with the treaty of 1846, including field sketches and manuscript and published detailed sheets. Maps of the areas adjacent to the boundary line—particularly that area now comprising the northern parts of Washington, Idaho, and Montana—showing information about topography, drainage, routes, trails, and Indian place names and tribal locations. Watercolor sketches of areas along the boundary line by James Alden, who accompanied the survey party. Published British Admiralty charts of the Straits of Haro, Rosario, and San Juan de Fuca, referred to in the protocol of 1873, showing the international boundary; and annotated and published maps of the boundary, resurveyed in accordance with the convention of 1908 and the treaty of 1915.

For the boundary between the United States and the Republic of Texas, settled by the convention of 1838, manuscript maps that resulted from a survey along the Sabine River to Logan's Ferry and then to a point due north on the Red River.

For the boundary between the United States and Mexico, records prepared in connection with the treaties of 1848, 1853, and 1882. Records concerning the treaty of 1848 include manuscript and published maps produced during the boundary surveys required by the treaties of 1853 and 1882. The conventions of 1884 and 1905 and the treaty of 1889 concerned the international waterways of the Rio Grande; the records include manuscript and published maps resulting from surveys and studies of the river in accordance with the convention of 1884 and the treaty of 1889, and maps showing the elimination of bancos (cutoffs) in the river, required by the convention of 1905.

For the Alaska-Canada boundary, published detailed maps of the southeastern segment surveyed in accordance with the convention of 1892 and photocopies of topographic sketches that accompanied a report. The photo-topographic technique was used during the surveys of the boundary; this was a map compilation process based in part on terrain photographs made from mountain peaks. Copies of the photographs, which may be considered early predecessors of aerial photographs, are preserved with the textual records of the surveys in the National Archives. Records illustrating the modus vivendi of 1899 include published maps showing the provisional boundaries and the claims of the United States and Canada along the southeastern segment of the boundary. The records of the convention of 1903 include published maps from the Alaskan Boundary Tribunal accompanying the case and countercase of the United States and the case of Great Britain relevant to the southeastern segment of the boundary; a published *Atlas of Award* showing the boundary established; and miscellaneous manuscript and published maps, some referred to as British Commission maps and some prepared by the U.S. Geological Survey. The records of the convention of 1906 include published atlases with detailed sheets showing the boundary established from Mount St. Elias to the Arctic Ocean and other manuscript and published maps.

For the cession of the Philippine Islands to the United States under the treaty of 1898, a number of published and annotated Coast and Geodetic Survey charts of the Islands. For the cession of the Virgin Islands to the United States according to the convention of 1916, several published Danish hydrographic charts of the Islands and a British map of the Islands, dated 1855, reproduced for the Department of State.

Also included are numbered planetable sheets, topographic field sheets, manuscript compilations, and drawings relating to the northeastern, northern, northwestern, and Alaskan boundaries with Canada.

The boundary maps are arranged in series by type of record or by area; thereunder the arrangement is generally chronological.

45. MISCELLANEOUS INTERNATIONAL AGREEMENTS TO WHICH THE UNITED STATES WAS A PARTY. 1854-1930. 272 items.

Maps illustrating the fisheries treaties of 1854 and 1871 with Great Britain, including hydrographic charts of coastal waters of the northeastern United States and eastern Canada annotated to show claims of the British and American Commissioners and numbered as Fishery Commission plans according to the treaty of 1854; and manuscript maps of the northeastern United States and eastern Canada showing rivers and river mouths reserved from common liberty of fishing under the treaty of 1871.

Maps illustrating the sockeye salmon treaty of 1930 with Canada, including hydrographic charts of the Straits of Georgia and San Juan de Fuca with overprints to illustrate the terms of the treaty.

Maps illustrating claims conventions with Mexico, including maps of Sonora prepared under the terms of the conventions of 1868 and 1871; manuscript, annotated, and published maps of Mexico and parts thereof relating to the Mexican Revolution, about 1910-20, showing revolutionary troop dispositions and military activities; and maps showing population, mining areas, land use, land values, and communications and transportation systems, prepared under the terms of the conventions of September 8 and September 10, 1923. Some of the maps show information about the particular claims for which they were used.

A published map of North Borneo used in the agreement of 1907 with Great Britain concerning the administration of certain coastal islands.

Arranged in series by subject.

46. ARBITRATIONS BETWEEN THE UNITED STATES AND FOREIGN POWERS. 1892-1926. 275 items.

Cartographic records of the dispute between Great Britain and the United States over fur seals in the Bering Sea presented before the Paris tribunal, 1892-93, following the convention of 1892. Included are charts showing tracks of American and British vessels in the Bering Sea. Some of the charts show locations and numbers of seals sighted, a few show whales sighted, and others show migration routes of the fur seal herd. There also are maps of rookeries showing breeding grounds and numbers of seals, 1872-91, and tables showing the fluctuations in numbers of seals taken. See entry 231 for other records relating to the fur seal arbitrations.

Also included are charts annotated to show coral fisheries in the Mediterranean Sea and pearl fisheries off the coasts of Panama, India, and Ceylon.

Maps used in the agreement of 1909 between the United States and Great Britain on fishing in the Atlantic coastal waters of the British Dominions and the United States. Included are British Admiralty charts and charts of the U.S. Hydrographic Office and the Coast and Geodetic Survey, some with annotations apparently showing fishing rights; Coast and Geodetic Survey maps of the coasts of Canada and Newfoundland showing areas in which American fishing rights dated from the treaty of 1818; and published volumes of outline maps of the east coast of North America identified as illustrating the case of Great Britain.

Maps and other sketches illustrating certain pecuniary claims arbitrations resulting from the agreement of 1910 between the United States and Great Britain. Some of these are unidentified as to specific claim. Other records included are sketches and hydrographic charts relating to claims of British vessels, published maps illustrating claims of the Cayuga Indians in the vicinity of Lakes Erie and Ontario, and maps of the Fiji Islands.

Published and certified photographs of maps of the Celebes Sea including hydrographic charts from official Government sources and privately published maps covering a wide range of dates. These maps were submitted by the Netherlands in the United States-Netherlands arbitration at The Hague over the Island of Palmas, under the agreement of 1925.

47. ARBITRATIONS BY THE UNITED STATES FOR FOREIGN GOVERNMENTS. 1876-1945. 15,230 items.

Cartographic records prepared during arbitrations of boundary disputes between countries in Latin America.

Maps submitted as evidence in the dispute between Argentina and Paraguay, under the treaty of 1876. Among them are early published maps of South America and parts thereof, charts of the Paraná and Paraguay Rivers, a map of Paraguay annotated to show the territory submitted to arbitration and the territories ceded by Paraguay to Argentina and to Brazil, and a published map of Bolivia, dated 1859.

Among the records used in arbitrating the boundary dispute between Argentina and Brazil under the treaty of 1889 are published maps of South America and parts thereof, some dating back to 1630, and manuscript copies of maps of South America and the territory in dispute, prepared from originals in the British Museum, the Archives of the Minister of Foreign Affairs in Paris, the Portuguese Archives in Lisbon, and the Archives of the Indies in Madrid; and Argentine maps of the territory in dispute, one showing Argentine land grants.

Maps used in the boundary dispute between Great Britain (British Guiana) and Venezuela under the treaty of 1896 include a map of part of South America, dated 1716, and a map of British Guiana, dated 1875.

Maps used in arbitrating the boundary dispute between Panama and Costa Rica under the convention of 1910 include published maps of the area, nautical charts issued by foreign governments, manuscript field maps and views from the boundary survey, tracings of United Fruit Co. location and railroad maps, maps of the boundary between Costa Rica and Colombia, a bound volume of maps and profiles accompanying the report of the Consulting Engineer of the Government of Costa Rica, and an atlas of historical and geographical maps of Costa Rica, 1890.

For the boundary dispute between Peru and Ecuador, under the protocol of 1942 and arbitration of 1945, aerial photographs of the disputed area and manuscript, published, and annotated maps showing the disputed boundaries, flight lines of the aerial survey, corrected boundaries, drainage features, railroads, and roads.

Arranged in series by date of treaty, convention, protocol, or other agreement.

RECORDS OF UNITED STATES PARTICIPATION IN INTERNATIONAL CONFERENCES, COMMISSIONS, AND EXPOSITIONS. RG 43

Since 1826 the United States has participated in numerous international conferences, committees, commissions, and other organizations concerned with social, economic, and political matters, and in international exhibitions and expositions. This participation usually has been carried on under the auspices of the Department of State pursuant to Congressional authorization.

48. INTERCONTINENTAL RAILWAY COMMISSION. 1890-98. 1,045 items.

The Intercontinental Railway Commission evolved from the First International Conference of American States, which convened at Washington in October 1889. The Committee on Railroad Communication presented a report recommending a railroad to connect all or most of the American nations. The report included recommendations concerning the surveying of a route and the construction and management of the railroad. It was submitted on May 12, 1890, by James G. Blaine, Secretary of State, to President Harrison, who recommended to Congress that the United States participate in this activity. In the appropriations act for the diplomatic and consular service of the United States for fiscal year 1891, provision was made for the United States to share in the costs of a preliminary survey for an intercontinental railway. The President was authorized to appoint three members to the International Railway Commission and to detail officers of the Army and the Navy to serve under the Commission in making the survey.

The Commission held its first meeting in Washington, D.C., on December 4, 1890. At this meeting the surveying parties were organized. Six field parties were planned but only three were organized, each as a corps. Corps I was composed almost entirely of officers of the U.S. Army; Corps II and III were under the direction of civilians.

These corps went into the field in 1891. Corps I surveyed in Guatemala, Salvador, Honduras, Nicaragua, and Costa Rica; Corps II, in Ecuador, Colombia, and Panama; and Corps III, in Ecuador and Peru. According to the ... *Condensed Report ... of the Commission ...*, vol. I, part 1, Corps I made more complete and detailed surveys than the other two corps and was therefore in the field longer. Corps II and III returned in 1892; and Corps I, in 1893.

Upon returning to the United States members of the three corps prepared their reports and cartographic exhibits. These were published in 1898 in several volumes with the maps folded loosely in separate volumes, one for each corps.

The cartographic records of the Commission are the manuscript maps, graphs, and profiles prepared for inclusion in the published reports. Included are large-scale maps of the areas surveyed showing existing and proposed routes for the railroad, topography and drainage, roads and trails, and boundaries. On many of the maps the scale is large enough to show cities and towns in some detail. Included also are profiles of the area covered by the proposed railroad routes and panoramic sketches of selected areas.

Arranged by volume and map number as they appear in the published report.

DEPARTMENT OF THE TREASURY

GENERAL RECORDS OF THE DEPARTMENT OF THE TREASURY. RG 56

The general records of the Treasury Department include those of the Office of the Secretary and its subdivisions and of smaller units, such as the former Office of the Chief Clerk and various research and statistical divisions. They also include the records of the Special Agents of the Department who functioned from 1861 to 1866 and were concerned with enforcing restrictions on commerce with the States declared to be in insurrection, with the collection of abandoned and captured property, and with carrying out the regulations for the welfare and employment of freedmen before 1865. Certain records of the Southern Claims Commission and of the Confederate States of America also are included.

49. GENERAL RECORDS. 1851-83. 6 items.

A published geological map of Wisconsin, Iowa, and Minnesota prepared by David Dale Owen, principal geologist of the "United States Geological Corps" and others, published in 1851 under instructions from the Secretary of the Treasury.

Published maps of the Eastern United States and adjacent areas in Canada prepared to accompany Israel Andrews' report to the Secretary of the Treasury, 1852-53; these maps show railroads, political subdivisions, and navigable waterways. A published map of the United States showing customs collection districts and ports of entry and delivery, 1883.

50. DIVISION OF CAPTURED AND ABANDONED PROPERTY. 1860-74. 12 items.

Manuscript, published, and annotated maps prepared or used by the special agents of the Department, including maps of land districts along the Mississippi River in Arkansas, Louisiana, and Mississippi showing plantations, abandoned plantations, and those abandoned plantations that were leased; miscellaneous maps of parts of Louisiana along the Mississippi River; published General Land Office maps of Louisiana and Florida; and manuscript maps showing the location of Government farms for freedmen in the First and Second Districts, Negro Affairs, Department of Virginia and North Carolina.

RECORDS OF THE BUREAU OF CUSTOMS. RG 36

The Customs Bureau, established in 1789, administers the assessment and collection of import duties and, in cooperation with other Government agencies, assists in the prevention of smuggling, espionage, and sabotage and in the physical control of persons and their effects entering and leaving the United States. In 1942 it was given certain functions, previously performed by the Bureau of Marine Inspection and Navigation, relating to the control of vessels, the collection of tonnage taxes, and the entrance and clearance of vessels and aircraft.

51. GENERAL RECORDS. 1929-54. 21 items.

A published map of the United States showing ports of entry and customs districts, headquarters, and airports, 1929. Published maps of the United States showing, respectively, customs districts and ports of entry, appraisers' districts and headquarters, comptrollers' districts and headquarters, laboratory districts and headquarters, and enforcement agency districts and headquarters. The maps in this series are undated but are believed to represent the 1954 administrative districts of the agency. A series of published charts, dated 1953 and 1954, showing the organization and functions of the Bureau of Customs and its component units.

RECORDS OF THE INTERNAL REVENUE SERVICE. RG 58

The Internal Revenue Service (IRS) was established in 1862 to administer, assess, and collect all internal taxes and to enforce all internal revenue laws.

The cartographic records of the IRS are from the Collector of Internal Revenue at Charleston, S.C., and consist chiefly of records of the Direct Tax Commission for the District of South Carolina. This Commission was created in 1861 to collect direct taxes levied on the States declared to be in insurrection. It was discontinued in 1870 and its functions and records were transferred to the Collector of Internal Revenue at Charleston.

52. COLLECTOR OF INTERNAL REVENUE, CHARLESTON, S.C. 1862-1912. 85 items.

Manuscript, annotated, and published maps and related records prepared or used by the Direct Tax Commission in the District of South Carolina, 1862-70. Included are maps of St. Helena's Parish and the cities of Port Royal and Beaufort that were used by the Commission in establishing the amount of taxes to be levied, and a manuscript map of St. Helena's Parish, about 1867, prepared at the direction of the Commission, showing the rectangular land subdivision carried out under provisions of the acts of June 7 and July 17, 1862, and February 6, 1863, relating to the collection of direct taxes and the confiscation of land, and of the acts of March 3, 1865, and July 16, 1866, creating and extending the Bureau of Refugees, Freedmen, and Abandoned Lands. Maps of St. Helena's Parish and of the cities of Port Royal and Beaufort showing property owners, school farms, and information relating to the sale of lands; a map of Beaufort, showing property ownership, about 1770, and a sketch of a land grant on Port Royal Island, dated 1785. Twenty-nine field survey notebooks relating to the surveys of sea islands in St. Helena's and St. Luke's parishes and to the survey of Port Royal, 1863-67.

Later records of the Collector of Internal Revenue for South Carolina related to the records of the Direct Tax Commission include five manuscript maps, 1873-74, of parts of St. Helena's Parish, including one of the city of Beaufort, showing land surveys; one annotated photostat of a map of St. Helena's Parish, about 1889; and one photostat of a Corps of Engineers survey of the Fort Fremont Quadrangle, 1912, annotated to show townships and sections used by the Direct Tax Commission.

Among these records are several undated manuscript and annotated maps of parts of St. Helena's Parish, a map of Port Royal, sketches of school farms on Port Royal Island, a sketch of the islands at the Port Royal entrance to Broad River, and a War Department map of North and South Carolina with unidentified annotations around Charleston and St. Helena's Parish.

RECORDS OF THE BUREAU OF MARINE INSPECTION AND NAVIGATION. RG 41

The Bureau of Marine Inspection and Navigation, established in 1932 and abolished in 1946, was responsible for the administration of navigation laws and the inspection of ships for seaworthiness and safety.

53. GENERAL RECORDS. n.d. 1 item.

A published map of the United States overprinted to show the boundaries of supervising districts and local districts of the Bureau and offices of supervising inspectors, local inspectors, and collectors of customs.

RECORDS OF THE UNITED STATES COAST GUARD. RG 26

The U.S. Coast Guard, established in 1915, was enlarged in 1939 by the addition of the Bureau of Lighthouses. The Coast Guard is responsible for the enforcement of customs and navigation laws, the supervision of the anchorage and movement of vessels, the reporting of marine casualties, the protection of life and property, and the installation, maintenance, and operation of lighthouses, lightships, buoys, and other aids to navigation. It operates under the Department of the Treasury in time of peace and under the Department of the Navy in time of war or when the President so directs.

For operational maps the Coast Guard depends primarily on the nautical charts issued by the Naval Oceanographic Office, the Coast and Geodetic Survey, and the U.S. Lake Survey of the Army's Corps of Engineers. Operating vessels of the Coast Guard using nautical charts issued by those three agencies are directed to report findings that necessitate changes in the charts. The records of the Archives Section of the Naval Oceanographic Office (see entry 186) include many annotated published charts and manuscript sketch maps furnished by Coast Guard vessels.

Bureau of Lighthouses and Its Predecessors

54. GENERAL RECORDS. 1858-1912. 36 items.

Published maps of the United States showing the boundaries of lighthouse districts and the locations of coast signal stations, principal lighthouses and light buoys; maps of the Atlantic and gulf coasts and the Pacific coast showing lighthouses, 1858 and 1861; maps of individual lighthouse districts showing lighthouses, light buoys, and light vessels, proposed facilities, and the ranges and types of lights; and a map of the Hawaiian Islands showing lighthouses and light buoys. A diagram in the form of a mariner's compass and a table of compass points.

55. MAP ENCLOSURES FROM CORRESPONDENCE OF THE
SUPERINTENDENT. 1921. 3 items.

Published charts of the Taunton River in Massachusetts, annotated to show corrections and information about lights and buoys.

56. AIRWAYS DIVISION. 1929. 3 items.

Published and annotated maps of the air route between Kansas City and Chicago showing ground aids to navigation, principally radio beacons and beacon lights; and a map showing the Los Angeles-Bakersfield segment of the Los Angeles-Seattle air route, with drawings and notations about existing and proposed sites for emergency landing fields and beacon lights.

57. CHIEF CONSTRUCTION ENGINEER. 1916. 1 item.

A photoprocessed plan of the Navassa Island Lighthouse Station between Jamaica and Hispaniola.

58. LIGHTHOUSE DISTRICTS. 1893-1939. 33 items.

Records of the Third Lighthouse District consisting of a series of published Coast and Geodetic Survey charts of the northeastern coast of the United States annotated to show harbor facilities, harbor approaches, lighthouses and light buoys, and changes in the positions of buoys, 1915-39. This series was continued by the Coast Guard (see entry 60).

A photoprocessed chart showing the line of electric buoys from Chicago to the World's Fair grounds prepared in the Ninth Lighthouse District, ca. 1893.

A published topographic map of the Hecata Head (Oreg.) Light Station, prepared in the Thirteenth Lighthouse District, 1894.

Arranged in series by district number.

United States Coast Guard

59. COAST GUARD VESSELS. 1920-41. 13 items.

Published and photoprocessed hydrographic and coast charts prepared by members of the Coast Guard sailing in arctic regions, particularly off the coasts of Alaska and Greenland. These charts were prepared upon base maps issued by the Hydrographic Office or by similar foreign agencies. Some of them show changes or additions made by members of the Coast Guard. Included is a unit of maps illustrating the route of the South Greenland Survey Expedition of 1941.

60. COAST GUARD DISTRICTS. 1940-41. 13 items.

Published Coast and Geodetic Survey charts of the northeastern coast of the United States annotated to show harbor facilities, harbor approaches, light-houses, and changes in positions of buoys. Several showing light buoys not in operation are identified as blackout charts for World War II. These appear to be a continuation of the charts prepared by the Third Lighthouse District (see entry 58).

DEPARTMENT OF DEFENSE

DEPARTMENT OF THE ARMY

RECORDS OF THE ADJUTANT GENERAL'S OFFICE. RG 94

The principal responsibilities of the Adjutant General's Office (AGO), established in 1813, have included the procurement, assignment, and discharge of all officers and enlisted men of the Army, the communication of all orders issued by the Department of the Army, and the compilation and issue of departmental manuals and other publications.

The Adjutant General's Office supervised the former Military Information Division until that unit was transferred to the General Staff in 1903. It inherited the records and functions of the former War Records Office and, as a part of its records management activities, it collected maps made by other units of the Army.

The Military Information Division was responsible for the preparation of intelligence maps of foreign areas. It also began the collection of maps that was later to become the General Staff Map Collection (see entry 128).

The War Records Office, established in 1875, was merged with the Record and Pension Office in 1899. The latter was then merged with the Adjutant General's Office in 1904. One of the major responsibilities of the War Records Office was the compilation of the multivolume *Official Records of the Union and Confederate Armies* and the *Atlas* accompanying that publication.

61. GENERAL RECORDS. 1853-1926. 39 items.

A group of published maps, chiefly of the Western United States, received in a portfolio marked "General McLellan's Portfolio." The maps were compiled during the Pacific Railroad Surveys (1853-55) and were published by the Office of Explorations and Surveys and the Bureau of Topographical Engineers. They show topography, routes of marches, military posts, and Indian reservations. Most of the items are published versions of manuscript maps in Record Group 48, Records of the Office of the Secretary of the Interior. Also in the portfolio are two general maps of Florida dated 1856. The maps are arranged in a numbered series; an accompanying list identifies each map by title and file number.

An alphabetical list, dated 1926, of provinces, arrondissements, cantons, and communes in Belgium.

62. MAP ENCLOSURES TO CORRESPONDENCE. 1875-90. 2 items.

A manuscript map dated 1875, bearing an AGO correspondence number, of parts of Kansas, the Indian Territory, Texas, and New Mexico showing routes, campsites, and sites of Indian battles.

A blueprint map, dated 1890, relating to Sioux disturbances in southwestern South Dakota and northwestern Nebraska, showing topography, roads, military posts, and Indian reservations.

63. WAR RECORDS OFFICE. 1861-95. 1,051 items.

An incomplete set of manuscript and annotated maps used in the compilation of the *Atlas to Accompany the Official Records of the Union and Confederate Armies* (Washington, 1891-95), copies of the two published volumes of the *Atlas,* and separately bound copies of some individual sheets. The *Atlas* contains 175 sheets, each of which includes several maps. Among them are general maps of the United States and of areas in the South showing topography and drainage, roads and railroads, and place names; maps illustrating specific campaigns and battles; and maps showing the military territorial divisions of the Union and Confederate forces. A number of sheets include plans and views of fortifications and pictures of unit flags and insignia.

The manuscript and annotated maps used in the compilation of the published maps were acquired from numerous sources. Maps prepared during the campaigns, manuscript and published copies of which may be found among the records of the Office of the Chief of Engineers (see entries 112-114) and among the records of United States Army commands in Record Group 391 and Record Group 393 (see entries 97 and 99), were a primary source. Maps showing battlefields and troop positions compiled after the war by the Office of the Chief of Engineers (see entries 112 and 113) were also used. Former military men from both the Union and Confederate Armies supplied records from their personal papers or annotated copies of published records with corrections or changes. Some of the maps supplied by such persons are in these files, others were returned, and some were retained in the correspondence files with the accompanying letters.

The manuscript and annotated maps used in the compilation of the published *Atlas* are arranged by plate number as the *Atlas* is organized. A complete index in Volume I serves as a finding aid to the maps and illustrations in the *Atlas* and also to the manuscript and annotated collection.

A blueprint copy of a map of Richmond and vicinity originally compiled under the direction of the Chief Engineer of the Department of Northern Virginia, C.S.A., in 1862 and copied in the War Records Office in 1890. The map shows drainage features, buildings, and the names of inhabitants.

64. MILITARY INFORMATION DIVISION. 1895-1902. 97 items.

Published maps including military maps of the United States, 1895-97, maps relating to military operations in Africa, Greece, Korea, and China, 1897-1900, and maps of Cuba, Puerto Rico, and the Philippines, 1897-1902. Among the latter, which were compiled during the Spanish-American War, are maps showing military facilities and maps pertaining to military engagements. A series of Hydrographic Office charts accompany a report on the Samoa Islands. Other records compiled by the Photo Room of the Military Information Division consist of views and sketches of areas in Cuba, 1898, an atlas containing plans of ports and cities in Cuba, 1898, and copies of maps and views of the Philippine Islands. Many of the manuscript maps compiled or collected by the Military Information Division of the Adjutant General's Office were incorporated into the files of the Military Intelligence Division of the General Staff (see entry 169) and into the General Staff Map Collection in Record Group 77 (see entry 128).

65. WORLD WAR DIVISION, AGO. 1918. 1 item.

Assembled sheets of the French "Carte de France et des Frontieres" showing, by means of colored pins and labels, the organization and disposition of the Allies and the Central Powers on the Western Front on Armistice Day, November 11, 1918. A letter from Capt. Thomas North, F.A., dated October 12, 1938, identifies this map as one reconstructed from two originals prepared in France during the war. The originals apparently were the one used in the Map Room of G-3, AEF General Headquarters, and the one prepared in Advance General Headquarters. Of those two the former was reported by North as having been sent to the Smithsonian Institution in Washington and the latter as having been sent to West Point. The records of the American Expeditionary Forces (Record Group 120) include two similar maps showing the positions of the opposing forces at the time of the armistice.

66. DEPARTMENTAL RECORDS BRANCH. 1941-45. 4,948 items.

Manuscript and annotated maps prepared by various army units during World War II and captured German, Italian, and Japanese maps. Few of these are identified by unit of origin. Included are annotated maps and photoprocessed copies of annotated maps showing military territorial commands and administrative divisions in the United States and overseas; a map showing the dates of Allied landings in the Southwest Pacific; and tables of organization of the Control Council for Germany, the Commanding General of a theater of operations, and the Middle East theater. There are maps relating to various theaters showing drainage and topography, troop dispositions and lines of march, defenses, canals, roads, and lines of communication. A large number of maps relate to the Allied landings in Sicily and Italy, including maps of beaches prepared in advance of the landings. There also are numerous maps prepared by the Sixth Army Group in a study of the Rhine River. Arranged in folders by area, with a list of contents for each folder.

The captured German maps include published maps and aerial mosaics of defenses in Germany, Italy, the Soviet Union, France, Belgium, Rumania, and the Netherlands; hydrographic charts of the English coast overprinted to show defenses; maps overprinted to show troop billeting capacities in Germany; reference maps of strategic countries; a series of maps from studies of German interests in Czechoslovakia; city plans; maps showing British resources; stereoptic views of mountain passes in Italy; and tactical and topographic maps of parts of Germany. The Italian records include maps showing defenses of Sicily, the defense systems of the XIV Corps in Italy, and maps relating to the Sino-Japanese War (1937-38). The Japanese maps include hydrographic charts of areas in the western Pacific, some of which were reprinted from American charts; miscellaneous published topographic maps and city plans of Japan, China, and certain islands in the western Pacific; manuscript and annotated maps showing military operations, particularly in China; and a series of Coast and Geodetic Survey charts of the Washington, D.C., area that were reprinted by the Japanese. Arranged by country of origin and thereunder in series by subject. An accompanying list describes the contents of each series.

RECORDS OF THE AMERICAN EXPEDITIONARY FORCES (WORLD WAR I), 1917-23. RG 120

The General Headquarters of the American Expeditionary Forces was established in France in the summer of 1918. The General Staff was organized into sections for Administration (G-1), Intelligence (G-2), Coordination (G-4), and Training (G-5). Division and corps organizations were formed as American forces and supplies in France were built up. By January 1918 an entire American division, the 1st, was able to occupy a sector of the line, and during the summer and fall of that year the independent American offensives of St.-Mihiel and Meuse-Argonne helped turn the tide of the war.

Following the armistice the American Third Army was designated the Army of Occupation and it proceeded to the Allied bridgeheads east of the Rhine. The Third Army was dissolved in July 1919; the remaining units were called American Forces in Germany, the last of which returned to the United States in January 1923. During and immediately after the war other American forces were engaged in Italy, North Russia, and Siberia.

Of the records in Record Group 120 slightly more than half are American in origin and of those about half are records of the General Staff. The most numerous of the foreign records are French, comprising about half, and German, comprising about a third. Many of the German records are manuscript and annotated maps captured in combat by American troops.

For detailed descriptions of the cartographic records in Record Group 120, see The National Archives, *Cartographic Records of the American Expeditionary Forces*, Preliminary Inventory No. 165 (Washington, 1966).

General Headquarters

67. GENERAL RECORDS. 1918. 18 items.

Maps of the St.-Mihiel and Meuse-Argonne offensives prepared to accompany the report of the Commander-in-Chief, November 20, 1918. Shown on 1:1,000,000 base maps are the daily lines of advance, divisions in the line, lines of French colonial troops, enemy defense lines, and railroads. A blueprint showing the telephone network in the Chaumont area. A group of processed and annotated 1:420,000 maps of the Archangel area in North Russia relating to Allied military operations. A 40-page booklet describing maps and aerial photographs and their use.

68. GENERAL STAFF. 1917-20. 5,484 items.

The description here given of the General Staff maps follows their arrangement, which is by organizational sections and subsections.

G-1 (Administrative Section). Printed sketch maps of France show supply facilities and a "Map Index of France" listing French towns (except those in Alsace-Lorraine and Corsica), the departments in which they are located, and the coordinates and sheet numbers for the 1:200,000 French sheets on which the towns are shown. The index is accompanied by a 1:1,265,000 Taride map of France overprinted with the grid coordinates of the 1:200,000 sheets.

G-2 (Intelligence Section). General records of the section include annotated maps similar to those accompanying the report of the Commander-in-Chief described above and maps forwarded with reports by American military attachés in various European countries.

G-2-A (Information). There are records produced by five of the nine numbered subsections of G-2-A. The records of G-2-A-1 (Order of Battle) are a large annotated map showing the enemy order of battle on the Western Front at 11 a.m. on November 11, 1918, sets of maps overprinted to show the enemy order of battle on the Western Front and on parts of it for particular days between August 14, 1917, and November 12, 1918, and a variety of printed, annotated, and manuscript maps and graphic material relating to enemy troop movements. A separate series shows similar information for the northern, central, and southern parts of the Eastern Front, the last of which is dated May 1919. A map of the Lorraine ironfield prepared by G-2-A-2 (Artillery Material, Economics, and Translations) shows underground and open mines and the 1913 production for individual mines and groups of mines. The records of G-2-A-3 (Enemy Works) are maps showing enemy defense organizations; frontlines for the German offensives in 1918; daily and weekly Allied and enemy activity, including raids, patrols, shelled and gassed areas, and aerial bombardment; and weekly summaries of enemy works showing depots, airdromes, cantonments, hospital units, battery emplacements, wire, bridges, tanks, and roads. Other maps show roads, bridges, railways, troop concentrations, water supply, geologic structure, and town plans. The records of G-2-A-6 (Radio Intelligence) are sets of maps which graphically summarize, usually at weekly intervals, the results of surveillance of enemy artillery and field radio stations, showing call letters, locations and types of stations, and for some dates message frequency and distribution. The records of G-2-A-7 (Air Intelligence) are maps of the enemy air order of battle, enemy airdromes and other installations, flights, and an incomplete set of exhibits made to accompany the report of the Air Order of Battle Section. Maps relating to bomb targets include printed, annotated, and processed maps showing bomb hits on various cities, charts showing targets and tonnages of aerial bombardment by American squadrons in August and September 1918 and by British squadrons for June through October, and material relating to Metz targets and reconnaissance flights. Also included are an incomplete set of exhibits made to accompany the report of the Bomb Target Section and printed aerial photomaps and aerial photomosaics, most of which are accompanied by French bombardment maps of industrial cities in France, Luxembourg, Alsace-Lorraine, and the Rhineland.

G-2-B (Intelligence). This organization, also referred to as the Secret Service Division, was assigned espionage and counterespionage functions. One annotated map, dated February 1, 1919, shows Bolshevist activity in selected German cities at weekly intervals during the period January 4-February 1.

G-2-C (Topography, Map Supply, and Sound and Flash Ranging). The records consist of general maps and maps of surveys, topographic compilations, and maps by the Mobile Topographic Unit. Some of the maps were made by the 29th Engineers under the direction of G-2-C. There are also general maps and reprints of foreign maps by the 29th Engineer Base Printing Plant, also under the direction of G-2-C.

The general records are principally base and outline maps of France and Europe and railroad maps of parts of France and Germany, but there are also annotated maps of the frontlines in Italy and a plan of Chaumont. The surveys by G-2-C are for airdromes, hospital sites, railroad yards, a tank field, and a camp; there is also one of Belleau Wood made in May 1919. Topographic compilations from French sources by the 29th Engineers include 1:20,000 and 1:50,000 sheets; maps of camps, practice grounds, and artillery fields; and a plan of Coblenz from German sources. Surveys by the 29th Engineers are principally of hospital sites. There are two topographic maps by the 109th Engineers. Two specially overprinted maps represent the work of the Mobile Topographic Unit, which was in operation after hostilities. Base Printing Plant general records include manuscript sheets outlining divisional training areas, photo visibility studies, photomaps of 1:50,000 topographic sheets, and other maps printed at the plant. The reprints include sheets of the French 1:200,000, 1:50,000, and 1:20,000 base maps and the same series with trench overprint, and 1:10,000 and 1:5,000 trench maps. Sheets reprinted from the German 1:50,000 and 1:20,000 maps are principally for the Rhineland area.

G-3 (Operations Section). These are general records and GHQ Map Room records. Among the general records are printed and annotated operations maps relating principally to the two major American offensives; maps of the frontlines, including the lines on November 11, 1918, and various maps showing successive daily lines; an annotated set of maps showing the length of front occupied by Belgian, British, French, and American forces beginning on January 31, on February 28 and March 21, and at 10-day intervals thereafter to November 11; and two volumes of material on the projected Metz offensive and the Metz fortifications. Map Room records—most of which were produced after the armistice—are printed and annotated operations, sector, and boundaries maps, many of which summarize in graphic form the major defensives and offensives and the American participation therein; a 34-volume set of annotated combined order-of-battle maps compiled from French sources daily from August through October 1914, weekly thereafter through March 1917, daily thereafter through May 14, 1919, and on additional days to June 22; sets of situation maps and maps showing the location and movements of American divisions; maps showing ground gained; graphic material tabulating activities of divisions in line; tracings showing the German lines of advance in 1918, studies of divisional frontlines and related material by Lt. Thomas North, and visibility studies.

G-4 (Coordination Section). This section exercised General Staff direction over Services of Supply activities. It produced general maps of supply facilities, a few plans for ammunition parks, and maps of hospital and transportation facilities. Other maps show administrative boundaries, regulating areas, progress for various services, and detailed locations of sections and facilities.

G-5 (Training Section). The records of this section include general maps of training areas, annotated sheets showing boundaries of divisional training areas, and a set of maps prepared by the AEF General Staff College for its training course.

In addition to the maps arranged under General Staff sections, there are other maps not identified as the products of particular sections. Annotated maps and a few manuscript and printed maps are arranged by subject matter as follows: information about the enemy, including location of units, sector organization, order of battle, defense lines, artillery, defensive works, camps, railroads, and other subjects; information relating mainly to American artillery and antiaircraft areas, zones, boundaries, and frontiers; sectors, objective lines, and maps to accompany field orders; frontlines, successive fronts, major operations, and divisional fronts; defensive lines and works; situations, positions, and operations; roads and railways; industries, mines, and industrial areas; combined order of battle; towns; bridges, depots, dumps, and salvage; technical matters, including communications, water supply, and defiladed areas; service and supply facilities; special reports, studies, and lecture material; and, for areas other than the Western Front, principally order-of-battle maps.

69. TECHNICAL STAFF. 1917-18. 102 items.

The cartographic records of the Technical Staff resulted from activities of the Chief Engineer not transferred to Services of Supply direction. They include a printed outline map of France and annotated maps showing roads, divisional training areas, and roads in the Italian-Austrian-Balkan area. Records of the

Geologic Section include printed geologic maps with color added to show surface formations, annotated maps showing quarries, a geologic cross section, and printed water-supply maps. There are also annotated maps of water-supply studies.

70. ADVANCE GENERAL HEADQUARTERS. 1918-19. 30 items.

Annotated situation maps from the G-3 Map Room showing division, corps, and army boundaries and headquarters on November 9, 10, and 12-16; December 5-24 and 26; January 20; and February 19.

Services of Supply

Under the provisions of paragraph 5, General Order No. 31, February 16, 1918, the chiefs of the administrative and technical staff services were directed to exercise all of their functions relating to procurement, supply, transportation, and construction under the coordinating direction of the Commanding General, Services of Supply (SOS). Most of the records described below are construction surveys or plans resulting from the activities of the Corps of Engineers. A few are by other technical departments.

71. SERVICES OF SUPPLY HEADQUARTERS. 1918. 1 item.

From the Chief Billeting Officer, Renting, Requisition, and Claims Service, SOS, an annotated 1:200,000 map showing the arrondissements of Tours and Blois.

72. SERVICES OF SUPPLY SECTION. 1918. 14 items.

A progress chart and map of construction in divisional areas by the Section Engineer, Advance Section; an annotated construction map of the St.-Nazaire area by the Chief Engineer of Base Section One; plans and layouts for the Talmont and Bassens docks and telephone installations at Pauillac Naval Air Station by the Chief Engineer and Base Signal Officer of Base Section Two; and plans of Camp Pontanezen, Brest, a drycleaning and salvage plant, and a barracks by the Chief Engineer Officer, Base Section Five.

73. SERVICES UNDER SOS. 1917-19. 150 items.

Engineer Department records consist of general maps and construction plans by the Chief Engineer; records of the Division of Construction and Forestry, which include plans for a rest camp, depots, terminal yards and docks, progress maps, and a forestry troop location map; and records of the Division of Light Railways and Roads, which include maps and plans of facilities and combat railway systems in various sectors. Some items are identified only by the regiment that produced them; included are records of the 13th, 15th, 16th, 17th, and 21st Engineer Regiments.

The Transportation Corps was organized as a department and a service under a Director General of Transportation before its corps designation became effective on November 12, 1918. Most of the material related to this organization consists of dock, port, and depot plans, and also tonnage routing maps by the Engineer of Construction. There is also a general map of proposed lines of communication. Some of the Corps' functions were taken over from the Chief Engineer of the AEF; others were returned to organizations in the Engineer Department; and the Army Transport Service, for which there is one map, was transferred to the Transportation Corps from the Quartermaster Corps on December 18, 1917.

Among the records of the Chief Surgeon are various hospital plans, including one from the Hospitalization Division showing the location of fixed Medical Department units at the time of the armistice.

Maps from the Office of the Chief Signal Officer show telephone and telegraph systems in France and England. A map from the Post Signal Officer at GHQ shows lines and stations in the Chaumont area.

An Ordnance Department map shows a depot layout near Jonchery-Villers-le-Sec.

A Motor Transport Service map shows truck routes, gasoline stations, proposed tank capacities, and oil depots.

Arms and Services

74. AIR SERVICE. 1918-19. 194 items.

A map showing Air Service stations; two sets of maps annotated to show movements of air units between January 17 and November 11, 1918; a bound volume containing principally annotated maps showing Allied airfields and locations of units; a bound volume of annotated, manuscript, and printed maps and graphic material showing German balloon ascensions, airfields and defenses, railways and base sections, bombardment objectives and lines of destruction, and the Allied situation and organization; and a similar bound volume of maps showing frontlines, German airfields, target distances, targets and tonnage of Allied serial bombardment, balloon observation areas and points of ascension, sectors and general areas of operations, and a sketch of river systems.

75. COAST ARTILLERY CORPS. 1917-18. 2 items.

Two blueprint plans of the camp near Haussimont: one dated December 18, 1917, showing building layouts and progress of construction; and one dated March 11, 1918, showing layouts and contours.

76. TANK CORPS. 1918. 10 items.

Maps showing the operations of the Tank Corps in the St.-Mihiel offensive, maps to accompany the report of operations from September 27 to October 1 around Le Catelet, and maps showing operations around Le Cateau on October 17 and 23, including a communications-system sketch and order-of-battle maps.

American Forces in Italy, Germany, and Siberia

77. AMERICAN TROOPS IN ITALY. 1918. 3 items.

Two annotated maps to accompany the report of the 332d Infantry on the campaign in Italy, October 28-November 18, and an annotated map of principal enemy roads copied from an Italian Fourth Army map.

78. AMERICAN FORCES IN GERMANY. 1919. 5 items.

Maps annotated to show the location of American units on June 26, July 19, and August 2; and two maps of the occupied areas annotated to show sector and administrative boundaries.

79. AEF, SIBERIA. 1918-19. 99 items.

Manuscript, blueprint, and photoprocessed maps by the Engineer Office, based on Russian General Staff maps of parts of Russia, Siberia, China, and Japan at scales of 1:1,680,315, 1:420,079, and 1:84,000. Shown are place names, roads, and hydrography, and in some instances topography. Included are a few items copied from maps by the Engineer Office of the Philippine Department. Other maps show the Volga Basin, Mesopotamia, and Vladivostok and vicinity.

Troop Organizations

80. ARMIES. 1918-19. 1,421 items.

Most of the maps of the First (814 items), Second (260 items), and Third (347 items) Armies originated in general staff sections and in the offices of the chiefs of technical services. Common to all three armies are serial publications containing information about the enemy by G-2, published or reprinted maps by G-2-C (primarily base or topographic), and situation maps prepared in the G-3 map rooms. The Third Army maps relate primarily to the occupation of Germany. The area covered by these maps coincides generally with army fronts and zones, and enemy areas under army responsibility.

First Army general records include an annotated map relating to the transfer of sector responsibility from the French and a printed map accompanying a report showing German defensive organization in the Meuse-Argonne. G-1 maps show roads, traffic, circulation, billeting areas, camps, zones of passage, various area organizations, and the locations of positions of command for some corps and divisions. G-2 maps are weekly or daily graphic summaries of enemy activity, periodic maps of the enemy order of battle, radio intelligence sketch maps showing enemy stations and call letters, maps showing frontlines for the St.-Mihiel and Meuse-Argonne operations, and maps showing enemy railways, dumps, works, and other features. G-2-C maps are base, trench, and other maps, including sheets showing the army front on November 11, reductions or editions of French maps, a map of divisional training areas, town plans, surveys of German positions made after the armistice, and a few printed maps showing information about the enemy. G-3 maps are operations maps (particularly defensive and offensive plans), maps to accompany field orders, and observations plans. There are similar maps from the Map Room. One set of maps issued daily shows the frontline during the period September 26-November 10 at 1100 hours and during the period October 20-November 10 at 2100 hours. Two files of daily situation maps, one sent to the GHQ Map Room and one to the Chief of Staff, First Army, show army and corps limits and positions of command, divisional command positions, and American and French divisional areas. Maps for some dates are missing from each of the files, but together they cover the period August 26-December 3.

First Army Artillery Information Service maps show enemy movements and works, Allied and enemy observation posts, artillery objectives, and areas visible from observation posts. Other artillery maps show enemy artillery activity, October 1-November 10, and various operations maps show battery positions and grouping, sectors of fire, and targets on maps accompanying field orders. Maps in a report volume show objectives of enemy batteries.

Maps from the Office of the Chief Engineer, First Army, show roads, railroads, mills, water-supply points, and dumps. There are also bridge maps and plans in the Meuse-Argonne region from the Bridge Section and water-supply maps from the Water Supply Service. Operations maps of the 1st Gas Regiment were made to accompany the report of the Chief Gas Officer, and other maps were made to accompany his lecture on January 13, 1919, on gas operations in the major American offensives. Communications maps from the Chief Signal Officer show command, artillery, and air networks.

Second Army G-1 maps show circulation and divisional police areas. One G-2 map shows enemy order of battle only, and a graphic summary-of-intelligence series shows enemy order of battle and other details of enemy activity, October 13-November 10. Other G-2 maps show radio intelligence data and details of German works and positions. G-2-C material includes a series of maps of the Rhine area enlarged from German maps and various editions and reprints of French artillery objective and trench maps. Special maps by G-2-C show roads and railroads, plans of Metz and Toul, divisional areas, German batteries, mines and works, and geodetic artillery firing data. G-3 Map Room material consists of various maps showing boundaries, limits, and areas, and situation maps showing army, corps, and division headquarters and boundaries, frontlines, and American and French divisional areas between October 12 and February 25, 1919. There are maps showing roads, waterpoints, and railways from the Office of the Chief Engineer. Other maps relate to instructions for the march into Germany, billeting areas, and observation posts.

Third Army G-2 maps show the enemy order of battle at the armistice and the assumed order of battle or German troop locations and movements on various dates up to June 20, 1919. G-2-C maps are reprints of German maps of western Germany, enlargements of German maps of the Rhine area, and reprints of British maps of northwestern and central Germany. There are also a few town plans, roadmaps and railroad maps, and maps of local political boundaries for the occupied area of Germany. G-3 Map Room situation maps are in two files, one of which was forwarded to GHQ. Together they cover the period November 17, 1918-June 30, 1919, at daily intervals until January and at weekly intervals thereafter, showing army, corps, division, and occasionally brigade headquarters, army and corps boundaries, and divisional areas. Other G-3 material consists of maps accompanying field orders related to the occupation limits and a volume showing limits and situations. Maps from the Office of the Chief Engineer include town plans and general roadmaps and railroad maps in the army area. Radio, telephone, and telegraph systems and circuits are shown on maps from the Office of the Chief Signal Officer. A map by the Information Section, Air Service, shows units assigned to the First Army during the Meuse-Argonne operations.

81. CORPS. 1918-19. 649 items.

The records of I-IX Corps are arranged by corps, thereunder by general staff section or technical service, and thereunder by general subject or type of record. The numbers of items for I-VI Corps, which were operational during hostilities, their general areas of operations, and the inclusive dates shown on the maps are as follows: I (118), Château Thierry-Belleau, Toul-Nancy, St.-Mihiel, and Meuse-Argonne, February 15-November 9; II (37), Ypres, Le Cateau, Le Mans, March 30-January 18; III (135), Aisne-Marne, Meuse-Argonne, and Germany, August 3-June 28; IV (136), St.-Mihiel and Germany, August 15-June 28; V (87), St.-Mihiel and Meuse-Argonne, September 12-January 27; and VI (10), Pont-à-Mousson and northwest of Metz, October 2-March 28.

The types of maps arranged under general staff sections and technical services for I-VI Corps are as follows: G-1, circulation maps for I, III (and billeting), IV, and V; G-2, enemy order of battle and other information for I (and frontlines), II, III, IV (and postarmistice survey of German defenses and a map of prisoner interrogation), V (and maps to accompany reports), and VI; G-2-C, base and other printed maps for all corps except II; G-3, maps to accompany field orders for all corps, frontlines for III and IV, operations for I, II, V, and VI, situation for I, II, IV, and VI, and progress for IV; artillery or Artillery Information Service for all corps except II and VI; Office of the Chief

Engineer powerlines for I, and Engineer School plans for I and II; and Office of the Chief Signal Officer communications systems for I, III, and IV.

Maps by VII Corps (116) show areas covered by the march to Germany and the occupation areas, including G-2-C roads, railroads, town plans, and other printed maps, G-3 situation, phase and operations maps, Office of Corps Engineers railroad map, and Chief Signal Officer communications systems maps.

Maps by VIII Corps (9) relate to divisional terrain exercises in France after the armistice. One map printed by IX Corps shows the St.-Mihiel operations of the First Army.

82. DIVISIONS. 1918-19. 1,459 items.

There are cartographic records for the 1st Division (176 items), the 2d Division (280 items), and for the other Regular Army, National Guard, and National Army divisions.

Manuscript, annotated, and printed maps by the 1st Division include various maps for the Royaumieux, Ansauville, and Cantigny sectors, operations and situation maps and a compiled battleline map, maps to accompany reports, and printed maps by G-2, Signal Office, and 1st Engineers.

Manuscript, annotated, and printed maps by the 2d Division include situation maps; maps to accompany reports; maps showing enemy order of battle, artillery, and communications; maps based on air photos; and annotated enemy activity, works, and movements maps.

Maps for the other divisions are arranged by unit and thereunder by subject or type. The material consists in general of situation maps showing the locations of units, most of which were sent to GHQ, G-3 Map Room; annotated and manuscript maps made after the armistice to accompany reports; other maps, principally by division G-2 or engineers; maps to accompany field orders; and maps of attached units. The numbers of maps extant for the respective divisions are as follows: situation maps for the 6th (7), 31st (1), and 88th (5); situation and report maps for the 3d (73), 27th (24), 29th (11), 30th (9), 35th (14), and 80th (25); situation, report, and other maps for the 4th (28), 5th (19), 7th (24), 26th (88), 28th (39), 32d (32), 33d (141), 37th (22), 42d (113), 77th (112), 78th (35), 81st (15), 82d (20), 89th (31), and 92d (12); report and other maps for the 36th (32), 79th (11), 90th (19), and 91st (16); and miscellaneous maps for the 41st (5).

AEF Historical Activities

These annotated and manuscript maps, relating to the records of troop organizations previously described, represent three stages of historical work with AEF records. Established as an adjunct to the AEF Historical Section, the Historical Archives worked closely with GHQ in France although it was under the direction of the Historical Branch of the War Plans Division of the General

Staff in Washington. After the closing of GHQ in France, the Historical Branch continued during 1919-20 to collect records of the AEF in Washington. Its functions passed to the Historical Section of the Army War College, in which were established working sections for the publication of materials relating to the 1st and 2d Divisions. The facilities of the Engineer Reproduction Plant at Washington Barracks were used for some of this work. Atlases accompanying the published records of the 1st and 2d Divisions are in Record Group 165.

83. HISTORICAL ARCHIVES. 1919. 116 items.

These maps, most of which were received by the Historical Archives in May 1919, are similar to maps made to accompany reports of troop organizations. There is material for the First Army and First Army Artillery, I, II, III, IV, and VI Corps, the Tank Corps, the 2d, 5th, 6th, 27th, 29th, 30th, 32d, 36th, 42d, 77th, 78th, 80th, 81st, 82d, 89th, 90th, and 92d Divisions, and the 56th Engineer Searchlight Regiment.

84. HISTORICAL BRANCH. 1919-20. 737 items.

Most of these maps are annotated, and they are arranged in a numeric classification system which indicates the troop unit, staff section, and the general subject matter of the map. In some instances the base or overprinted portion of the map was classified, and the annotations show information not included in the classification. There are a few general maps showing facilities and a few for the First and Third Armies. Much of the corps and division material consists of operations maps, maps showing troop locations, and maps of defensive plans and organizations. There are maps for all corps except IX, for the regular divisions except the 6th and 8th, and also for the 26th, 29th, 30th, 36th, 42d, 76th, 77th, 89th, and 92d Divisions. There are in addition maps apparently of French and Italian origin similarly classified.

85. HISTORICAL SECTION. 1918-32. 1,125 items.

Maps of the 1st Division consist of a variety of annotated maps of the Cantigny, Ansauville, and Meuse-Argonne sectors, 1st Field Artillery Brigade firing plans, maps of the occupation of Germany, and other miscellaneous items, including reproduction media and tracings of German maps and of maps in other files.

Maps of the 2d Division consist of folders of situation and artillery maps, maps for the Château-Thierry, Soissons, St.-Mihiel, Somme-Py, and Meuse-Argonne sectors, maps related to the occupation of Germany including situation maps, and tracings of maps in Marine Corps files.

Maps copied by the Engineer Reproduction Plant are principally situation maps for the 1st and 2d Divisions.

Allied Organizations

86. BELGIAN. 1911-19. 479 items.

General maps showing roads, railroads, and navigable waters, printed maps by the Military Cartographic Institute, large-scale *plans directeurs* by the Army Topographic Service and the Ground Survey Group, various General Staff maps, and manuscript maps of industrial complexes.

Among the records of the Military Cartographic Institute are a 1911 map of Belgium showing railroads, roads, and navigable waters, and a partial set of Belgian 1:40,000 topographic maps and 1:20,000 topographic sheets, some with artillery grid. Most of the *plans directeurs* of Belgium are 1:5,000 and a few are 1:10,000 and 1:20,000.

Maps from the Belgian General Headquarters General Staff are by the Second Section. They include 1:200,000 enemy order-of-battle maps dated January 30-October 1, 1918; 1:20,000 maps for various parts of the Belgian front dated December 2, 1917-September 11, 1918; maps showing enemy artillery activity; various situation maps relating to German troop locations in 1914, 1918, and 1919, and to Bolshevik, anti-Bolshevik, Ukrainian, and German troops in Russia in 1918; and other maps showing information about the enemy, including batteries, works, defenses, communications, supply facilities, railways, bombardment objectives, aviation signals, and zones.

An undated annotated map shows details of the German occupation of Belgium, and manuscript 1:100,000 maps show roads, railways, and navigable waters. There are eight general 1:320,000 maps and 245 detailed 1:20,000 sheets for Belgian industries, which show the locations of blast furnaces, railway rolling stock plants, chemical industries, timber and bridge shops, steel works and rolling mills, and powder and explosive plants.

87. BRITISH. 1908-19. 1,720 items.

Topographic and subject matter maps by the Geographical Section of the General Staff, maps showing the distribution of enemy forces on various fronts, General Headquarters maps of the enemy order of battle and other subjects on the Western Front, maps by armies and other organizations, and a few maps of undetermined origin, some of which are annotated.

Parts of the 1:1,000,000 (International Map of the World) series by the Geographical Section, General Staff, including sheets covering much of Europe and parts of Asia and Africa. There are also 1:420,000 sheets of Russia, particularly the Murmansk-Archangel region, 1:250,000 sheets covering parts of England, France, the Rhineland, and northwest Europe, and 1:100,000 sheets covering parts of the Balkans and Turkey, Belgium, the Netherlands, France, and the Rhineland. Maps on a larger scale include 1:40,000 trench maps of parts of Belgium, the Netherlands, and northeastern France, 1:25,000 sheets of the Rhineland, 1:20,000 topographic and trench maps of parts of Belgium, the Netherlands, and France, and 1:10,000 and 1:5,000 trench maps.

Also from the Geographical Section, General Staff, are maps at various scales showing sequential frontlines in British sectors of the Western Front and in Palestine; town plans and town bridge maps; roadmaps and bridge maps, principally for Belgium, showing span lengths, road widths and surface, and railway and foot bridges; railway maps for various parts of the Western Front, Germany, Poland, and Palestine; water-supply maps for Belgium showing wells, springs, reservoirs, pumping stations, daily capacities, and depth of wells; maps prepared for night use by aviators; maps of the Balkans, northwestern France, part of Belgium, and the Vladivostok area in Siberia; a map showing German army corps districts; and an ethnographic map of central and southeastern Europe.

Serial maps prepared at GHQ show the distribution of enemy forces during late 1917 and 1918 on base maps prepared by the Geographical Section, General Staff, on the Western, Italian, Russian, and Balkan Fronts, and in southern Russia, Turkey, and Persia. Maps from the War Office show the situation in Russia and Siberia during the period July 29, 1919-August 4, 1919.

Enemy order-of-battle maps for the Western Front were made by various units of the Royal Engineers at General Headquarters and Advance General Headquarters; they are 1:1,000,000 maps showing the entire front for days between July 1, 1917, and November 11, 1918, and 1:250,000 maps for specific segments of the front. There are also 1:100,000 sheets showing German railways, defensive lines, headquarters, ammunition dumps, and other details for parts of the front.

An Air Ministry map shows the organization and location of German aviation training establishments on September 3, 1918, and another shows areas, groups, and RAF stations in the British Isles on November 16, 1918.

A Tank Corps Headquarters map shows operations, August-November 1918, with locations and numbers of tanks and lines of advance for the First, Third, and Fourth Armies.

Maps from GHQ show billeting areas and boundaries, the grouping of German guns around Ypres, Lille, and Cambrai, German and Belgian town plans, frontlines on the Western Front and in Italy, the battles in Flanders in 1917, German troop movements by rail to and from Flanders in 1917 and during the spring offensives in 1918, the distribution of German forces and order of battle, enemy wireless station activity for the period March 14-October 25, 1918, and hostile airdromes, night lighting, and signal lights.

Dated maps at various scales show information overprinted by the First through Fifth Armies along the front, and maps and diagrams by the Army of the Rhine show areas, routes, and telephone circuits for the Cologne bridgehead.

Other maps with information overprinted by field survey units of the Royal Engineers and by unidentified organizations show enemy organization, order of battle, artillery positions, targets, trenches, and other information.

An annotated map shows Second Army area water supply in the Ypres area, and a bound volume of annotated maps illustrates boundaries north of Lens, defenses east of Arras, boundaries and objectives near Langermarck, and other information.

88. FRENCH. 1871-1920. 5,742 items.

More than half of these are printed *plans directeurs* by the Ground Survey Groups and printed topographic maps on various scales by the Army Geographical Service. There are a few items by the Finance and Interior Ministries and by services attached to General Headquarters. Maps by the General Staff, Second Bureau, and by French armies constitute about a fifth of the material, and there are also maps by French corps, other printed maps, and a series of annotated and manuscript maps.

Maps by the Ground Survey Groups consist of 1:50,000 base and trench maps for the Vosges region and for other areas, sets of *plans directeurs* for most of the Western Front, both base maps and dated editions with trench overprints, on scales of 1:20,000, 1:10,000, and 1:5,000, and also panoramic sketches showing views from observatories, aerial photomaps, industrial target maps, "night maps" made for the use of aviators, and town plans.

A few of the maps by the Geographical Service are 1:1,000,000 sheets of southern and eastern Europe, but most are of France (incomplete sets on scales of 1:600,000, 1:500,000, 1:320,000, 1:200,000, 1:80,000, and 1:50,000). There are also reprints of Italian and German maps, notably sets of 1:300,000 and 1:20,000 German maps, the latter of the Rhineland, and other maps of German postwar boundaries, troop movements on the Eastern Front, and camps.

A reprint of the "Carte Cantonale de la France" and sheets of the 1:100,000 map of France prepared by order of the Minister of the Interior.

A few maps made by GHQ services show railroads, enemy communications networks and airfields, and supply and transportation zones. One item from the General Artillery Reserve relates to the movement of American gun carriages.

General Staff maps by the Second Bureau are enemy order-of-battle maps, most of which show 1918 information, for the Western Front and also for Turkey and the Near East, Russia, the Balkans, and Italy. The Second Bureau or its sections, alone or in cooperation with railroad commissions, prepared for bombardment purposes a variety of maps showing industrial targets, such as railways, stations, factories, and bridges, for cities in Belgium, Luxembourg, France, Alsace-Lorraine, and the Rhineland provinces. Other maps include aerial photo target maps, an ethnographic map of Austria-Hungary, railway maps, and a map of German troop organization in 1920. A few maps showing the order of battle on the Italian Front were made under the direction of the General Staff of the Advance Group.

Maps dated 1917 and 1918 showing by overprinting a variety of information about the enemy, artillery in general, and French supply and communications were produced by various organizations, principally the Second Bureau of the General Staff, of the French First through Eighth Armies and the Tenth Army. Most of these maps are from the Second and Eighth Armies, mainly for areas where American units served under French command. Twenty-four French corps and corps topographic sections maps show information about the enemy and other details. About two-thirds of the maps not identified by organization show information about the enemy, and there are also maps showing French activities, bombardment maps of railways and industrial cities, and a map showing the First American Army camps. There are a few maps for other fronts, principally Palestine, the Caucasus, northern Russia, and Italy.

A series of annotated and manuscript maps is arranged in two groups, each with more detailed subject matter classifications, and there is a third group for French troop units, most of which is related to XXI Corps and the 65th Division. Classifications include enemy information, mines, situation, lines, zones and sectors, artillery, towns and ports, camps and training areas, order of battle, air bombardment, communications and supply, railways, and areas not on the Western Front, principally the Balkans, Siberia, and the Rhineland.

89. ITALIAN. 1895-1919. 531 items.

Topographic maps by the Military Geographical Institute, special printed maps by the Supreme Command and by Italian armies, various other printed maps, and a few annotated maps.

Among the records of the Military Geographical Institute are 1:500,000, 1:200,000, and 1:100,000 topographic maps of northern Italy, incomplete sets of standard maps of Italy and adjacent regions on scales of 1:500,000, 1:200,000, and 1:100,000; a set of 1:200,000 maps of central Europe reprinted from an Austro-Hungarian map, and a few special maps relating to operations in northern Italy.

Maps from the Supreme Command are situation maps for the Italian Front dated between October 4, 1918, and May 26, 1919, and enemy order-of-battle maps dated between February 15 and November 1, 1918. There are a few other items, among which are maps of the battle of Vittorio Veneto and a photograph of Val Lagarina.

Of the maps specially overprinted by cartographic sections or information offices of the Italian armies, most numerous are those by the Third Army. There are also maps by the First, Second, Fourth, Sixth, Seventh, and Eighth Armies, and by the Gorizia Zone Command. The material in general includes maps showing information about the enemy, particularly defenses and positions, panoramic sketches and photographs prepared for artillery use in the mountain areas, and 1:25,000 and 1:10,000 base and trench maps.

Other printed maps, not identified by unit of origin, are: panoramic sketches; maps and photomaps; general operations and battleline maps for the Italian Front, the Western Front, and fronts in Siberia, North Russia, Palestine, Persia, Mesopotamia, and the Balkans; and various plans and sketches, including port plans of Genoa, Italy.

Annotated maps show artillery positions along the Piave, general frontlines, zones for Italian divisions south of Asiago, and zones assigned to British, French, and American troops east of Lake Garda.

Enemy Organizations

90. AUSTRO-HUNGARIAN. 1894-1917. 134 items.

A set of printed 1:200,000 topographic maps of parts of Austria-Hungary, northern Italy, and adjacent Balkan States and printed 1:75,000 topographic maps of parts of south-central Europe, both by the Military Geographical Institute.

91. GERMAN. 1848-1920. 3,325 items.

Topographic maps by the Cartographic Section of the Prussian Land Survey, the Baden and Bavarian Topographical Bureaus, and the Cartographic Section under the Deputy Chief of the General Staff, and reprints of maps from other sources. There are a few items from German Railway Offices, the Marine Office, the Air Force, and the postwar Troop Office. Maps by German troop organizations and a series of manuscript and annotated maps complete this subgroup.

Prewar maps by the Prussian Land Survey include 1:1,000,000 Mukden, Peking, and Vladivostok sheets, 1:300,000 sheets of Memel and parts of central Europe, and 1:200,000 and 1:100,000 sheets of Germany. War-period maps include 1:300,000 sheets of Belgium, France, western Germany, and Lithuania, 1:200,000 sheets of France and western Germany, 1:100,000 sheets for various parts of the Western Front, Russia, and Poland, and 1:80,000 and 1:50,000 sheets of Western Front areas. There is an incomplete set of 1:25,000 maps of the Rhineland and Alsace-Lorraine compiled during the period 1880-1915, and there are German reprints of 1:60,000 sheets of Belgium and 1:80,000 sheets of France.

Topographic maps by the Baden Topographical Bureau at 1:25,000 show that part of Baden bounded by Alsace, the Bavarian Palatinate, and the Rhine River from Worms to the Swiss border.

Topographic maps by the Topographical Bureau of the Bavarian General Staff show the region around Abbeville, Montreuil, and along the Meuse at 1:50,000. Other maps from the Bureau, dated 1848-67 and 1907-13, show parts of the Palatinate.

Topographic maps by the Cartographic Section under the Deputy Chief of the General Staff are 1:300,000 sheets of areas in Poland, Russia, France, and western Germany, and 1:200,000, 1:100,000, 1:80,000, and 1:25,000 sheets of areas along the Western Front.

There is a railway map made for furlough purposes from the General Staff railway office, a 1914 railway map from the German railway office, annotated billeting and garrison maps of 1920 from the Troop Office showing proposed areas and distributions of German armies, and 1:10,000 and 1:5,000 aerial photomaps from the Commanding General of the Air Force.

Topographic base maps, trench maps, and other special maps are among the items produced by the First, Second, Fourth, Fifth, Sixth, and Isonzo Armies, and "Detachment C." Groups Maas-West and Gorz are principally represented in the dated maps relating to enemy artillery activity and battery positions, but there are also maps by Groups Argonnen, Metz, Mihiel, Oise, and Py, some of which also show communications, railroads, camps, and sector boundaries. Various overprinted maps from Army and Reserve Corps show details of trenches and technical works and information about the enemy on the Western Front. There is also a map showing camps around Treviso and the enemy situation around Riga. Maps by 12 artillery commands relate principally to target zones. Maps by 24 divisions show a variety of information. There are topographic base, trench, and special maps, principally at scales of 1:25,000, 1:10,000, and 1:5,000 for American sectors of the Western Front, prepared by 18 survey units attached to German armies. There are also a few items showing enemy artillery activity, flash and sound ranging units, maps by regiments and engineer companies, and other printed and processed maps and graphic material.

A large group of manuscript and annotated maps of the Meuse-Argonne and St.-Mihiel areas relating to infantry and defensive positions, artillery operations, communications and technical services, and other subjects are arranged on a sector and subject basis. A smaller group of similar maps covers other areas of the Western Front, northern Italy, and the Kolditschewo area; and other annotated and manuscript maps not identified by area complete the series.

RECORDS OF THE CHIEFS OF ARMS. RG 177

The Chiefs of Arms included the Chiefs of Coast Artillery and Field Artillery (formerly a single Chief of Artillery), and the Chiefs of Infantry and Cavalry. Each was responsible, under the direction of the Chief of Staff, for the supervision of schools, the formulation of tactical doctrine, and the preparation of manuals and training literature for his arm.

During the 1942 reorganization of the War Department the functions of the Chiefs of Arms were transferred to the Commanding General, Army Ground Forces.

Chief of Artillery

92. THE ARTILLERY SCHOOL. 1880. 1 item.

A photoprocessed map of Yorktown, Va., and vicinity showing the area of the siege of 1781.

Chief of Coast Artillery

93. GENERAL RECORDS. 1908-13. 3 items.

Published topographic maps of Fort Adams, R.I., and vicinity and Fort Morgan, Ala., and vicinity, and a map of the artillery district at Narragansett Bay.

94. THE COAST ARTILLERY SCHOOL. 1926. 1 item.

A photoprocessed map of Yorktown, Va., and vicinity showing the earthworks constructed during the Civil War.

Chief of Infantry

95. THE INFANTRY SCHOOL OF ARMS. n.d. 12 items.

A published multisheet topographic map of the area around Columbus, Ga.

Chief of Cavalry

96. THE MOUNTED SERVICE SCHOOL. 1908. 1 item.

A published topographic map of the military reservation at Fort Riley, Kans., compiled for the maneuvers of 1908.

RECORDS OF UNITED STATES REGULAR ARMY MOBILE UNITS, 1821-1942. RG 391

The cartographic records in Record Group 391 include maps compiled by Regular Army mobile (tactical) units during training operations of the approximate period 1905-42.

97. GENERAL RECORDS. 1905-42. 300 items.

Maps compiled by infantry, cavalry, and artillery regiments, chiefly photoprocessed copies of topographic quadrangles that had been annotated to show military information; most of these are from the period about 1905-12.

Post-World War 1 records of various corps and divisions, including chiefly topographic quadrangles of areas near military posts or areas used for training exercises, about 1920-42.

RECORDS OF UNITED STATES ARMY COAST ARTILLERY DISTRICTS AND DEFENSES, 1901-42. RG 392

In 1901 the U.S. Army Artillery was reorganized into field artillery batteries and coast artillery companies, and the coast artillery district was established as the standard geographical command for that branch; it was subordinate to the Army division or department within which it was located. Each district consisted of one or more forts and the related minefields and other land defenses. After several reorganizations the coast artillery districts were abolished in the major Army reorganization of 1942.

98. GENERAL RECORDS. 1906, 1927. 2 items.

A photoprocessed diagram of a temporary fire-control system for the Artillery District of New London, 1906, and a photoprocessed plan of Fort Adams, R.I., 1927.

RECORDS OF UNITED STATES ARMY CONTINENTAL COMMANDS, 1821-1920. RG 393

In 1821 the United States was divided into two territorial commands by the Army: an Eastern Department and a Western Department. Between 1821 and 1920 there were numerous changes in the names and geographical jurisdiction of the commands, together with an increase in the number of commands necessitated by America's westward growth. At times the United States was divided only into departments; at other times, into military divisions and thereunder into departments; and during some periods there were also independent departments not subordinate to any division. At times the departments also were subdivided into districts.

99. GENERAL RECORDS. 1836-1920. 1,984 items.

Seminole War records of the Army of the South, including two general published maps of Florida dated 1836 and 1839; a 10th Military Department map showing General Riley's route through the mining districts of California, 1849; and a Department of Utah map showing routes reconnoitered to the east and south of Great Salt Lake, 1858.

Records of the Army of the West, including published maps showing Civil War operations in Alabama and Mississippi.

Civil War records compiled by the Divisions of the Gulf, the Mississippi, the Missouri, and the Tennessee; by the Departments of the Cumberland, the Gulf, the Mississippi, the Ohio, the South, the Tennessee, and West Virginia; and by the Middle Department. Included are general maps of the South and of individual Southern and border States, detailed maps of smaller regions and local areas, plans of specific towns and cities, strategic maps showing the overall dispositions and movements of armies, tactical maps showing in detail the disposition and movements of troops in specific battles, and plans of fortifications.

Civil War records of the Army of the Ohio, showing operations in Tennessee and Mississippi; records of the Army of the Cumberland including fortifications plans, city plans, and general regional maps, and maps illustrating operations in Kentucky, Tennessee, Alabama, and Georgia; and records of the Army of the Potomac including general regional and local maps of areas in Virginia,

Maryland, West Virginia, and the District of Columbia, and maps illustrating the Peninsular Campaign, the siege of Petersburg, and the battles in northern Virginia. For detailed listings, see The National Archives, *Civil War Maps in the National Archives* (Washington, 1964).

Records of post-Civil War divisions and departments chiefly in the Western United States for the period about 1865-1900. Included are maps of entire departments and divisions and of individual States, detailed maps of smaller regions and local areas, maps showing the routes of exploring expeditions, maps showing operations against hostile Indians, maps and plans of military posts and reservations, and maps of Indian agencies and reservations. Records of military departments and districts of the period about 1900-20 include chiefly large-scale topographic and tactical maps of areas near military posts and areas used for training maneuvers; among these are sheets from the Progressive Military Map of the United States. Also included are a few plans of military posts and reservations.

Maps compiled by units of the National Army (World War I) including chiefly plans of camps and military reservations in the United States where National Army units trained before their movement overseas. (Records of the American Expeditionary Forces are in Record Group 120.)

RECORDS OF UNITED STATES ARMY CONTINENTAL COMMANDS, 1920-42. RG 394

In 1920 the Army abolished departments as the basic units of territorial organization and replaced them with nine corps areas. The corps areas were responsible for the administration, training, and tactical control of troops assigned to their jurisdiction. During the period 1920-42 the corps area boundaries remained essentially unchanged, except for the creation of the Military District of Washington, which was separated from the Third Corps Area. In 1942 the corps areas were succeeded by armies and other commands under the Army Ground Forces.

100. GENERAL RECORDS. 1921-42. 895 items.

Records of the corps areas, including maps showing military activities, maps of military reservations and camps, strategic and tactical maps, topographic maps, and parts of the Progressive Military Map of the United States. The records of the Eighth Corps Area also include maps of parts of Mexico and the United States-Mexican border.

Records of the First and Fourth Armies, dated 1942, including topographic maps and photomaps of military reservations and training areas.

RECORDS OF UNITED STATES ARMY OVERSEAS OPERATIONS AND COMMANDS, 1898-1942. RG 395

The cartographic records of U.S. Army commands in Record Group 395 include maps from both tactical and territorial units, relating chiefly to the Spanish-American War and the Philippine Pacification, and to peacetime military activities in overseas possessions of the United States.

101. COMMANDS IN CUBA. 1898. 7 items.

Maps prepared under the direction of the Chief Engineer of the Fifth Corps, including a map showing roads traveled by the Fifth Corps from Daiquiri to Santiago de Cuba in June 1898, maps showing American, Cuban, and Spanish positions along the southern coast of Cuba and in the vicinity of Santiago, July 14, 1898, and plans of the Punta Gorda batteries. Records of volunteer Engineer units include a plan of the second floor of the Castillo de Severino and a survey of a site for a proposed national cemetery. There is also a map showing routes surveyed for a railroad in eastern Cuba, reproduced by the Chief Engineer of the Headquarters of the Army.

102. COMMANDS IN THE PHILIPPINES. 1870-1941. 1,703 items.

A series of large-scale manuscript maps prepared by Spanish troops to show routes during the campaigns of the period 1870-92. These maps were forwarded to Army headquarters by American Engineer officers in the Philippines.

After the acquisition of the Philippines from Spain the U.S. Army established a Division of the Philippines; this was superseded in 1915 by the Department of the Philippines. Among the records of the Division are a 51-sheet map of Iloilo Island from surveys of 1900, a few route sketches, and a map of part of northern Luzon showing the flight of the rebel leader Aguinaldo.

The largest group of records is from the Office of the Chief Engineer Officer. These include blueprint copies of maps from the numbered files of the Office, among them plans of battlefields, maps showing operations against insurgents, maps of individual islands, maps and plans of military posts and reservations, and maps showing land claims, boundaries of military reservations, and proposed reservations. Other records include unnumbered maps of the Philippines showing boundaries of the military departments, stations occupied by troops, military operations against the insurgents, and general maps of the Philippines and maps of the individual islands and provinces.

Many maps were prepared from surveys made by Engineer units. Among them are maps from surveys of proposed fortified sites, plans of forts and military reservations, maps from general reconnaissances of selected areas and individual islands, large-scale topographic maps of Luzon, progressive military maps, maps from surveys of railroad lines, roads, and trails, and a few manuscript maps from a military survey of Luzon.

The records of the Military Information Division include maps compiled by, numbered by, or traced in the Division. Among these are a map of Manila, maps showing the movements of Aguinaldo from November 13, 1899, to March 23, 1901, plans of posts, maps showing telegraph and telephone lines, general maps of selected areas or individual islands, and sketch maps of routes of expeditions. Other maps, compiled from studies of the Russo-Japanese War, show operations of the opposing armies and plans of Chinese forts. There are several maps of defended areas in Siam.

Records of Signal Corps units assigned to the Philippine Division include sketch maps of some of the smaller islands and a map showing the route of the cable expedition up the Lintogup River and Panquil Bay, 1900-1901.

Records of the Medical Reserve Corps of the Philippine Division include maps of the District of Infanta, one in several sheets.

Many records are from the territorial departments within the Division, including the Departments of Mindanao, Luzon, the Pacific, the North Philippines, the Visayas, and Southern Luzon. The records for the Department of Mindanao are the most voluminous, including maps showing positions of Army units, plans of posts and reservations, maps of special areas and individual islands, and maps showing routes followed by military expeditions. The records of the other departments are similar but less comprehensive.

There is a 15-sheet map, identified as having been compiled by the Engineer of Moro Province, showing construction details of a proposed railway from Camp Overton to Marahui and a map showing the territory covered by General Wood's expedition. The records of the post at Jolo, on Jolo Island, include a plan of a four-company infantry post; a plan of Camp Jossman is from the records of that camp.

Among the records of troop commands within the Division are records of the Eighth Corps including maps showing the field of operations of the Corps and its components, maps showing positions of troops, maps of parts of provinces, districts, and islands, and a few maps showing routes of expeditions.

The records of the various infantry, artillery, and cavalry regiments consist chiefly of sketches of territory covered by expeditions and of local areas in which the regiments were stationed, some showing operations or maneuvers of the troops, and plans of camps or reservations. There are a few records from General Schwan's expeditionary brigade showing the area of operations and unit positions.

Among the records of the Philippine Department, successor to the Philippine Division, are maps by G-2 showing communications facilities in the Department and a map showing stations and the troop organization of French forces in Indochina in 1939.

Among the records of the Military Information Division of the Department are reconnaissance maps of the Manila-Subic Bay area and the Manila-Batangas area. There are also a map of Europe, dated 1914, and a few maps of parts of French Indochina. The Signal Corps records consist of maps showing the telephone project at Corregidor and radio, telephone, and telegraph circuits on Luzon.

The records of the Department Quartermaster Construction Division include a map of the Philippines showing military reservations, forts, and camps in 1925 and plans of Forts Hughes and Mills. There is an operations map of Corregidor showing the emergency defense system, 1941, prepared by the Harbor Defense Office.

Among the records of the Department Engineer are maps of Luzon, including a set of topographic maps from the military survey of 1915-16; a set of the same maps corrected to 1937; enlarged military maps of areas of strategic importance; a maneuver map of Fort William McKinley; a tactical map of Baler; and maps of several of the islands, including Corregidor. Other records include topographic and tactical maps of Guam and a map of China.

103. COMMANDS IN HAWAII. 1912-42. 30 items.

Records of the Department of Hawaii, consisting of terrain maps, 1930-42; maps of individual islands, 1942; maps showing the inshore hydrography of Oahu, 1925; a map showing potential sites for military installations on Ford Island, 1914; fire-control maps, 1930-42; and a map of the Schofield Barracks Military Reservation and vicinity, 1912.

104. COMMANDS IN PUERTO RICO. 1898-1941. 39 items.

Maps from Spanish-American War troop commands, including a map showing positions defended by the Spanish at Aguadores on the San Juan River; a map of the battle of August 10, 1898, between U.S. troops under General Schwan and Spanish troops under Colonel Villanueva; a map of Guayama and vicinity showing routes of forces under General Brooke; and a preliminary survey of Ponce Bay and vicinity.

Records of the Department of Puerto Rico, which also included the Virgin Islands, include an undated and incomplete series of aerial photos of Puerto Rico; a few topographic quadrangles of Puerto Rico, 1940-41; a photomap of the Salinas training area, 1941; and roadmaps of Puerto Rico and the islands of St. Thomas, St. Croix, and Antigua, 1941.

105. COMMANDS IN THE CANAL ZONE. 1916-42. 293 items.

Maps prepared by U.S. troops in the Canal Zone, 1916-18, consisting of reconnaissance maps of Panama and of the Canal Zone, a plan of the town and post of Corozal, and a map of Quarry Heights.

Maps prepared under the direction of the Panama Canal Department, consisting of a map of the Canal Zone, 1925; roadmaps of Ancon, Balboa, and Panama, 1927; a map of the world centered on the Canal Zone, 1940; a map of the Pacific terminal cities of the Canal Zone, 1941; and topographic quadrangles of parts of Panama.

106. CHINA RELIEF EXPEDITION. 1900-1901. 24 items.

Photoprocessed maps showing the defenses of Peking and the siege of Pei-Tang, plans of forts located around the Gulf of Chihli, maps showing sites for proposed camps for U.S. troops and the operational areas of the troops, and cross sections of the Great Wall and of other walls surrounding Chinese cities, showing their composition.

107. U.S. TROOPS IN MEXICO. 1916. 15 items.

Photoprocessed copies of maps made by the 2d Engineer Battalion, assigned to the Mexican Punitive Expedition under the command of General Pershing. These include maps of Chihuahua showing operations of the expeditionary forces and the Villa forces, maps of Sonora showing troop positions, and miscellaneous position and route sketches. Manuscript maps compiled by units of the Punitive Expedition are in the General Staff Map Collection (see entry 128).

RECORDS OF UNITED STATES ARMY COMMANDS, 1942-. RG 338

In 1942 the Army's nine corps areas were succeeded by nine service commands as the basic units of territorial organization; the boundaries of the new commands were identical with those of the old corps areas. In addition to the records of the service commands, Record Group 338 includes cartographic records from the California-Arizona Maneuver Area, certain overseas commands, and a few tactical units stationed in the United States.

108. TERRITORIAL COMMANDS. 1942-52. 194 items.

Published records of the First, Fifth, Sixth, Eighth, and Ninth Service Commands, including an index to topographic maps of the First Service Command area, 1943; topographic maps of the areas around Camp Campbell, Ky., and Camp Atterbury, Ind., 1943, Camp McCoy, Wis., and Camp Ellis, Tex., 1942, and Fort Riley, Kans., and Camp Carson, Colo., 1944-46; topographic maps of parts of Texas and Arkansas, including some of areas near Camp Chaffee, 1942-46; a map showing military installations in the Eighth Service Command area, 1942; and photomaps of parts of California, 1942.

Records of the California-Arizona Maneuver Area, including topographic maps of parts of the Hawaiian Islands, 1943-51; and records of the Panama Canal Department, including topographic maps of parts of Panama, 1943-49, a roadmap of the Canal Zone, 1947, and a map of the Pacific terminal cities of the Panama Canal, 1952.

109. TACTICAL COMMANDS. 1942, 1953. 19 items.

Records of the Fifth Army, including topographic maps of parts of Missouri, 1953; and records of IX Corps including planimetric tactical maps of parts of Oregon and California, 1942.

RECORDS OF HEADQUARTERS ARMY SERVICE FORCES. RG 160

The functions of the Army Service Forces, created in 1942 to succeed the Services of Supply, were to provide services and supplies to meet Army requirements except those peculiar to the Army Air Forces. Record Group 160 contains the records of the Headquarters Staff. The Army Service Forces were abolished in the War Department reorganization of 1946.

Office of the Director of Personnel

110. INFORMATION AND EDUCATION DIVISION. 1942-46. 97 items.

The Army Information Branch in this Division supervised the preparation and production of several Army publications disseminated to the troops during World War II. The cartographic records of the Branch consist of an incomplete series of the published *Newsmap*, which included maps with related pictures and descriptive text illustrating military and civilian activities during the war. Among the records are maps of the United States showing Army areas and installations, maps of the world showing Allied, Axis, and neutral countries, maps showing the status of the territories under Axis control, maps of strategic areas, and maps of the various combat areas showing the status of the campaigns. Arranged chronologically by date of publication.

Office of the Director of Military Training

111. ARMY SPECIALIZED TRAINING DIVISION. 1943. 1 item.

An *Atlas of World Maps* issued by the Division as Army Service Forces Manual M-101. Included are 30 world maps, among them a general reference map and maps showing landforms, ocean currents and sea ice, climatic regions, vegetation types, soils, drainage basins, distributions of population, languages, and religious groups, predominant types of economic activity, major agricultural regions, fuel and power production and consumption, iron and steel production and trade, major transportation facilities, overseas shipping routes, railroads and their relationship to population distribution, and areas owned or controlled by the major powers.

RECORDS OF THE OFFICE OF THE CHIEF OF ENGINEERS. RG 77

The production and distribution of maps for the Army is, overall, the responsibility of the Office of the Chief of Engineers. Except for certain matters of policy, administration, and liaison, this responsibility is detailed in large part to the Army Map Service. A large number of operational maps and plans, however, are prepared in the field agencies of the Corps of Engineers responsible for local civil and military works and by Engineer topographical units which can be assigned to any project, area, theater, or command to assist in the accomplishment of cartographic and surveying missions.

The military and civil duties of the Office of the Chief of Engineers and of the former Corps of Topographical Engineers (1838-63) at various times in their history have included the surveying and construction of military camps and fortifications, military reconnaissance and exploration, the maintenance of river navigation and the improvement of harbors, surveying for other Government agencies, planning and constructing flood-control projects, operating locks and dams, approving plans for construction and maintenance of roads in Alaska, and maintaining public buildings and grounds in the District of Columbia. Mapping has been an important part of all these activities.

The cartographic records of the Office are composed of two major bodies: the records of the Office of the Chief of Engineers (the Engineer headquarters records) and the records of the field offices which function as the Corps of Engineers. Each of these bodies is divided into subgroups based on the administrative origin of the records.

Office of the Chief of Engineers

112. GENERAL RECORDS. 1804-1960. 853 items.

The principal series of general records is the Published Record Set, consisting of maps published by the Office of the Chief of Engineers. This series does not include maps compiled or published by specific offices under OCE; those are arranged and described as separate subgroups in Record Group 77, Records of the Office of the Chief of Engineers. Also included in the general records of Record Group 77 are a few miscellaneous maps collected by OCE.

The earliest maps in this group, dating from 1804 to about 1850, are primarily surveys for internal improvements in the eastern United States. Among them are maps showing routes surveyed for national and mail roads, surveys of rivers and harbors, surveys for locating canals, and plans of canals as constructed. Other maps show the surveys of the international boundaries with Canada and with Texas, the Ohio-Michigan boundary, the Northwest Territory, the lands assigned to emigrant Indians west of the Mississippi River, the States of Texas and Florida, the Territory of New Mexico, campaigns of the Mexican War, the Fort Smith-Santa Fe route, and the Oregon Trail from the Fremont surveys.

The maps for the period 1850-60 concern primarily the territories west of the Mississippi River. They include general topographic maps of the United States west of the Mississippi River, editions of 1850 and 1857; maps of western territories and military departments; maps from reconnaissances of routes and surveys for military roads; and maps prepared from surveys by expeditions assigned to explore or survey particular areas. Other maps for this period include a few river and harbor surveys, particularly of Chicago harbor, and a map of the State of Florida.

Most of the maps from the Civil War period, 1861-65, show military departments in the central and southeastern parts of the United States; parts of Virginia and Maryland in the vicinity of the District of Columbia, the Potomac River, and Richmond, Va., showing drainage and topography, roads and railroads, and often the boundaries of farms with the names of inhabitants; battlefields, generally showing topography and drainage, wooded areas, roads and railroads, and troop positions; and defenses, particularly those around Washington, D.C., Richmond and Petersburg, Va., and Mobile, Ala. Other maps show General Grant's campaigns in central Virginia, General Sherman's campaigns in Georgia and North Carolina, and census statistics by county in Louisiana. For detailed lists of these and other Civil War maps, see The National Archives, *Civil War Maps in the National Archives* (Washington, 1964).

The maps published during the period 1866-90 cover many subjects. Immediately after the Civil War the Engineers renewed their internal improvement activities relating to harbors and navigable rivers, and many maps were published in connection with those surveys. They also renewed their exploration and survey activities in the West and in Alaska and published maps of the regions they surveyed and of the States, territories, and military departments. In 1869 they began publishing a standard map of the United States showing military divisions, departments, and posts; new editions of this map were published at frequent intervals.

During this period the Engineers surveyed many of the Civil War battlefields and prepared detailed topographic maps showing the dispositions of Union and Confederate troops. In 1867 Maj. Nathaniel Michler headed surveys and compiled maps of the battlefields between Gettysburg and Appomattox Courthouse. Many of the maps compiled from these surveys were published in 1869 in an atlas illustrating the campaigns of the Army of the Potomac; two different versions of this atlas are included among the records. From 1872 to 1879 maps of the battlefields were published by the Office, among them a set of three maps showing the troop positions on each of the 3 days of the Battle of Gettysburg.

The Office also compiled and published or reprinted maps of foreign areas. Among these are topographical maps of Cuba, topographical maps of Turkey and vicinity identified as maps of "the Seat of War in Asia," maps of Mexico showing the Mexican National Railroad, maps of northern Egypt with part of Palestine, a map of the Egyptian Sudan, a map of Turkestan, a map of Central America, and a map of Manitoba Province in Canada showing railroad and telegraph lines.

Four extensive surveying expeditions operated in the Western States and territories during this period. Records of two of these expeditions, the United States Geological and Geographical Survey of the Territories (the Hayden Survey), 1867-69, and the United States Geographical and Geological Survey of the Rocky Mountain Region (the Powell Survey), 1869-79, are among the records of the Geological Survey (see entries 238 and 239). The other two expeditions—the United States Geographical Surveys West of the One Hundredth Meridian (the Wheeler Survey), 1869-79, and the Geological Explorations of the Fortieth Parallel (the King Survey), 1867-80—were sponsored by the War Department. The records include published atlases and other maps compiled from both of these surveys.

Included are two atlases from the King Survey—one composed of topographic and geological maps and cross sections of the area surveyed, and the other identified as *Atlas Accompanying Volume III on Mining Industry*. The latter includes a general map of the area along the 40th parallel showing mining districts, geological maps of the Washoe, Toyabe Mountains, and White Pine mining districts, and maps showing the horizontal extent of the mine shafts, longitudinal elevations, cross sections, and horizontal sections of parts of the Comstock Lode.

Among the published records from the surveys under the direction of Lieutenant Wheeler are pages from several editions of the topographical and geological atlases consisting of title sheets, legend sheets, sheets showing conventional signs, maps of the Western United States showing the annual progress of the surveys, index maps, outline maps of the United States, maps of the Western United States showing drainage basins, and topographic sheets overprinted to show land classification and geological formations. Other records include maps appearing in the annual reports and other reports compiled by Wheeler. Among these are a series of maps of North America from the period 1508-1782; a map of the Antilles, 1463; maps of forts, camps, or cities showing the sites of astronomical stations; maps showing triangulation; maps showing camps, distances, and routes, among these a map showing routes followed while surveying the Grand Canyon; a model topographic map; maps of Southern California including a map showing mounds and burial places and a map of the topographic depression in the Colorado Desert; maps of sites where river current observations were made; maps of the United States including one showing the progress of military and public land surveys in 1879, one showing the locations of hot springs, and one showing the United States divided into regions for Government surveying purposes; maps of the Washoe Mining District showing locations of claims and the Sutro Tunnel; topographic maps of Lake Tahoe, Lake Bonneville, and Yosemite Valley; a map showing the Continental Divide in parts of Colorado and New Mexico; and profiles of routes crossing the Continental Divide and of routes in southern California.

Beginning with the year 1890 and through 1960 when the series currently ends most of the maps are of the United States and show primarily administrative-type information. Among these are maps showing the navigable waterways and the tonnages carried on navigable rivers; maps showing Army activities, the older ones showing divisions, departments, camps, and posts and the more recent ones showing corps areas or service commands and Army installations by type; maps showing lines of communications; maps showing railroad systems, the project for the development of a national highway system, and military and priority railroads and highways; maps showing Engineer divisions and districts and river and harbor divisions and districts; maps showing Civilian Conservation Corps camps and the Government agencies administering them; and maps showing flood control, navigation, irrigation, and power projects planned by the Engineers. Most of these maps are in several editions.

With the maps published from 1890 to 1955 is an atlas showing troop dispositions at the battle of Antietam, Md., during the Civil War; a 1911 edition of a map showing Civil War forts and roads in Washington, D.C., and vicinity; a 1912 reprint of a set of three maps originally published in 1876 showing troop dispositions at Gettysburg for each of the 3 days of battle; a map of the "Seat of War in the East" (Turkey) in 1897; a plan of Government-owned lands at Fort Wadsworth, N.Y.; a map of Rhode Island, Connecticut, and Massachusetts; terrain, tactical, and special military maps of military reservations and other Army-owned lands in the United States dated from 1923 to 1945; a map of the United States summarizing information from the electric power survey of 1931; tactical maps of Unalaska Island in the Aleutians, 1940-41; a map of the Bermuda Islands, 1941; a map of central North Africa, 1941; city plans of Safi, Morocco, and Dakar, French West Africa, 1942; maps showing the distribution of mineral resources in Yugoslavia and mineral fuels in Bulgaria, 1943; maps of the Belgian Congo, 1943; a map of Wake Island, 1943; and topographic quadrangles of Celebes Island in the Netherlands East Indies compiled from Dutch maps dated 1927.

Also in this group are three maps and a chart from a special study of the moon published in 1960 by the Military Geology Branch of the U.S. Geological Survey for the Office of the Chief of Engineers. The chart is a verbal description of the moon's surface. One map shows lunar rays (grooves in the lunar surface radiating from craters), another is a generalized photogeologic map of the moon, and the third shows the physiographic regions of the moon.

Arranged chronologically by date of publication, when known. Undated maps have been placed in what appear to be their approximate chronological positions.

In addition to the Published Record Set, the general records of the Office of the Chief of Engineers include a few manuscript, annotated, and published maps received from the Office without file number or other identification. Many are similar to items in the two principal divisions of Record Group 77; the Headquarters (Civil Works) Map File and the Fortifications Map File, described in entries 113 and 114. File numbers were not assigned to these maps, although many bear correspondence numbers. Among them is a published map of the Pacific Ocean annotated to show areas involved in acts of King George III of England relating to whaling ships and areas under charter to the East India Company and the South Sea Company; a map of the Arkansas River used in a report of Lt. T. S. Brown, 1833; a map of Grand Traverse Bay, Mich., showing the encampments of Lt. J. N. Macomb and others, 1843-44; a tracing from one of the sheets from the 1857 survey of the southern boundary of Kansas; a map of the area around Vicksburg, Miss., similar to some Civil War maps in the

Headquarters Map File; sketches and plans of harbors on the Great Lakes, 1865-68; an undated, unidentified map of the Western United States showing locations of forts during the Indian Wars; an 11-sheet map of the Mississippi River between the mouths of the Illinois and the Ohio compiled from surveys under the direction of Colonels Raynolds and Simpson, 1870-75, with three sheets of drawings illustrating the construction of dams and dikes; a series of published maps of the Mississippi River from the Illinois River to New Orleans, dated 1870-78, annotated with changes and additions to place names and other corrections; a map of the Western United States annotated to show principal mail routes, railroads, and the route of General Rusling in 1866-67; a proposed plan of the Tortugas Lighthouse, 1856; plans of Fort Assiniboine, Montana Territory, dated 1879 and 1883; maps accompanying a report on a survey of St. Augustine, Fla., 1880, and a plan of Pensacola, Fla., traced in 1881; a plan of the Italian port of Malamocco, 1872; maps of Pointe du Bler, France, and a plan of the city of St. Hyacinthe, traced in 1897; maps showing properties surveyed on the Camp Bullis Military Reservation in 1919; tracings of the Civil War battlefield at Pea Ridge, Ark., accompanying a report of the Pea Ridge Battlefield Commission dated 1926; and a base map of the United States annotated to show numbers of short tons of freight carried in 1934 on streams in the Mississippi River Basin. There is also a bound volume of maps of parts of Canada in the vicinity of the St. Lawrence River, including both published and manuscript maps, dated from 1790 to 1843.

113. HEADQUARTERS MAP FILE. 1800-1935. 32,438 items.

Among its other duties the Office of the Chief of Engineers, until about 1890, served as a central repository for maps prepared or acquired by Army units. The cartographic records of the Corps of Engineers and the Corps of Topographical Engineers (1838-63) were placed in the Headquarters Map File, except that maps relating to fortifications were kept in a separate Fortifications Map File (see entry 114). The Headquarters Map File also includes manuscript maps forwarded by territorial and troop commands; published versions of many of these are in Record Group 393, Records of United States Army Continental Commands, 1821-1920.

This file includes many maps reflecting the explorations in the West and the territorial growth of the United States. An example is the body of manuscript maps prepared from surveys west of the 100th meridian made under the direction of Lt. George M. Wheeler, 1871-79. The original drawings from these surveys and the manuscript compilations used for the published maps are included. These and many other maps from surveys and explorations show topography and drainage, vegetation, roads and trails, Indian tribal locations, settlement patterns, and military camps and forts.

Among the early records are numerous military maps from campaigns conducted during the Seminole Wars in Florida, the wars with the Indian tribes of the West, the Mexican War, and the Civil War. The records pertaining to these campaigns include topographic maps of strategic areas, maps showing routes of military units, maps showing troop dispositions and illustrating the conduct of campaigns, and maps and plans of battlefields.

The early records also contain maps from surveys for internal improvements, including surveys for national roads, canals, and railroads, and surveys of rivers and harbors. Some of the maps show the general routes surveyed and others show details of the surveys. Other early maps include manuscript compilations later incorporated in maps published by the Engineers and many manuscript maps that were never published. There are also many manuscript compilations that were sent to the Headquarters Office by the Lake Survey.

Manuscript and annotated maps forwarded to the Engineers from sources outside the Army appear in the files. There are some maps from early harbor and coastal surveys conducted by members of the U.S. Navy and the Coast Survey, and maps captured by Army personnel during the military campaigns. A number of Confederate Army maps are among the records, as well as other maps acquired by the Union Army in occupied areas during the Civil War.

Maps of foreign areas show military operations and civil engineering activities that were observed by American officers.

Originally the maps in the Headquarters Map File were given alpha-numeric file numbers and were arranged in a system that was based primarily on geographic regions but also included a few subject classifications. Maps placed in the Headquarters Map File after about 1890, however, were given strictly numerical designations unrelated to geographic regions. After a file number was established for a map of a specific area, subsequent maps of that area were filed under the same number and assigned subnumbers. The finding aid to the Headquarters Map File is a card catalog prepared in the Office of the Chief of Engineers. The cards are arranged by State or region, or by subject, and thereunder chronologically. Many of the maps are cross-referenced by author and subject.

Many of the maps, particularly those compiled after about 1870, are stamped with correspondence numbers that relate them to correspondence files in the textual Engineer records in the custody of other branches or divisions of the National Archives.

114. FORTIFICATIONS MAP FILE. 1790-1941. 57,000 items.

Manuscript, annotated, and published and photoprocessed maps and plans of forts and camps in the United States and in U.S. territories and possessions. The records relating to the coastal forts, most of which were elaborate permanent installations, are voluminous. The records of one of these forts may consist of two or three hundred individual items including general maps predating the establishment of the fort and showing proposed fort locations and purchases of land, proposed plans for the initial construction of the fort, plans of the fort as constructed, plans of specific buildings and gun emplacements, plans of proposed and completed changes or repairs, plans for additional armament, maps showing arrangement of batteries and fields of fire, maps and plans showing progress of construction or condition of the fortification, armament reports, and other records. Most of these records date from the early 19th century to about 1920; for a number of specific forts the records cover a span of more then 100 years.

The plans of the inland forts are not as extensive as those for the coastal forts, nor are there records for all the forts that were constructed during the settlement of the interior of the United States. For the most part the existing records consist of reconnaissances for the purpose of selecting construction sites, topographic maps of individual reservations, and ground plans of the forts; for a few forts there are plans of individual buildings.

Some of the forts for which there are maps and plans were constructed and used during the Civil War. There is an extensive list of fortifications and defenses in and around Washington, D.C. Others were Union fortifications in the Border States and Union-held areas along the Atlantic and gulf coasts. There are a few captured plans of Confederate forts and defenses, some compiled by Confederate units and others by Union forces.

There are maps and plans relating to fortifications, defenses, and military operations in the U.S. territories and possessions. Puerto Rico is well represented with records pertaining to fortifications, defenses, and military operations during the Spanish-American War, including copies of Spanish plans of fortifications. A number of maps show the establishment of defenses in the Hawaiian Islands and in the Philippines.

Among the other records in this file are harbor charts showing various components of existing and proposed defenses; city plans; special maps showing areas of strategic interest; maps relating to the Mexican War including plans of Mexican defenses, maps of battlefields, and campaign maps; maps and plans relating to troop activities in the United States during the Spanish-American War; plans of Government buildings; maps and plans of the Washington Aqueduct, Washington, D.C.; maps and plats of tracts of land ceded to the United States for defensive purposes, 1775-1810; miscellaneous construction plans of standard equipment for forts, guns, floating batteries, scows, fixed bridges, pontoon bridges, barracks, officers' quarters, channel obstructions, construction equipment, experimental firings, hospitals, torpedoes, and torpedo vessels; maps and plans of Cuba showing defenses and military campaigns during the Spanish-American War; maps and plans of China showing defenses and military activities during the China Relief Expedition of 1900-1901; and maps of other foreign areas showing defenses and defense plans and internal improvements.

Arranged numerically by assigned drawer and sheet number. A list describes the records dated to about 1902 by name of fortification or by subject entry. A card catalog lists the records in the same manner and includes records dated since 1902.

115. MISCELLANEOUS FORTS FILE. ca. 1840-1920. 7,000 items.

Manuscript maps of military reservations, ground plans of forts and other military posts, and plans and views of individual buildings. Prepared by officers and men of tactical units stationed at the posts.

116. MILITARY DIVISION. 1917-41. 303 items.

The Military Division was composed of several sections concerned with problems of supply, transportation, military construction, training personnel, and intelligence. The two sections for which there are cartographic records are the Intelligence Section and the Military Construction Section.

The Intelligence Section was responsible for military mapping, map reproduction and supply, and studies of military engineering and history, a function later transferred to the Intelligence and Mapping Division in the Office of the Director of Military Operations. The records of this Section include a published set of the Harriman Geographic Index System maps covering the United States. This system was adopted by the War Department in 1919 and used for keying to the earth's surface a system of coded grids to permit the rapid and accurate location of any part of the world.

Other records of this Section consist of a map of the military reservation at Indiantown Gap, Pa., published by the Telegraph-Press, Harrisburg, Pa., and annotated to show a different version of the boundary of the reservation and uses of the areas within the reservation; maps of Camp Bragg, N.C., one annotated to show the reservation boundary and the triangulation net and the other, published from surveys of 1918, annotated to show survey points of the Coast and Geodetic Survey and the Geological Survey and suggested future work; and an uncontrolled map with superimposed transit and triangulation controls, compiled from aerial photos and drawn by Company A, 17th Engineers, Camp Meade, Md., in 1923.

The Military Construction Section was, until 1941, responsible for any activities the Engineers undertook relating to construction on military reservations. The records of this Section include photoprocessed plans of military reservations in the United States and its territories prepared by the Quartermaster General's Office and annotated to show new or proposed railways, railway facilities, warehouses, highways, and waterways in the reservations. Arranged alphabetically by name of State or territory and thereunder by name of reservation.

Other records of this Section consist of various revised editions of published maps of the United States overprinted to show boundaries and headquarters of Engineer divisions and districts for 1940 and 1941 and the jurisdiction of the Mississippi River Commission. The edition of 1940 shows for each district the number of officers, classified and unclassified civilians, and the funds available for various military and civil activities.

117. TROOPS DIVISION. ca. 1941-43. 1 item.

This Division was established during World War II to supervise the research and development program of the Corps of Engineers, the organization and training of Engineer troops and troop units, the technical Engineer intelligence program, and the Engineer mapping and map service programs. In December 1943 the Division was renamed the Office of the Director of Military Operations.

The only item included for this subgroup is a record of the Operations and Training Branch, one of whose functions was the preparation of logistical plans and studies affecting the supply and movement of Engineer units overseas. It is a published map of the Northwest Pacific area and eastern parts of Siberia and China, showing ports by class, airdromes, and river anchorage depths.

Corps of Engineers

The Corps of Engineers is composed of the field agencies of the Office of the Chief of Engineers (OCE). These agencies are responsible for carrying out military surveys and internal improvement activities assigned to OCE. Most of the actual mapping and map reproduction work originates with the Corps of Engineers, chiefly at the Army Map Service. Engineer topographical units working under various commands in the United States and in numerous foreign countries are equipped to produce maps relating to specialized activities peculiar to their assigned tasks. Maps and plans for various projects are drawn up in the Engineer divisions located throughout the country. Other maps may be prepared by the Boards and Commissions that are responsible to OCE.

118. GENERAL RECORDS. 1842-1943. 928 items.

Included are Corps of Engineers maps not identified by unit of origin and maps that were prepared by two or more subordinate units of the Corps. Records prepared by specific subordinate units of the Corps are described in subsequent entries.

The main body of records consists of an incomplete set of maps published under the authority of the Corps of Engineers. Among these is an early chart of the Detroit River; two Civil War maps of fortifications in the Gulf of Mexico area; detailed maps of surveys of navigable rivers, principally the Mississippi River and its tributaries; maps from the reconnaissances of the lava beds at Tule Lake, Calif.; a plan of Mackinac National Park; a plan of Custer's battlefield; a map of part of Arizona; a map of the southeastern coast of the United States showing locations of public works, examinations, and surveys, 1887; maps of historic grounds in the Maumee Valley of Ohio, surveyed in 1888; a few harbor plans and plans for improving harbors and waterways; plans of the Illinois and Mississippi Canal; a survey of lands at Hull, Mass., made for fortification purposes; maps of military reservations, grounds, and campsites, including many from the World War 1 period; a map of Mount Rainier National Park; miscellaneous quadrangles published as progressive military maps; tactical maps, special military maps, terrain maps, and fire-control maps, usually topographic quadrangles, of areas under military control; a base map of the United States; a map of the United States showing railway artillery routes, 1920; sheets from the 1917-18 military survey of the Philippines (see records in Record Group 395, Records of United States Army Overseas Operations and Commands, 1898-1942) with roads revised to 1933; a map of the United States showing Army facilities; an index map to aerial tri-lens photographs of Camp Meade, Md., and vicinity; atlases of the United States showing information about potential waterpower; one sheet of a two-sheet map of Tientsin, China, 1927; photomaps of military reservations, some overprinted with gridlines; flood-control plans for the Mississippi, Missouri, and Ohio River Basins; a special highway map of the United States showing the relative importance of main traffic routes to the military establishment; maps relating to plans for developing water resources in the Missouri River Basin, about 1930-39; diagrams of terrain features by type; roadmaps of North and West Africa; aviation route maps for parts of the United States; and sketch maps of possible landing fields in Greenland, 1941.

Arranged chronologically by date of publication or information.

The maps not identified by unit of origin include a group of planimetric quadrangles of parts of California in the vicinity of San Francisco and a group of planetable sheets and paper and cloth tracings of possible and proposed landing sites and airbases in Greenland, 1941.

119. MISSISSIPPI RIVER COMMISSION. 1876-1954. 1,333 items.

The Mississippi River Commission, established in 1879, was given responsibility for flood-control projects on the Mississippi and its tributaries. It is composed of three civilians, appointed by the President of the United States, and representatives from the Corps of Engineers and the Coast and Geodetic Survey. The President of the Commission is also the Division Engineer of the Lower Mississippi Valley Division, one of the several field agencies of the Corps of Engineers.

The cartographic records of the Commission consist of large-scale manuscript and published maps and charts of the Mississippi River and its tributaries and their surrounding areas. Among these are series of charts, some in bound volumes, of parts of the river and its tributaries showing the channel, aids and dangers to navigation, soundings, bridges, and distances. These charts also show features of the adjacent shore areas along the rivers, such as topography, natural vegetation, crops, bridges, railroads, transmission lines, and towns and settlements. In addition there are general maps of the river and its tributaries showing alluvial areas, alluvial deposits, proposed flood-control projects, and changes in the course of the river, 1765-1932. Other records include photomaps from a survey of the river between St. Louis, Mo., and Cairo, Ill., 1925; topographic quadrangles of areas adjacent to the river in Louisiana, Mississippi, Arkansas,

Tennessee, and Missouri showing cultural features, 1932-55; a bound volume of maps pertaining to the Intracoastal Waterway along the gulf coast, 1954; and reports relating to river heights and velocities.

Arranged in series by general subject of map. The several series from the river surveys, drawn at varying scales, cover the entire river, the upper river (above Cairo, Ill.), the lower river (below Cairo), and shorter segments of the river. The quadrangles are arranged by State and thereunder alphabetically by sheet title. Index maps to the quadrangles are among the records of the Geological Survey (see entry 242) and the Army Map Service (see entry 130).

120. MISSOURI RIVER COMMISSION. 1889-96. 286 items.

The Missouri River Commission was established in 1884 to superintend and direct improvements to the river, make appropriate surveys, and carry out plans for creating and maintaining a channel for commerce and navigation. It was composed of five members appointed by the President: three members of the Corps of Engineers and two civilians. It was abolished in 1902.

The cartographic records of the Commission consist of large-scale published maps of the river in multisheet series. These maps show the channel, aids and dangers to navigation, and soundings, and also natural vegetation, crops, and roads and railroads along the adjacent shores. A few maps show proposed improvements to the river.

The detailed survey sheets are arranged chronologically by date of publication and thereunder numerically by assigned sheet number. Index maps show the coverage of individual sheets.

121. SPECIAL BOARDS. 1901. 1 item.

A photoprocessed copy of a map showing pierhead and bulkhead lines recommended for the New York City waterfront by the New York Harbor Line Board in 1901.

122. BOARD OF ENGINEERS FOR RIVERS AND HARBORS. 1940-49. 10 items.

This Board was established in 1902 and assigned the functions of reviewing all reports on the preliminary examination and survey of river, harbor, and flood-control improvements approved by Congress; advising and assisting local port authorities in planning the layout and equipment of terminal facilities; and compiling, publishing, and distributing statistics and information about ports and inland water transportation. The Board is composed of seven Engineer officers detailed by the Chief of Engineers.

The records include published plans of the ports of Saginaw and Detroit, Mich., and Charleston, S.C., showing port facilities; maps of the Great Lakes showing information relating to shipping between Detroit and other lake ports; a bound volume from a study by the Board of Engineers for Rivers and Harbors and the U.S. Maritime Commission concerning the ports of Philadelphia and Camden and Gloucester, N.J., with maps and plans of the ports and their facilities and related textual descriptions; a bound volume from a study of the ports of Duluth and Two Harbors, Minn., and Superior and Ashland, Wis., with maps and plans of those ports and their facilities; a map of the Alabama-Coosa branch of the Mobile River system showing existing and proposed improvements; and a map of the Chesapeake Bay area showing transportation lines serving Baltimore.

123. BEACH EROSION BOARD. 1941-42. 35 items.

This Board was established in 1930 to initiate investigations and studies of coastal areas for the development of methods of preventing shore erosion due to wave and current action. These functions are carried out cooperatively with State agencies located on the Atlantic, Pacific, and gulf coasts, on the Great Lakes, and in the territories. During World War II the Board collaborated with the Military Intelligence Division of the Office of the Chief of Engineers in preparing studies of foreign beaches and ports.

The records consist of published maps of strategically located beaches and shores in foreign areas. These records are security classified and may be used only with proper authority.

124. INTEROCEANIC CANAL BOARD. 1929-31. 75 items.

In 1929 Congress authorized an investigation and survey to determine the practicability and cost of constructing an interoceanic ship canal across Nicaragua. The survey was made under the direction of the Secretary of War and the supervision of the Chief of Engineers with the aid of civilian engineers. The field survey was undertaken by the 29th Engineer Battalion (Topographic).

The records consist of manuscript, published, and annotated maps showing world trade routes; proposed canal routes across Mexico, the Isthmus of Darien, and Nicaragua; and camps, depots, gages, and the progress of the survey along the Nicaragua route finally selected. Two series of detailed manuscript maps of the survey of the Nicaragua route show topography, river soundings, and drainage; and there are plans of dams and lock sites along the Nicaragua route. Other records include maps from surveys of Lake Nicaragua and of Nicaraguan rivers; a plan of Managua showing the effects of an earthquake; a profile of the canal railroad location; miscellaneous topographic maps of Nicaragua; and series of manuscript maps relating to a proposed project for a third set of locks and for a sea-level canal at the Panama Canal.

Arranged in series by subject or type of map; those maps assigned numbers by the agency also are arranged numerically.

125. ENGINEER DIVISIONS AND DISTRICT OFFICES IN THE
     UNITED STATES. 1829-1958. 14,325 items.

The internal improvements and construction activities of the Corps of
Engineers in the United States are decentralized regionally to divisions, each of
which has jurisdiction over several district offices. The cartographic records of
the divisions and district offices consist of maps prepared by or gathered in the
individual offices, relating chiefly to activities carried on within their respective
jurisdictions.

Among the records are manuscript, published, and photoprocessed maps
and plans of harbor defenses and other fortifications, and of military
reservations; manuscript, published, and photoprocessed maps from river surveys
showing aids and dangers to navigation, channel improvements, and shoreline
features; manuscript and published maps of river basins showing existing and
proposed flood-control systems, reservoirs, dams, and locks; maps and plans of
coastal waterways; plans of proposed military and national parks; an incomplete
set of the hydrographic charts published during the period 1850-1958 by the
U.S. Lake Survey, a part of the Great Lakes Division; and manuscript maps of
proposed canals. In addition, there are plans of levees, dams, and reservoirs, and
of snag boats and other military engineering equipment.

Arranged by division and thereunder by district office; some of the maps are
further arranged by file numbers assigned in the agency.

126. ENGINEER UNITS. 1904-43. 168 items.

The cartographic records of Engineer units assigned to territorial and troop
commands are maintained with the records of those commands, principally in
Record Groups 120, 393, 394, and 395. The Army Map Service (AMS) assigned
series numbers to many maps compiled by Engineer units before AMS was
established; these maps appear as first editions of many of the AMS series.

Among the records of Engineer units not filed under specific troop or
territorial commands are published maps of Army maneuver areas in the United
States, 1904-18; plans of forts, camps, and military reservations in the United
States, 1904-43 (most of which are from the World War 1 period); maps from
surveys of the boundaries and original plots of land at Fort Belvoir, Va.,
1922-23, and of the lands adjacent to the Tobyhanna (Pa.) Government Reserve,
1923; a series of topographic quadrangles of parts of California annotated
to show benchmarks, with attached data relating to the recovery of the
benchmarks by the 29th Engineers, 1939; a series of charts of project areas in
California showing triangulation established by the 29th Engineers, 1939; special
military maps of areas in California compiled by the 29th and 30th Engineers,
1939; index maps to the topographic map coverage of Oregon and Washington,
showing the progress of mapping by the Geological Survey and the 29th
Engineers; an index map to wide-angle photographs of Willapa Bay, Wash., made
by the 69th Engineers, 1942; and a maneuvers map of the Wichita Mountains at

Fort Sill, Okla., compiled by the Engineer detachment at Wright Field, Ohio. The maps are arranged by unit of origin.

127. THE ENGINEER SCHOOL. 1918-27. 3 items.

Maps compiled from surveys made at The Engineer School, Fort Belvoir, Va., including outline and topographic maps of the Fort Belvoir reservation showing the locations of buildings on the post and a plan of sections D, E, F, V, and W. The School also has published a number of maps from compilations made by other Army commands. Most of these are filed with the records of those commands; a few are in other subgroups of Record Group 77.

The Army Map Service and Its Predecessors

The Army Map Service originated in 1942 through the merger, in the Office of the Chief of Engineers, of the War Department Map Collection and the Engineer Reproduction Plant. The AMS records are described in three separate entries—one for each predecessor unit and one for the Army Map Service itself.

128. WAR DEPARTMENT MAP COLLECTION. 1836-1942. 2,770 items.

The War Department Map Collection, originally the General Staff Map Collection, was initiated about 1895 in the Military Information Division of the Adjutant General's Office. This Division apparently succeeded the Office of the Chief of Engineers as the Army's central map repository. In 1903 it was transferred to the Military Intelligence Division of the General Staff and later it was attached to other organizations in the Army before its transfer to the Office of the Chief of Engineers in 1939.

In addition to its map-collecting functions, the staff concerned with the War Department Map Collection was responsible from 1939 to 1941 for compiling and publishing maps under its own imprint. The collection includes an incomplete set of these, in addition to other maps from a wide range of sources.

When the Army Map Service was organized in 1942 its library reviewed the former General Staff Map Collection, retaining some of the records and transferring the remainder to the National Archives. At the National Archives duplicates of published maps issued by other Federal agencies and general published maps issued by foreign governments or private publishing concerns were removed. The General Staff Map Collection as it now exists in the National Archives consists of manuscript and annotated maps compiled by Army staff units and Army commands that were forwarded to the various headquarters of the Army; manuscript, annotated, and published maps accompanying reports of military attachés and observers; maps received as gifts, usually from heirs of prominent military men; and a number of unidentified manuscript and annotated maps. They are arranged geographically by continent and thereunder by country and are described herein in the same manner.

Maps of the world show daily sources of earthquake relief for Japan during part of September 1923 and submarine cables, 1898 and 1923, and a map of the North Atlantic Ocean, dated 1919, shows routes of organized mercantile convoys, apparently used during World War I. With these are a series of manuscript topographic sheets of parts of Canada and Mexico at varying scales and large-scale maps of counties and plans of cities in Nova Scotia.

Maps pertaining to the United States and to individual States include maps of military departments, 1870-90; a map showing the stages of American territorial expansion west of the Mississippi, 1803-67; maps showing Indian and military reservations and proposed reservations, forts, and camps; and maps relating to Indian campaigns, including maps showing routes of march and plans of battlefields. Maps of the United States show Army installations and territorial commands, 1904-22. Maps relating to the mobilization plans for World War I show mobilization and concentration points, locations of supplies, and transportation facilities. A series of maps relating to the industrial unrest in 1915 and in the 1920's, prepared by the Military Intelligence Division of the General Staff, show strike areas and threatened areas, tranquil areas, unionized and nonunion areas, areas of unemployment, and areas where communists, socialists, anarchists, and members of the International Workers of the World were active. Other maps of the United States consist of miscellaneous indexes to different series of maps published by units of the Army and by other Federal agencies, and maps showing transportation facilities, airways, telegraph lines, operating zones for electric companies, congressional districts in 1915, and the route taken by Hon. W. Frank James investigating housing conditions in the U.S. Army in 1927.

Maps filed by State include those relating to the Seminole campaigns in Florida, 1836-38, those showing routes taken by the Army in Arizona in the 1860's and '70's, plans of military reservations, 1870-1940, a few maps relating to military operations during the Civil War in Virginia, Maryland, and Georgia, and maps relating to Army training maneuvers, particularly before World War I.

Maps pertaining to Mexico and the individual states in Mexico include maps of the United States-Mexican border area showing communications lines, roads and railroads, and patrol districts, general maps of miscellaneous index maps, maps showing communications, railroads, and air routes including those taken by Colonel Lindbergh, about 1928, maps showing foreign economic interests by nationality of ownership, maps showing natural resources, maps showing military zones, maps showing American consular districts and consulates, maps showing locations of disturbances and the distribution of military forces, 1910-19, and plans of cities.

Maps of the State of Chihuahua pertain, for the most part, to the Pershing expedition in 1916. Included are route and terrain sketches and maps showing military operations and the disposition of forces. Other records include a 49-sheet map of the State, corrected to 1928. Maps of other Mexican States include general maps, route sketches, plans of cities, plans of railroads, a map of Tabasco showing rebel activities during World War I, maps showing the extent and capacity of the Tuxpan and Panuco oilfields, and maps of Vera Cruz showing military activities in 1914.

Among the maps pertaining to Central America and to the individual countries in that region are maps showing disputed boundaries and the routes of the Inter-American Highway, general topographic maps, plans of cities, a map showing the conflicting interest of the United and Cuyamel Fruit Companies in Guatemala (1908), plans of the Panama Canal and of American properties and facilities in the Canal Zone, and maps showing routes taken by military units.

Among the maps pertaining to South America are a map showing Bolivian and Paraguayan forts in the Gran Chaco (1908), general topographic maps, maps showing airline routes and landing fields including one of the entire continent showing airline routes by nationality of ownership, maps showing defenses, maps showing known and probable oilfields in Colombia and Venezuela, and a map of Venezuela showing aerial photo coverage (1940).

Among the maps relating to the West Indies are two showing the cruise of the U.S. fleet during the maneuvers of 1902. The other maps pertain to the individual countries. Most of the maps of Cuba relate to the Spanish-American War and the American occupation and pacification of Cuba. Included are plans of defense works, plans of battlefields, route sketches, maps showing troop positions and movements, maps showing lines operated by the Army Signal Corps, general maps, maps of railroads, and city plans. The other West Indian countries are represented by general maps, route sketches, and maps showing communications and transportation facilities. The records pertaining to Puerto Rico consist largely of maps relating to the military activities during and after the Spanish-American War and a number of city plans prepared in 1908.

The maps pertaining to Europe are primarily pre-World War 1 maps prepared by military observers showing the training maneuvers of various European armies; maps relating to World War 1 showing the theaters of operations, the frontlines, troop dispositions, defenses, and communications facilities; maps relating to the "Bolshevist" unrest in various countries, particularly in Eastern Europe; and maps prepared during the postwar period showing conflicting boundary lines and locations of ethnic groups. There are maps showing the disposition of troops in Ireland, 1921-22; foreign claims in Spitsbergen, in the Arctic Ocean; and maps of the Soviet Union showing the distribution of various economic activities and the territorial-political reorganization and military operations during the Russian civil war.

The maps pertaining to Africa consist of base maps of each of the Canary Islands, 1898; a map of the area involved in the Ashanti War, 1900; a map showing the areas controlled by the various colonial powers in 1918; a railroad map of West Africa, 1920; and maps of Egypt showing railroads and distances and a plan of the defenses of the Suez Canal.

Maps of China include those relating to the military situation in 1900 showing troop dispositions, routes of American forces, and plans of Chinese forts; those relating to the Russo-Japanese War showing defenses, battlegrounds, routes of marches, and troop dispositions; and those relating to military activities from 1905 to 1915 showing defenses, locations of Chinese revolutionary forces, and German and Japanese troop activities. Other records consist of a map showing the boundaries of the new Manchurian Province, 1913; a plan of Canton, 1939; and plans of the defenses of Formosa and the Pescadores Islands, 1909-12.

Records relating to other Asian countries include a map showing the seat of war on the northwest border of India, 1897; maps of Japan showing military and administrative subdivisions, 1910-20, and military maneuvers, 1907-33; indexes to land survey maps of Japan and Korea; maps of Siberia, including a plan of the defenses of Vladivostok, a map showing locations of Japanese troops in 1920, and a volume of maps identified as a geographical and economic revue of Siberia by Louis de Maier, Colonel of the Russian General Staff, 1920; a map of Bangkok and vicinity, showing roads, 1941; and maps of Turkey showing military activities, 1919-22.

A map of New Zealand shows mineral resources, 1918.

Maps of the Philippine Islands pertain primarily to the Spanish-American War and the Philippine Pacification. Included are maps showing operations against the Spanish forces and against the Filipino insurgents, route sketches, and plans of forts and camps. Other records include railroad maps of Luzon, maps showing defenses of Manila and Corregidor Island, plans of U.S. military reservations showing boundaries and the acquisition of properties, and maps of the islands showing the distribution of Japanese inhabitants in 1920 and landing fields in 1932.

Other items include plans of the areas used to house the General Staff Map Collection, showing the locations of map cases and the headings for the categories of maps filed in the cases; plans of native signals used in the Philippines and a view of an insurgent position; a plan of a pontoon bridge constructed in Japan; plans used in training for military operations, including a plan of a trench system, an artillery net, and a mobile barrage; and materials used in a War College map problem.

The maps published by the War Department Map Collection (WDMC) include base maps of the world and of individual countries; index maps showing the coverage of maps issued by foreign governments; air navigation and airstrip maps of Latin America; a map of the Pacific Ocean showing mandates and spheres of influence; a map of China showing Japanese airbases in 1940; maps compiled from military surveys of Latin American countries; a series of large-scale topographic maps of Central America, Iceland, Greenland, and Africa; and reproductions of Australian city plans and topographic and railroad maps.

Arranged numerically by assigned WDMC map number or by area if no number was assigned.

Other published maps bearing the War Department Map Collection designation may be found among the records of the Army Map Service, since AMS continued publication of many of the same series.

129. THE ENGINEER REPRODUCTION PLANT AND ITS PREDECESSORS. 1910-42. 577 items.

In 1910 a map-producing unit was established at the former Washington Barracks, now Fort Leslie J. McNair, in Washington, D.C. Although no maps are maintained as records of this unit, maps bearing the credit line "Washington Barracks" may be found among the cartographic records of other Army commands.

In 1917 this map-producing unit was named the Central Map Reproduction Plant and was enlarged to supply maps needed by overseas units during World War 1. However, AEF facilities proved adequate for AEF map requirements [see Record Group 120, Records of the American Expeditionary Forces (World War 1), 1917-23]. The plant was generally concerned with printing or reproducing training, tactical, and special military maps and maps of camps and reservations prepared by the territorial and troop commands. It also reproduced special maps compiled by other Army offices, particularly the Office of the Chief of Engineers and the General Staff. Copies of many of the maps printed by this plant may be found in other record groups containing Army maps. Five items are arranged as records of the Central Map Reproduction Plant because no other authority for their production is given. These are: two maps of the maneuver grounds at Chickamauga Park, Ga., one with a woodland overprint; the northeast part of a railroad map of the United States; a topographic map of Camp Sevier, S.C., and vicinity; and a map of part of Alexandria, Va., showing railroads.

Shortly after World War 1 the Central Map Reproduction Plant was renamed the Engineer Reproduction Plant (ERP), although it continued to function as the Army's central mapmaking agency. The Engineer Reproduction Plant, like its predecessor, printed the maps compiled by many different Army units; therefore its maps may be found among the records of other Army commands. They include topographic quadrangles, tactical and terrain maps, and special military maps. The plant began the production of several series of maps that were continued as Army Map Service series. These maps are usually the earliest editions in such series and are arranged with the appropriate series in the AMS files, though the AMS number is not printed on them.

The maps that are maintained as records of the Engineer Reproduction Plant consist of maps printed by the plant that are not identifiable as records of a specific command; maps compiled and printed by the plant that were not incorporated into Army Map Service series; and ERP reprints and revisions of maps that were issued originally by specific commands. Among the records is a list of tactical and terrain maps of the United States that were published by the Engineer Reproduction Plant, the Eighth Corps Area, and the Mississippi River Commission in 1941; and a volume of 17 maps representative of those published by the plant in 1919 and 1920. The maps in this volume include a map indexing special military maps of Oahu; a map of the Eastern Department of the United States; a map and computations relating to the channels in New York harbor; a map of part of Europe and Asia; a map showing the "Bolshevist" situation in

Europe and Asia; a plan of Fort Sill's Apache Gate firing range; a sample topographic map; a plan of the Accotink Creek Reservoir, Va.; a sketch map of an unidentified area to be used for the disposal of hospital sewage; a group of maps and plans, published in 1948, showing the master construction program for Fort Monroe, Va.; a general map of Mexico; and a map of the area northwest of Baltimore, Md.

Other ERP records include maps of the United States showing boundaries of Corps areas, infantry division areas, and areas of the Organized Reserve and the National Guard; topographic quadrangles of the Gettysburg-Antietam area; general maps of military reservations in the United States; training, topographic, and special military maps; maps prepared for use in Staff College problems; and other miscellaneous maps. There are maps of Latin America showing airline routes and landing fields; general maps of individual countries; and maps compiled from military surveys of specific countries, 1939-41. Maps of Europe include a base map showing the theater of operations in western Europe, World War 1; a general map of the Meuse-Argonne operation; a map showing boundaries of the First and Second Armies, August 29-November 11, 1918; and a 1937 highway map of France showing the battleline of March 20, 1918. There are parts of a topographic map of Australia; five airstrip maps of Australia, 1928-34; a map showing railways in South Australia, 1929; and reproductions of five commercial highway maps of parts of Australia. An incomplete series of unnumbered topographic maps of India and Asia is arranged by area.

130. THE ARMY MAP SERVICE. 1942-66. 136,500 items.

The Army Map Service, formed in 1942 as a field installation under the Chief of Engineers, is responsible for the compilation, reproduction, and distribution of maps required by the Army. Its headquarters offices are located in Washington, D.C., and it has several field offices across the United States, each of which, like the headquarters, is capable of performing all of the operations required in the production of maps. Engineer mapping units attached to troop and territorial commands receive technical direction from the Army Map Service in the performance of command duties and are often responsible for certain phases of mapping related to the overall program of AMS.

The military requirements of World War 11 caused the Army Map Service to expand rapidly. Between 1941 and 1945 more than 40,000 different maps of all types covering nearly 400,000 square miles of the earth's surface were prepared; many of them were completely new maps of areas never before mapped in detail. Approximately 500 million copies of these maps were produced for distribution during the war. Since World War 11 further expansion of cartographic activities has taken place to meet the military requirements of the United States. In addition to its extensive topographic series AMS produces roadmaps, special strategic planning maps, plastic relief maps, and related cartographic materials for use by the Department of Defense. It also is responsible for the development of improved mapping techniques, procedures, and materials.

The records of the Army Map Service that are now in the National Archives include a number of manuscript and annotated maps from the AMS Library; some were gifts and some accompanied reports of military attachés. The AMS Library stamp and file number appear on some of the maps, but others are completely unidentified. Included are several index maps of the Aleutian Islands annotated to show areas photographed by date and by type of camera; maps of several cities in the United States showing public buildings and roads, 1940-41; a topographic map of the Blue Beaver area in the vicinity of Mount McKinley, Alaska, annotated to show triangulation stations; a map showing proposed military roads across Oahu Island, Hawaii; preliminary maps of the Norman Carcajou Basin, Canada, compiled in 1944 from aerial surveys; maps of Central America consisting of a reconnaissance of the San Juan River in Costa Rica and Nicaragua, 1944, a series of plans of cities and of river and mountain crossings in Costa Rica, 1915, a reconnaissance of the Nicoya Peninsula, Costa Rica, 1943, a map of Nicaragua showing a proposed canal route and radio stations, and a plan of Chinandega; maps of South America consisting of one showing the positions of Ecuadorian troops during a conflict with Peru, 1941, an outline map of Brazil, a plan of Niterói (Nictheroy), Brazil, 1941, a map of Ecuador showing road conditions, a map of the Rio Caribe area, Venezuela, showing dispositions of troops, antiaircraft units, guard posts, and cyclone fences, 1943, and a plan and profile of the Andean National Corporation pipeline in Colombia; maps of the West Indies consisting of a base map of Aruba Island, a map of Havana, Cuba, annotated to show gun emplacements and roads leading to the Military Camp of Columbia, 1937, and a map of Mona Island, near Puerto Rico, annotated with information about Mona Light.

Maps of Europe consist of a map of Berlin showing railroad stations and a map of the Zuider Zee area in the Netherlands. Maps of French Equatorial Africa show passable roads, water and air routes, Axis airfields, areas captured by the French, tribal locations, and areas infected with sleeping sickness, 1942. There is a plan of the city of Douala in the Cameroons. A map of an unidentified Chinese city, probably Shanghai, shows the native city, foreign concessions, and the retreat of the Chinese forces. Maps of Japan consist of maps of the prefecture of Ryu Kyu (the Ryukyu Islands), maps of Nagoya and Yokosuka annotated apparently to show target areas, 1942, and a series of small sketches of Japanese cities and a few harbor plans showing defenses. A map of Formosa shows roads and territorial-political subdivisions. Maps of Thailand show new boundaries, 1942. Maps of the Philippine Islands consist of maps of Fraile and Corregidor Islands and Manila Bay annotated to show soundings, maps of Luzon annotated to show the Peñaranda River Irrigation Project, a map of Samar annotated to show place names, and a map showing routes between Camp Stotsenberg and Manila. Maps of the East Indies include a map of Borneo showing landing fields, oilfields, pipelines, and coal and iron mines; a map of Bali showing land use, roads, and temples; and a plan of Cheribon, Java.

Other AMS Library records include a 1942 mimeographed provisional edition of the "Guide to the Williams Subject Classification and Cataloging in

Use at Map Library, The Army Map Service" and a series of monthly "Library Accessions Report[s]," June 1946 through July 1948. In addition to maps these reports include lists of monthly book and pamphlet accessions. The records also include copies of the third edition of the map indexes to the holdings of the library, 1944-45, and supplemental sheets issued in 1947 and 1948. These show the coverage of the holdings by continent and by region. Arranged by geographical area.

The cartographic records of the Army Map Service consist chiefly of (1) the maps published by AMS, its predecessors, and its field offices; (2) maps produced for AMS by commercial or governmental contractors; (3) maps compiled and produced by foreign mapping agencies under agreement with AMS, in accordance with joint and mutually accepted specifications; and (4) maps produced by foreign mapping agencies, primarily as a part of their own mapping program, that have been adopted by AMS with or without variations.

The AMS maps are arranged in series established by the agency. A map series, as defined by AMS, consists of maps of a common scale or consistent format which collectively cover all or part of a specified area. Exceptions to this definition exist, and some series have been established to include maps in which scale and format differ but which were designed to serve a common purpose, such as city plans of a specific area. Odd or isolated sheets may be grouped with a series for a given area if the scales are nearly the same.

Each series is identified by a numerical or an alpha-numeric symbol which indicates the scale and the geographical area covered. More detailed information about the classification of AMS map series may be found in *Map Identifications and Other Marginal Information*, AMS Technical Manual No. 22 (February 1951). A copy of this manual is included in the records of the agency.

Among the records is a set of the various editions of the index maps, which are frequently revised; these indexes date from 1942 to 1960.

The records also include a set of published index maps, compiled by AMS in 1942, covering the British Geographic Section General Staff (GSGS) maps available to AMS for distribution during World War II. Most of these GSGS maps were later assigned AMS series numbers and were reprinted in revised editions by AMS. The indexes to the AMS series also show the original file numbers for those GSGS series incorporated into AMS records. A copy of the catalog of index maps to GSGS series is annotated to show which series were adopted by AMS.

Other index maps consist of catalogs of maps of the United States indexing the topographic maps published by other Federal mapping agencies, one set with annotations showing the editions of each sheet and with overlays to show the coverage of special military maps; and the other set with annotations to show the coverage of military photomaps.

The military maps issued by AMS or considered to be AMS records are revised frequently and each new edition is identified by its edition number and the date of issue. The earlier editions of many of the sheets were published by predecessors of AMS, by American topographic units in the field, by other

Government agencies, or by foreign governments, principally the British GSGS. These editions are maintained with the regular AMS series, although they do not bear AMS series numbers.

The small-scale maps of the world and of continental or subcontinental areas include outline, topographic, transportation and communications, and planning maps, and maps showing climatic zones and clothing allowance zones. The maps of the regional and subregional areas include the same kinds of maps listed for the continental areas and in addition photomaps and city plans.

Most of the AMS maps are large-scale topographic sheets of areas in all parts of the world. Among those pertaining to the United States are many topographic quadrangles similar to those issued by the Geological Survey. There is little duplication of effort between the two agencies, however, because specific assignments are made regarding areas to be mapped. The Army Map Service prepares topographic quadrangles principally of areas under military control or interest and is responsible for the preparation of topographic sheets of the United States at the scale of 1:250,000. The Geological Survey reprints these topographic sheets for civilian use, omitting the military grid.

AMS records in the National Archives include a representative sample of plastic relief maps of areas throughout the world.

Aerial Photographs

131. GENERAL RECORDS. 1918-38. 53,000 items.

Prints of aerial photographs of parts of France, 1918, apparently taken by American aviators. The photographs show military fortifications, and they are grouped by the following town designations: Bouillonville, Essey, Jaulny, Limey, Rembercourt, Remenauville, Thiaucourt, and Vieville. Scales vary.

Film negatives from aerial photography of the lower Mississippi River and its tributaries in Arkansas, Missouri, and Tennessee, 1929-38. The surveys are identified and indexed as follows: Alluvial Valley Survey, Mississippi River, 1929; Alluvial Valley Survey, St. Francis River, 1930; Low Water Surveys, Mississippi River, 1930-34 and 1937-38; St. Francis River Flood Survey, 1930; Wolf River and Nonconnah Creek Survey, 1931; New Madrid Floodway Survey, Mississippi River, 1935; Wappapello Reservoir Survey, St. Francis River, 1935; Wolf River Survey, 1935; and Mississippi River Flood Outline Survey, 1937. They are accompanied by incomplete indexes. Scales vary.

Prints of aerial photographs of parts of Central America from the Inter-American Highway Survey, 1932. These are grouped by the following series: (1) Costa Rica, (2) Nicaragua, (3) Honduras and Nicaragua, (4) unidentified, (5), (6), and (8) Guatemala, (7) Costa Rica and Nicaragua, (9) Nicaragua and Guatemala, and (10) Panama. They are accompanied by indexes. Scales vary.

RECORDS OF THE BUREAU OF INSULAR AFFAIRS. RG 350

The Bureau of Insular Affairs, established in the War Department in 1898 and abolished in 1939, was responsible for all matters pertaining to civil government in island possessions of the United States that were under the jurisdiction of the War Department.

132. GENERAL RECORDS. 1902-4. 2 items.

Published maps of the Philippine Islands. One, dated 1902, shows schools, military posts, military telegraph lines and cables, other cables, open and coastwise ports, lighthouses, post offices, provincial boundaries, and the distribution of Moro (Moslem) and other non-Christian tribes. The other, published in 1904, differentiates the Christian and the non-Christian provinces.

133. MAP ENCLOSURES TO CORRESPONDENCE FILES. 1911-34. 55 items.

Manuscript and annotated maps of the Philippine Islands and Puerto Rico stamped with correspondence numbers of the Bureau of Insular Affairs. Those relating to the Philippines include a series of maps annotated to show radio, telephone, and telegraph facilities, their ownership or control, and their service areas, 1931; a map annotated to show the reorganization of the Courts of the First Instance, about 1914; maps showing roads, trails, and railroads and their condition; a map showing suggested projects for the port of Manila; a corrected forestry map of the Islands; a map of the Islands showing constabulary stations, dispensaries, and hospitals; a map showing the survey of property for the National Guard in the Barrio of Tamba, annotated to show areas to be expropriated and areas to be returned; a map showing waterfront lands required for the port reservation at Manila; and a plan of property surveyed for a General Land Registration Office in the Barrio of Santa Elena, Calanbayungan Island.

The records pertaining to Puerto Rico include maps of San Juan showing harbor developments and approved developments, a proposed site for the Muñoz Rivera Park, and swamp areas east of the city proposed for reclamation.

RECORDS OF THE OFFICE OF THE JUDGE ADVOCATE GENERAL (ARMY). RG 153

The duties of the Judge Advocate General include supervision over the system of military justice throughout the Army, the furnishing of legal service for the Army, and, through its Lands Division (formerly the Military Reservations Division), the maintenance of records relating to the title to and the acquisition, administration, possession, and disposal of real property under the control of the Army and the Department of the Army.

134. LANDS DIVISION. 1840-1930. 347 items.

Manuscript, published, and photoprocessed maps and plans of former military reservations and other Army-held lands within the United States that were relinquished by the Army to other Government agencies, principally to the Department of the Interior. Included are maps of military reservations and related hay and timber reserves showing boundaries, drainage, and topography; additions of lands; roads and trails entering and crossing the lands; and connections with public land surveys. Many of the maps contain brief histories of the reservations and descriptions of their natural resources. Ground plans of the forts or camps identifying the buildings, often showing the kinds of building materials used in their construction, are included, sometimes as a separate map but more often on the same sheet with the map of the reservation.

Also included in this file are manuscript maps of the mouth of the Columbia River, one showing sites for possible fortifications; an undated map of the route of Captain Lyons' command to Pit River, Calif.; a plan of the Rancho Corte Madre del Presidio, San Francisco; a plan of Coronado Heights, San Diego; plans of St. Paul, Minn., 1889; plans of a few Indian reservations; an undated map of the Arkansas Military Road; and a plan for a proposed military post on the Des Moines River, 1838.

Arranged by name of fort or under the title "Miscellaneous." A card catalog lists the records by area.

135. COURTS OF INQUIRY. 1880. 5 items.

Maps published for inclusion as part 3 of the published report on the G. K. Warren Court of Inquiry. These maps relate to the Battle of Five Forks, Virginia, April 1, 1865. Included are a map of Five Forks and vicinity compiled by order of the Court of Inquiry from official maps and maps prepared by J. E. Cotton, a civil engineer; copies of maps by Cotton, one of the battlefield and one of the White Oak Road area which General Warren's Corps was to have secured during the battle; a map showing the formation of the 5th Army Corps south of Gravelly Run Church on the afternoon of April 1, 1865; and a published copy of the photographic map exhibited in the Court and referred to by General Warren in his testimony.

RECORDS OF THE MILITARY GOVERNMENT OF CUBA. RG 140

Under the treaty of peace signed between the United States and Spain on December 10, 1898, Spain relinquished all claim to sovereignty over Cuba. Three days later the Adjutant General of the Army, by direction of the President of the United States, established a Division of Cuba, later designated the Department of Cuba. This command existed until 1902 when the United States yielded sovereignty over the country to the newly established government of the Republic of Cuba.

136. DIVISION OF CUBA. 1899-1900. 24 items.

Records of the Civil Division, consisting of a map of Havana annotated to show the boundary of the municipality of Regla as approved by the Civil Governor on April 4, 1881. This map was enclosed with the second endorsement of the Civil Division, Division of Cuba, No. 3747, dated July 11, 1900.

Records of the individual departments within the Division including the Departments of Havana, Santiago, Matanzas, Santa Clara, and Matanzas and Santa Clara. Those of the Department of Santiago include manuscript plans of fortifications and batteries within the Department. Among the records of other departments are topographic surveys of fortified sites, maps of strategic shorelines, plans of jails in Santa Clara Province, maps of the provinces, and plans of cities and harbors. The records of the Department of Havana include maps showing the progress of a survey of Spanish fortifications in the vicinity of Havana.

Arranged in series by department of origin.

137. DEPARTMENT OF CUBA. 1900-1902. 26 items.

Records of the Office of the Chief Engineer of the Department, including published maps of Santa Clara Battery and Rowell Barracks annotated to show the limits of U.S. jurisdiction. Other records consist of a map showing government lands and military zones near Forts Cabana and Morro; a map showing the progress of a topographic survey of Havana and vicinity; a chart of Havana harbor showing bulkhead lines proposed for the improvement of Atarés Bay; a map showing locations of gun pintles of modern coast batteries defending Havana; a map of areas in Vedado and Carmelo reserved for U.S. troops; and an incomplete set of drawings of modern coast batteries defending Havana, with index maps showing their fields of fire.

A photoprocessed map showing artillery defenses of Havana prepared by the quartermaster headquarters of the Artillery Corps, and a map of Columbia Barracks Reservation near Havana prepared by the Quartermaster Corps.

Records of the Chief Engineer of the City of Havana, including a city map annotated to show an ideal plan for tracks of the Havana Electric Railway Company and two published maps of the city showing the frequency of street cleaning and sprinkling.

Arranged in series by unit of origin within the Department.

RECORDS OF THE NATIONAL GUARD BUREAU. RG 168

The National Guard Bureau, established in 1908 as the Division of Militia Affairs in the Office of the Secretary of War, is responsible for all matters pertaining to the development and maintenance of the National Guard. The cartographic records of the Bureau consist of maps that have been compiled by State units to show their training reservations and maneuver grounds.

138. CONNECTICUT NATIONAL GUARD. 1897. 1 item.

A published topographic map of the State Military Reservation and vicinity at Niantic, Conn.

139. MICHIGAN NATIONAL GUARD. 1924-28. 2 items.

Published topographic military maps of Camp Graling and vicinity, Hanson State Military Reservation.

140. MINNESOTA NATIONAL GUARD. 1936. 1 item.

A published topographic training map of Camp Ripley Military Reservation.

141. NEW MEXICO NATIONAL GUARD. 1911. 1 item.

A photoprocessed map of the maneuver ground and target range of the New Mexico National Guard.

142. NEW YORK NATIONAL GUARD. 1927. 1 item.

A published topographic map of Peekskill, N.Y., and vicinity enlarged for the command and staff course of the New York National Guard from the West Point and Carmel Quadrangles prepared by the Geological Survey.

143. OHIO NATIONAL GUARD. 1936. 1 item.

A photomap of Fort Knox, Ky., and vicinity compiled by the 37th Division, Aviation, Ohio National Guard.

RECORDS OF THE PROVISIONAL GOVERNMENT OF CUBA. RG 199

In 1906, in response to an appeal by the President of Cuba, the United States established a Provisional Government of Cuba for the purpose of maintaining order in the face of an insurrection. The Provisional Government exercised its authority largely through the existing departments of the Cuban Government; therefore when it was terminated in 1909 most of the records it had created were left in the custody of those departments.

The cartographic records in this record group were compiled by the Army of Cuban Pacification.

144. GENERAL RECORDS. 1906-8. 58 items.

A bound volume of photoprocessed plans of cities and towns in Cuba showing buildings occupied by the Army of Cuban Pacification, plans of military posts, and tabular descriptions of facilities in the cities and on the military posts that pertained to the billeting of men. The descriptions include the names or designations of units occupying specific areas, the numbers of men, the names of the commanding officers, descriptions of the sanitary facilities, and comments on the water supplies.

A photoprocessed map of Cuba showing railroad and steamship connections and posts of the Army of Cuban Pacification.

145. CHIEF ENGINEER AND ENGINEER UNITS. 1906-9. 82 items.

A manuscript military map of Cuba prepared under the direction of the Chief Engineer from reconnaissances by Army detachments, 1906-8. This map, in 70 sheets, shows trails, roads, railroads, settlements, ruins, blockhouses, churches, working and ruined sugar mills, and many other cultural and physical features. Insets show details of specific towns in the area covered by the map. Six supplementary sheets show plans of the larger cities.

A separate manuscript map of the city of Marianao, 1908; a published map showing the temporary fieldworks erected by the Spanish forces for the land defenses of Havana, 1897-98; photoprocessed maps from surveys by the Corps of Engineers including a map of part of Havana Province; plans and cross sections of fieldworks, particularly along the Mariel-Artemisa Trocha (road); a survey of the Jucaro-Marón Military Trocha; and a plan of Camp Columbia.

146. OFFICE OF THE CHIEF SIGNAL OFFICER. 1907. 1 item.

A published map of Cuba showing telephone and telegraph lines and offices, cable lines, and railroad lines and stations.

147. MILITARY INFORMATION DIVISION. 1907-8. 3 items.

A published map of Cuba showing sugar mills; a photoprocessed map of a part of Cuba showing public and privately owned railroads and telegraph, telephone, and cable lines; and a copy of a map showing routes followed by the Bailen Battalion in the Cárdenas-Matanzas area during the period April 1896-February 1897.

148. TROOP COMMANDS. 1908. 1 item.

A photoprocessed map from a reconnaissance of the four eastern Cubitas Mountain passes and lateral communications by Captains Hardesty and Smith of the 17th Infantry.

RECORDS OF THE OFFICE OF THE CHIEF OF ORDNANCE. RG 156

The Office of the Chief of Ordnance, established in 1812, is responsible for the design, procurement, storage, supply, and maintenance of weapons, munitions, vehicles, and other combat equipment for the Army.

149. GENERAL RECORDS OF THE OFFICE OF THE CHIEF OF
ORDNANCE. 1845. 1 item.

A published map of the mineral lands adjacent to Lake Superior that were
ceded to the United States by the treaty of 1842 with the Chippewa Indians.
The map shows sections leased and sections located under "permits" or
applications. Shown on the tracts are lease numbers and agency numbers.

150. GENERAL RECORDS OF THE ORDNANCE DEPARTMENT (FIELD).
1908. 4 items.

Blueprints, including two undated plans of parts of the Edgewood Arsenal
Experimental Grounds, N.J.; a map showing the boundaries of the Sandy Hook
Proving Ground, N.J., 1908; and a plan of the Sandy Hook Proving Ground
identifying each structure at the installation.

RECORDS OF THE OFFICE OF THE QUARTERMASTER GENERAL. RG 92

The mapping activities of the Office of the Quartermaster General are
limited to the preparation of maps necessary to facilitate its assigned functions,
which relate chiefly to the construction and maintenance of military installations and the development of military equipment. Included among the
Quartermaster cartographic records are administrative maps, maps and plans
showing the location and arrangement of U.S. Army reservations, ground plans
of Army posts and cemeteries, construction plans and drawings, and supply and
transport maps.

151. GENERAL RECORDS. 1820-1951. 1,336 items.

A set of published maps including maps of the United States showing
military posts and land-grant and bond-aided railroads; a bound volume of
photoprocessed maps and charts relating to the production and consumption
and the exportation and importation of food supplies in the world, 1921; a map
of the world showing proved and probable oil deposits; a map of metropolitan
Washington, D.C., showing commissary zones; and landform maps of Alaska,
Southeast Asia, and the European part of the Soviet Union. The landform maps
were prepared for the Quartermaster General by other Government and
non-Government agencies. Arranged in series by subject.

Processed plans of military reservations and national cemeteries in the
United States and its territories and possessions, 1903-17. These plans show
boundaries of the reservations or cemeteries, relief, and buildings and other
facilities. For many reservations there are several plans, including revisions of the
original plans. Arranged alphabetically by name of State, territory, or possession
and thereunder by name of installation.

Manuscript and annotated maps and plans, known as the "Post and
Reservation File," 1820-1905, including maps and plans of military installations,

buildings, and equipment; maps showing routes of military expeditions in the continental United States; maps showing Indian lands and cessions; and a number of general military maps. Representative of these records are plans of military posts in the Territories of Michigan, Wisconsin, and Minnesota, dated about 1820; plans of military posts in the West, particularly in California, dated about 1872; and plans of quartermaster installations in use during the Civil War, including a group of detailed plans of installations in Washington, D.C., and vicinity showing their precise street locations and layout.

Other records include a map of the Eastern and Western Military Departments showing the location of forts, about 1820-30; a map of Texas and Mexico, about 1820; a map of the route from Fort Laramie to Fort Pierre, 1849; a sketch of St. Thomas' Manor at Chapel Point near Port Tobacco, Md.; a sketch of a proposed road through the Choctaw country in the Indian Territory; and a map showing landholdings and land cessions of the Sac and Fox Indians. Arranged by numbers assigned in the agency. A card catalog lists these items by subject or area.

152. CONSTRUCTION DIVISION AND PREDECESSORS. 1917-41.
179 items.

Published and photoprocessed maps of the United States showing the activities of the Construction Division, 1918-19. Bound volumes of photoprocessed maps and plans of National Army and National Guard camps in the United States, prepared by the Cantonment Division, the predecessor of the Construction Division, 1917. Photoprocessed copies of maps and plans of military reservations in the United States and its territories and possessions. These maps and plans, showing changes and proposed changes in facilities at the individual reservations, were prepared by the Constructing Quartermasters assigned to the reservations, 1917-19. A map showing proposed wells and dams at Killeen Armored Division Camp (Fort Hood), Tex., 1941. Arranged in series by type of map.

153. MILITARY PLANNING DIVISION. 1943-52. 93 items.

A set of published maps including a map showing mountain regions of the world; maps of Canada, the Near East, Arabia, Australasia, and parts of northern and eastern Africa showing landforms; a map of the world showing clothing allowance zones for the Army; maps of Arabia, Canada, Japan, Alaska, and the Near East showing clothing zones or requirement areas; graphs showing combat clothing to be issued monthly in certain areas; and maps of each of the continents, eastern Asia, and the United States showing monthly climatic zones.

These maps were prepared by or for the Research Development Branch. Those showing landforms were prepared for the Environmental Protection Section of that Branch by other institutions, principally universities. The series showing monthly climatic zones of the continents was prepared by the Climatology and Environmental Protection Section.

Arranged in series by subject.

154. AMERICAN GRAVES REGISTRATION SERVICE. n.d. 8 items.

A series of published ground plans of American cemeteries established during World War 1 in France, England, and Belgium showing tree and shrub plantings, flagpoles, walks, and locations of graves. Figures for the approximate numbers of graves in each cemetery are included on the plans.

155. TRANSPORTATION SERVICE. 1920-21. 2 items.

A published map of the 5th Corps Area with headquarters at Fort Benjamin Harrison, Indianapolis, Ind., showing a model study of motor transport service, 1921; and a diagram showing trunk railroad lines in the United States.

RECORDS OF THE OFFICE OF THE CHIEF SIGNAL OFFICER. RG 111

The Office of the Chief Signal Officer and its field offices and units that function as the Signal Corps were established during the Civil War and are concerned with military signal communications and photographic duties not otherwise assigned. Past functions of the Signal Corps that were transferred to other agencies and for which there are cartographic records include meteorological observation, assumed by the Weather Bureau in 1890, and military aviation operations, which were transferred to the Air Service when it was separated from the Signal Corps in 1920.

Office of the Chief Signal Officer

156. GENERAL RECORDS. 1879-1927. 15 items.

Maps published under the direction of the Chief Signal Officer consisting of a contour map of the United States showing signal stations, 1879; a map of a part of northwestern Alaska showing explorations conducted by an expedition to Point Barrow, 1881-83; a map of Puerto Rico showing lines of communication operated by the Signal Corps, 1900; a series of maps showing the Signal Corps' progress in erecting telegraph lines and laying cables in the Philippine Islands, 1899-1904; a map of the United States showing departmental boundaries and establishments of the Signal Corps, 1921; maps of Alaska showing the Army telegraph and cable systems and lines connecting them with the continental United States, about 1904-20; and maps of the United States showing the Army-Navy radio network and radio traffic stations, 1923 and 1927.

157. SUPPLY DIVISION. n.d. 1 item.

A photoprocessed plan and utilities map of Camp Alfred Vail, N.J., prepared by the Engineering Section.

158. COMMUNICATION AND LIAISON DIVISION. 1942. 1 item.

A photoprocessed map of the United States showing full-period telephone circuits leased by the U.S. Army.

159. METEOROLOGICAL SERVICE. n.d. 2 items.

Published maps of the United States showing reporting stations for meteorological data.

160. PLANT AND TRAFFIC DIVISION. 1934. 1 item.

A photoprocessed diagram of the Army radio system showing the various military networks in the United States and its territories, and commercial and governmental radiotelephone and radiotelegraph stations in Alaska.

Signal Corps

161. GENERAL RECORDS. 1898-1945. 7 items.

Published and photoprocessed maps consisting of a map of the northeastern United States showing the routes of balloons in the international race of 1907; a map showing lines of the Mountain States Telephone and Telegraph Co. and connecting lines along the southwestern border of the United States; maps and diagrams showing Signal Corps administrative boundaries, line routes, and teletype traffic lines in France, 1945; a map of the United States showing facilities of the Signal Corps Aviation Section, 1918; and a map of Camp George H. Thomas, Chickamauga Park, Tenn., showing telephone lines, 1918.

162. SIGNAL CORPS SCHOOLS. 1918-24. 4 items.

Published maps of Camp Vail and Fort Monmouth, N.J., 1924; a terrain map of Fort Monmouth, 1924; and a photoprocessed plan of the Signal Corps Aviation School, Fairfield, Ohio.

RECORDS OF THE OFFICE OF THE SURGEON GENERAL (ARMY).
RG 112

Although a permanent peacetime medical service for the Army was provided for in 1802, the Medical Department of the Army had no chief until the creation of the Office of Physicians and Surgeon General in 1813. An act of April 14, 1818, gave the Department a permanent chief with the title of Surgeon General.

163. GENERAL RECORDS. 1914. 4 items.

Photoprocessed maps of the United States showing the mobilization schemes for sanitary equipment individually for the Regular Army, the Organized Militia, and the U.S. Volunteers; and a map showing the general mobilization for all three groups.

RECORDS OF THE WAR DEPARTMENT GENERAL AND SPECIAL STAFFS. RG 165

The War Department General Staff was established in 1903 to assist the Chief of Staff in preparing plans and policies and gathering information pertinent to the national defense. Subsequent reorganizations created within the General Staff a number of functional divisions.

No one division or office has had sole responsibility for the mapmaking activities of the General Staff. Most of the surveying and mapping has been accomplished by Engineer units attached to the various Army schools supervised by the General Staff. From 1903 to 1939 the General Staff Map Collection was under the supervision first of the Military Intelligence Division and its predecessors and then of the War College Division and the Army War College; these units compiled many additional maps and placed them in the collection. In 1939 it was transferred to the Office of the Chief of Engineers, as was the Engineer Reproduction Plant; in 1942 the ERP became the Army Map Service (see entry 128). Other divisions and offices within the General Staff also have, on occasion, engaged in mapmaking or map-collecting activities related to their assignments.

164. GENERAL RECORDS. 1927-39. 6 items.

Miscellaneous annotated maps for which a specific authority is not designated. Included is an undated map of the United States annotated to show the coverage of airstrip and sectional maps issued by the Air Corps and by the Department of Commerce (Coast and Geodetic Survey); an undated map of Japan annotated to show priority areas for mapping, areas for which translations of the 1:50,000 maps were available, and areas for which there were no maps on file; a map of the Panama Canal Zone annotated apparently to show areas mapped in 1927, those remaining to be mapped in the 1927 project, and those to be mapped in fiscal years 1928 and 1929; and maps of Europe annotated to show the availability of map coverage in 1939.

Office of the Chief of Staff

165. GENERAL RECORDS. 1912-35. 2 items.

A booklet published by the Office of the Chief of Staff in 1912 showing conventional signs for mapmaking as adopted by the U.S. Geographic Board.

A published map of the United States showing military priorities of the national highway system, approved by the Chief of Staff in 1935.

166. CENTRAL STATISTICAL OFFICE. 1941-46. 6 items.

Photoprocessed copies of maps of the world overprinted to show administrative boundaries for the various American theaters of operations.

167. NATIONAL LAND DEFENSE BOARD. 1915. 42 items.

Photoprocessed and annotated maps of the Panama Canal Zone showing locations of defenses; and plans of forts and military reservations in Hawaii giving the numbers of troops stationed at each fort or reservation.

Personnel Division (G-1)

168. STATISTICAL BRANCH. 1922-33. 25 items.

Two versions, one of them incomplete, of a published map of the Meuse-Argonne offensive, September 26-November 11, 1918, enlarged from a map accompanying General Pershing's final report with additional information and colors to denote positions occupied and territory covered by the American divisions.

Photoprocessed maps of the United States, Hawaii, the Philippine Islands, the Panama Canal Zone, and Puerto Rico showing Army installations and the units assigned to them. Maps of the United States showing proposed military construction projects, corps area quotas, and emergency construction work capabilities in each corps area for 1933; and an undated map of the United States showing the number of surplus men that could be moved from other corps areas to the Ninth Corps area.

Intelligence Division (G-2) and Predecessors

This Division is responsible for the collection, evaluation, and dissemination of military information. In 1885 a Military Information Division was organized in the Adjutant General's Office (see entry 64). In 1903 this Division was transferred to the newly organized General Staff where it was made a section in the War College Division. In July 1918 it was reorganized as the Military Intelligence Branch and placed under the supervision of the Executive Division. In August 1918 it was given separate divisional status as the Military Intelligence Division and in 1946 it was renamed the Intelligence Division.

169. GENERAL RECORDS. 1904-44. 2,000 items.

Maps compiled and published by the Military Intelligence Division and its predecessors in the General Staff and maps of undetermined origin reproduced by the Division. Among the earliest are general maps of Cuba, the Philippines, Hispaniola, and Panama showing topography, drainage, railroads, and roads and trails. Other maps show the strategy of the Russo-Japanese War, 1904-5, as reported by American military observers.

A number of maps of Europe and countries in Europe were prepared during World War 1. Among these are maps showing the theaters of operations, order of battle, railroad lines, navigable waters, and political boundaries. Maps of the U.S.S.R. show railroads and military operations during the Russian Civil War.

A large group of maps pertaining to Mexico, about 1916-22, includes outline maps and maps showing communications, political boundaries, strategic information, density of rural population, the political situation in 1920, and the Tuxpan oil regions.

The largest single group of maps is a set of the 1:50,000 Japanese Imperial Land Survey maps overprinted by the Military Intelligence Division, 1925-35, with English translations of place names.

Other records include general maps of foreign countries; index maps of the United States and its territories and possessions showing the status of surveying for the Progressive Military Map of the United States; a topographic map of Rock Creek Park, Washington, D.C., 1910; strategic maps of the Gettysburg area; maps of China showing forest and mineral resources, 1918; maps of the United States-Canadian border areas; maps of the United States showing Army corps areas, training camps in 1918, communications facilities, and a plan for coastal defense; railroad and airlines maps of Turkey, 1934; maps of the world showing time zones and the status of topographic mapping; a special airfield map of the Far East prepared in 1944 for G-2 by the Assistant Chief of Air Staff, Intelligence, Air Movements Branch; and a map of the area in the vicinity of Suva and the lower Rewa River, Viti Levu Island, Fiji Islands. Arranged in series by area.

There are a few map enclosures to G-2 reports, including a photoprocessed map of Mexico showing airway routes, 1934; a photoprocessed map of Costa Rica showing landing fields, 1935; a map of Barcelona, Spain, annotated to show properties; and a map of Cuba annotated to show telephone lines, 1940. (Most of the map enclosures were filed with the General Staff Map Collection in Record Group 77; see entry 128.)

170. GEOGRAPHIC BRANCH. 1927-46. 163 items.

Published maps of areas of strategic interest throughout the world. Included is a set of 1:50,000 sheets of the United States and Canada adjacent to the boundary; a set of 1:250,000 sheets of Central America; part of a set of 1:100,000 maps of Cuba; and sets of 1:250,000 maps and air navigation charts of Mexico.

Other maps include a time zone map of the world; a base map of Africa and a map of Africa showing transportation facilities; maps of Cuba including an outline map, a map showing airplane facilities, and a map showing long-distance circuits of the Cuban Telephone Co. in the Western and Santa Clara Districts; a map of the Philippine Islands showing air facilities; maps of Mexico including an outline map, a map showing military territorial jurisdictions, maps showing railroads, a topographic map of Vera Cruz and vicinity, and a plan of Coatepec; a topographic map of Ethiopia published originally by the National Geographic Society and reprinted with additions by the Geographic Branch; an outline map of the United States and a map showing military posts; and a plan of Inchon, Korea.

There is also a map of Europe annotated to serve as an index to airways maps on file in the Geographic Branch in 1932.

171. MILITARY INTELLIGENCE SERVICE. 1942-45. 25 items.

The Military Intelligence Service was established in G-2 in March 1942. In the fall of 1943 it was discontinued and its functions were handled by other units in G-2. In June 1944 the Service was reactivated. The Service was continually undergoing internal administrative changes. The cartographic records are described in series corresponding to the offices or units within the Service that were responsible for compiling and publishing them. They are:

A map of the Middle East showing railways and canals, compiled by the Theater Intelligence Section.

Map records of the Intelligence Group including railway maps of Burma and Assam and of Mexico, a map of northeastern Siberia, and a map of Bougainville Island.

A map of Cayenne Island, French Guiana, compiled by the Cartographic Section.

A series of manuscript, annotated, and printed map studies of Korea compiled by the Training Branch in 1943. These maps show topography, defenses, roads and railroads, vegetation, predominant crops, and languages spoken by the inhabitants.

An outline map of Burma compiled by the Map and Photo Branch of the Information Group.

A plan of Tampico, Mexico, and vicinity compiled from American intelligence sources.

Maps compiled by the Dissemination Branch including a roadmap of Java and an outline map of Borneo.

A strategic map of South-Central Europe showing railroads and navigable waters. The unit of origin is unidentified.

172. MILITARY MONOGRAPHS SUBSECTION. n.d. 3 items.

Published maps showing the route of the Murmansk Railroad, in the Soviet Union, and a published map showing the routes between Tampico and Tuxpan, Mexico.

173. TOPOGRAPHIC DETACHMENT. 1948-50. 2 items.

An outline map of Africa and adjacent parts of the Mediterranean Sea and the Near East, and a relief map of Iceland.

174. LATIN AMERICAN SECTION. 1924. 1 item.

A map of Cuba showing the distribution of sugar-producing areas and the comparative production of sugar by provinces.

Organization and Training Division (G-3)

Before 1942 this Division was known as the Operations and Training Division. In 1942 it was renamed the Organization and Training Division and those functions relating to operations were transferred to the Operations Division, the successor of the War Plans Division (see entry 181).

The Organization and Training Division is responsible for supervising training throughout the Army, including training at the United States Military Academy, the service schools of the arms and services of the Army, the Command and General Staff School, and the Army War College. It also supervises the training programs for the National Guard, the Organized Reserves, and the Reserve Officers Training Corps (ROTC). The records in this Division include those of the former War College Division, the Army War College, the United States Military Academy, the Command and General Staff School and its predecessors, and training courses of the ROTC. Records from schools under the jurisdiction of the arms and services and the National Guard are arranged in separate record groups according to the arm or service immediately responsible for their supervision.

175. WAR COLLEGE DIVISION. 1911-17. 275 items.

The War College Division was established in 1911 to supervise the activities of the Army War College and other service schools. It was also responsible for the collection and dissemination of military information through its subordinate unit, the Military Information Section. In 1917 this Division was abolished and its functions were transferred to other divisions in the General Staff.

Maps published by or for the War College Division include maps of the United States showing railroads, radio stations, military reservations, divisional districts of the National Guard, and posts occupied by the Army; a set of maps of the United States-Mexican border area compiled by the Intelligence Officer of the Southern Department for the War College Division; topographic and strategic maps of Cuba, Panama, and Puerto Rico, including a published version of the detailed map of Cuba in 70 sheets compiled under the authority of the Army of Cuban Pacification in 1906-9 (see Record Group 199), and published with some corrections by the War College Division in 1913; a series of progressive military maps of Puerto Rico; maps of Mexico including general maps, railroad maps, an index to railroad maps, and maps of individual states; and maps of Europe, including outline maps and maps showing railroads, political boundaries, the Franco-German frontier, and the ethnography of the Balkans. Other records include a topographic map of Rock Creek Park, Washington, D.C., and plans of model entrenched zones, an entrenched line, and typical supporting points.

176. ARMY WAR COLLEGE. 1910-45. 800 items.

General records of the Army War College include photoprocessed maps of central Mexico and the Dominican Republic; a map illustrating the Serbian campaign of 1915; a map showing strategic areas in Korea; a map of the United States illustrating a problem of routing regular, militia, and volunteer Army units to the Pacific coast in 1909-10; photoprints of the Army War College command course in 1922-23; a map of the theater of operations in the war games of 1914; a map of the Western Front in Europe showing the main river systems and railroads used by the French and the Germans in 1914; and a series of plans of typical command posts, supporting points, and entrenched lines, 1917.

Among the records of the Historical Section of the Army War College are maps relating to World War 1, including maps annotated to show frontlines; a series of annotated maps of Europe identified as "Colonel Price's Lecture Maps: Mineral Resources of the German Defense System," showing iron and steel works, furnaces, petroleum, iron, coal and salt deposits, transportation routes, industrial areas, and navigable waterways; maps showing major offensive and defensive operations and the Allied order of battle on November 11, 1918; maps of France, Italy, and Belgium showing provinces; maps annotated to show the relation of the operations of the 1st, 2d, 3d, 4th, 26th, 28th, 32d, and 42d U.S. Divisions to the general advance in the Second Battle of the Marne; a map study of the Meuse-Argonne operation; and atlases accompanying published records of the 1st and 2d Divisions.

Other records of the Historical Section include manuscript maps showing campaigns and battles of the Revolutionary War compiled for the Washington bicentennial atlas (see entry 7); manuscript maps illustrating the history of the area encompassed by the Shenandoah National Park and vicinity, including maps showing the extent of Washington's travels, the chain of frontier forts, and the Civil War campaigns and battlefields; and a series of strategic and tactical maps of the Fredericksburg campaign of 1862, compiled in 1933.

177. UNITED STATES MILITARY ACADEMY. 1916-21. 5 items.

Published maps compiled by units of the Academy, including topographic maps of West Point and vicinity, provisional maps of the West Point Military Reservation, and a special military map of Camp Dix, N.J., and vicinity.

178. COMMAND AND GENERAL STAFF SCHOOL AND PREDECESSORS. 1904-43. 333 items.

Published maps compiled by the Command and General Staff College and its predecessors, the Army Service School, the Army Staff College, the Signal School and Staff College, and the General Service and Staff College. The records include numerous topographic and strategic maps and a few aerial mosaics of Fort Leavenworth, Kans., and vicinity, at varying scales. There are also numerous topographic and strategic maps of the Gettysburg-Antietam area in Maryland, Virginia, and Pennsylvania prepared for war games and other training purposes.

Other maps compiled and published by these schools include maps of the European theater during World War I. Among these are maps of the western and eastern theaters compiled and published before the United States entered the war and map studies made after the war of the military operations in which U.S. troops participated.

Special maps compiled by the schools include an early airways map of the northeastern United States, a map of Asiatic Turkey, a map of Kansas and Missouri showing highways, a map of the Pacific Ocean showing the organization of U.S. forces in 1932, a special military map of Fort Riley, Kans., and maps of eastern and western Europe in 1943.

179. RESERVE OFFICERS TRAINING CORPS. 1921-33. 2 items.

A published special military map of Princeton, N.J., and vicinity, compiled by the ROTC at Princeton University in 1933; and a published plan of part of San Marino, Calif., compiled by the ROTC at the California Institute of Technology in 1921.

Service, Supply, and Procurement Divison (G-4)

180. GENERAL RECORDS. n.d. 1 item.

A map of the United States overprinted to show first-priority railroads in the emergency plan, prepared by the Office of the Chief of Engineers.

Operations Division

The Operations Division, which succeeded the War Plans Division in 1942, was the wartime command post of the Chief of Staff in directing the theaters of operations.

181. ASIATIC SECTION. n.d. 1 item.

An outline map of the area between the Salween River in Burma and the Brahmaputra River in India, showing roads and railroads.

Aerial Photographs

182. GENERAL RECORDS. 1916-18. 1,100 items.

Prints of aerial photographs of World War 1 combat areas in France and bombardment objectives in Germany. Approximately 900 are mounted in photograph albums; the remainder are filed individually. Accompanied by publications in French, English, and German pertaining to the military use of aerial photographs. Scales vary.

DEPARTMENT OF THE NAVY

GENERAL RECORDS OF THE DEPARTMENT OF THE NAVY. RG 80

The general cartographic records of the Department of the Navy consist of miscellaneous groups of maps acquired or prepared to meet special needs rather than the requirements of a systematic mapping program.

183. OFFICE OF THE SECRETARY OF THE NAVY. 1908-13. 9 items.

Maps forwarded with correspondence to the Secretary of the Navy. Among these are a map of the lands of the Richardson Construction Co. in the Yaqui River Valley, Sonora, Mexico, annotated and forwarded by the U.S.S. *Buffalo* in 1913, and blueprints of maps of Guam showing lands purchased at Sumay for a coaling station, transportation and communications systems, schools, and technical information about naval facilities on the island.

184. OFFICE OF THE DIRECTOR OF NAVAL PETROLEUM AND OIL SHALE RESERVES. ca. 1932. 2 items.

Published Geological Survey topographic sheets of McKittrick and Buena Vista Lake, Calif., mounted together and annotated to show the flight lines for the air mapping strips of Naval Oil Reserves 1 and 2, Calif.

RECORDS OF THE HYDROGRAPHIC OFFICE. RG 37

The Hydrographic Office, established as a separate agency in 1866, succeeded the Depot of Charts and Instruments, which had been established in 1830; before 1866 it had been associated with the Naval Observatory in a single agency. In 1962 it was redesignated the U.S. Naval Oceanographic Office.

The Naval Oceanographic Office is responsible for providing navigational aids to vessels of the Navy and the Merchant Marine, and to Naval aircraft. In fulfilling this duty it plans and conducts oceanographic research and surveying programs and issues numerous charts and other publications. In general, agreements on a division of geographical areas to be surveyed are worked out with other countries in order to avoid a duplication of effort. The Office ordinarily does not survey coastal waters of the United States; those areas are primarily the responsibility of the Coast and Geodetic Survey.

In addition to compiling nautical and aeronautical charts, the Naval Oceanographic Office conducts research in geodesy, nautical astronomy, navigation, terrestrial magnetism, geophysics, and related fields. These activities result in the production of a wide variety of maps and charts not directly related to the standard nautical and aeronautical series.

Hydrographic Office

185. GENERAL RECORDS. 1890-1945. 58 items.

Maps and publications prepared to illustrate or facilitate the activities of the Hydrographic Office. Included are technical manuals and general publications describing methods of hydrographic surveying and charting, 1930-45, gazetteers giving variants of foreign place names, chiefly in the Pacific Ocean, 1941-45, and manuscript maps of the oceans showing known soundings, about 1910.

186. ARCHIVES SECTION. 1838-1952. 17,091 items.

The Archives Section maintained the records of surveys conducted by the U.S. Navy and the chart enclosures from Hydrographic Office correspondence. The areas surveyed most extensively by the U.S. Navy for charting purposes are the coasts of Central and South America and the island areas in the Pacific Ocean. The records of these surveys are chiefly manuscript and include "boat" or work sheets, "smooth" or compilation sheets, topographic sheets, planimetric sheets, running survey sheets, reconnaissance sheets, rough field sheets, and sketches or views of land areas and rocks or shoals. Records from other Navy surveys include maps compiled by exploring expeditions, such as the Page survey of the La Plata River and its tributaries (1848-52), the Ringgold-Rodgers or North Pacific Surveying Expedition (1852-58), and the Perry expedition to Japan (1854-55). There are also records from surveys for the laying of cables, the most important historically being the survey of the Atlantic by the U.S.S. *Arctic* in 1855. Other records pertain to special sounding surveys, including the first sonic sounding survey made around the world by the U.S.S. *Stewart*, 1922-24, surveys made to determine the most practical location for an interoceanic canal across Central America, surveys made for coaling stations to be used by the U.S. Navy, surveys made for such reported dangers as shoals and rocks in navigable waters, and surveys for speed courses.

Among the chart enclosures to Hydrographic Office correspondence are manuscript and annotated maps forwarded to the Office for information purposes, including published charts annotated with corrections or additional data observed by navigators at sea; map reports from the North Atlantic ice patrol; maps made by private explorers, including maps made by Adm. R. E. Peary during his Arctic explorations of 1893-1903; track charts of naval and merchant vessels showing winds, currents, and other weather data recorded on voyages; and maps from privately compiled studies of ocean weather.

Other records include published charts of harbors and coastal areas annotated to show anchorages for ships of the fleet and charts prepared from inquiries into ship disasters, particularly the *Jeannette* in the Arctic Ocean, 1881, and the S.S. *Titanic* in the North Atlantic, 1912.

187. DIVISION OF OCEANOGRAPHY. 1944-51. 7 items.

The Division was responsible for conducting research on a wide range of oceanographic problems now studied by several divisions of the Naval Oceanographic Office. Its records include seven published monographs relating to physical oceanography and ocean dynamics; these were based chiefly on research conducted jointly by the Hydrographic Office and various private oceanographic institutes.

Naval Oceanographic Office

188. NAUTICAL CHART DIVISION AND ITS PREDECESSORS. 1868-1966. 37,244 items.

This Division is responsible for the production of most of the nautical charts and related publications issued by the Naval Oceanographic Office. Some of its publications are described under the organization responsible for compiling the data shown on these charts. The records of the Division include manuscript, published, and annotated nautical charts. The charts published before about 1920 were annotated with corrections and editorial changes for the purpose of bringing them up to date. Since 1920 only published charts have been added to the files. A small group of manuscript compilation sheets for some of the published charts also is included.

Other series of published maps include anchorage charts, which are Coast and Geodetic Survey charts of harbors and ports in the United States and its territories and possessions overprinted in the Hydrographic Office to show areas where ships of certain sizes may anchor; emergency reproduction charts, which are photolithographic reproductions of foreign charts covering areas not yet charted by the Hydrographic Office; field charts, which are nautical charts prepared and published aboard field survey ships; miscellaneous charts, which include preliminary charts, emergency reproductions, charts showing unsounded areas, charts showing naval facilities, training charts, preliminary charts, special regional charts, and maps prepared and published by the Hydrographic Office for other bureaus or offices within the Navy; mobilization charts, which show anchorage positions for ships of a fleet; position-plotting contoured charts, showing known contours of ocean bottoms, issued for the use of ships in reporting soundings; naval operations charts, used by ships in reporting their positions; current-plotting charts, used by ships to report currents encountered on their voyages; route charts, showing nautical routes; provisional (or temporary) charts, issued before final verification of the data can be made; and standard view charts, containing views of coastlines in addition to hydrographic data.

Finding aids include lists of charts published by the Hydrographic Office, 1866-1954; catalogs of index maps showing the coverage of the numbered nautical charts, with lists describing special nautical maps and related publications, 1884-1962; and loose maps indexing the coverage of the numbered nautical charts and special series of charts, 1916-57.

189. AERONAUTICAL DIVISION AND ITS PREDECESSORS. 1928-65. 2,350 items.

This Division is responsible for the production, or procurement, and distribution of all aeronautical charts and related air navigation publications required by the U.S. Navy. Its records include published aeronautical charts at varying scales covering strategic areas, chiefly in the polar regions, the Southwest Pacific, and the Gulf of Mexico-Caribbean Sea area. These charts show radio and visual navigation aids, isogonic lines, aircraft facilities, relief, and spot elevations. Some of the earlier editions also include plans and photomaps of airfields on the reverse sides of the charts.

Other records include several editions of an index map of the United States showing U.S. Navy aviation facilities; and a number of volumes of index maps to Hydrographic Office aeronautical charts, with lists describing special aeronautical charts and related publications, 1952-54.

190. NAVIGATIONAL SCIENCE DIVISION. 1945-61. 545 items.

This Division is responsible for compiling navigational manuals and tables and various specialized charts, and for developing and constructing navigational devices. Much of the data resulting from research undertaken by this Division is incorporated in the nautical and aeronautical charts issued by the Nautical Chart and Aeronautical Division.

The records of the Navigational Science Division include LORAN (long-range navigation) charts, published at various scales, which are designed for the use of marine and air navigators in determining exact geographic positions. They show, by periodic curves of equal time, differences in synchronized radio impulses, measured in seconds, that are transmitted by LORAN stations. There are a number of catalogs in index maps to the LORAN charts, and these include maps showing LORAN service areas and lists of related publications, 1946-54.

191. MARITIME SAFETY DIVISION AND ITS PREDECESSORS. 1852-1950. 86 items.

This Division is responsible for collecting and preparing for publication nautical data necessary for the safety and efficiency of U.S. Naval and Merchant Marine operations. It cooperates with other divisions in the preparation of charts and other publications and is responsible for the pilot charts and for revisions of the *Ice Atlas of the Northern Hemisphere*.

The Division's records include published copies of the Maury wind and current charts, 1852, and meteorological charts, 1853-54, which were predecessors of the pilot charts; an incomplete set of pilot charts, 1895-1946; an atlas of pilot charts of the upper air, 1945; current charts of the oceans, 1946-50; sea and swell charts, 1943-50; and the *Ice Atlas*, 1946.

Aerial Photographs

192. GENERAL RECORDS. 1923-50. 8,848 items.

Negatives (65 rolls) from photography covering areas in the Aleutian Islands, 1943.

Negatives from photography covering coastal areas in the eastern United States (7 rolls), about 1927-35; parts of Cuba (2 rolls), 1923; and certain islands in the Pacific Ocean (8 rolls), about 1941-43.

Negatives from photography of the Marianas Islands (4 rolls), about 1943-44; and the area occupied by the Hydrographic Office buildings at Suitland, Md. (1 roll), 1950.

One hundred and thirty-five cut negatives from World War II photography of certain Pacific Ocean islands (oblique) and Bermuda (vertical).

Mosaic prints from photographs of La Guaira, Venezuela (1937), San Juan Island and San Juan, Puerto Rico (1924), Midway Island in the Pacific (1924), and areas in the Hawaiian Islands, including Pearl and Hermes Reef (1924), French Frigate Shoal (1924), and Kaneohe Bay, Oahu (1924).

RECORDS OF THE UNITED STATES MARINE CORPS. RG 127

For its map requirements the U.S. Marine Corps depends primarily on the principal Federal mapping agencies. Maps to meet specific needs are produced by mapping units in the Intelligence Section of Marine Corps Headquarters and at the Marine Corps Schools, and by mapping units with the tactical forces in the field.

For a detailed listing of the records in Record Group 127 see The National Archives, *Cartographic Records of the United States Marine Corps*, Preliminary Inventory No. 73 (Washington, 1954).

193. GENERAL RECORDS. 1885-1939. 58 items.

Parts of a map of the battlefield of Gettysburg published by the Marine Corps Schools at Quantico, Va., in 1932, apparently for training purposes. Manuscript and annotated maps and plans of Marine Corps installations in the United States; maps showing properties acquired, or to be acquired, and proposed construction; fire-control maps; and ground plans of target butts, rifle ranges, and ammunition depots.

Maps relating to island possessions of the United States include maps of Guam showing topography, volcanic formations, vegetation, municipal boundaries, and a plan of the Marine barracks at Sumay; a map from a survey of the harbor of Apia, Samoa; a plan showing the defenses of Subic Bay, Philippine Islands; and a plan of the Marine Corps rifle range and machinegun range at Christiansted, Virgin Islands. A strategic chart of the Pacific Ocean shows possible anchorages.

Arranged in series by area. A card catalog lists the records by area.

194. RECORDS RELATING TO PEACETIME ACTIVITIES OF THE CORPS. 1904-43. 729 items.

In time of peace the Marine Corps is empowered to enter foreign lands to assist in quelling revolutions, to secure redress for crimes committed upon U.S. citizens in those lands, and to assist in times of disaster. These records reflect those tasks. They are primarily manuscript and appear to have three distinct origins; some were prepared in the Washington headquarters under the direction of the Intelligence Section of the Division of Operations and Training; others were prepared in the mapping sections of the individual units in the field; and the remainder were prepared by the F-2 Mapping Section of the Marine Corps Schools.

The areas represented by these maps are the islands in the Atlantic Ocean and the Caribbean Sea, Central and South American countries, and China. Among the records are outline and topographic maps at various scales, with particularly detailed coverage of Nicaragua and the Dominican Republic; general maps showing transportation facilities and maps from surveys of specific routes; maps showing communications facilities; plans of cities; maps showing international and internal boundaries and disputed boundary areas; maps showing troop movements and dispositions of forces during military operations; and maps prepared from military reconnaissances.

Arranged by area number. A card catalog lists the maps by area and thereunder by subject or kind of map.

195. FOURTH BRIGADE. 1918-19. 212 items.

The 4th Brigade, composed of the 5th and 6th Regiments and the 6th Machine Gun Battalion, was one of the two infantry brigades of the U.S. 2d Division fighting in France during World War 1. It was engaged in eight distinct operations, of which four were major operations. After the armistice the Brigade remained in Europe, taking a position north of Coblenz on the Rhine where it remained until the middle of June 1919 when it was ordered to an advanced position within Germany for the signing of the peace treaty.

The cartographic records of the Brigade consist largely of published topographic maps of France and Germany annotated during the operations of June 6, 1918-June 19, 1919. Among the records are maps showing boundaries of areas occupied by the Brigade, dispositions of forces and locations of headquarters, military objectives, jumpoff lines, order of battle, positions of relief, frontlines and successive lines of advance, lines of communication, billeting areas, and lines of resistance in Germany faced by the Brigade after the armistice.

Arranged chronologically by date of operation. A card catalog lists the maps by operation.

RECORDS OF THE BUREAU OF MEDICINE AND SURGERY. RG 52

The Bureau of Medicine and Surgery was established in the Navy Department in 1842 to maintain the health of the Navy and to care for the Navy's sick and wounded. It manages naval hospitals, medical supply depots, medical laboratories, the Naval Medical Center, and technical schools, and it supervises the professional education of Medical Department personnel.

196. DIVISION OF PREVENTIVE MEDICINE. 1946. 1 item.

A published atlas entitled *Distribution of Mosquitoes of Medical Importance in the Pacific Area.* It was prepared in the Bureau from research conducted in the Pacific during World War II. It contains 26 maps of the Southwest Pacific, each of which shows the distribution of a different species of mosquito. Related descriptions give pertinent information about the biological classification, life cycle, and disease-transmission characteristics of each species.

RECORDS OF NAVAL OPERATING FORCES. RG 313

This record group was established for the control of records created by mobile units of the U.S. Navy including fleets, squadrons, individual vessels, and other operating forces.

The Naval Oceanographic Office (formerly the Hydrographic office) is responsible for the overall mapping program of the U.S. Navy; therefore records of vessels assigned to that Office for surveying purposes are in Record Group 37 (see entry 186). From time to time, however, fleets, squadrons, vessels, and other operating forces of the Navy have prepared maps for special purposes.

197. U.S. ATLANTIC FLEET. 1907-18. 24 items.

Published charts of harbors and ports throughout the world annotated to show anchorages used by the fleet on the Around-the-World Cruise, 1907-9; charts of the Hudson River, N.Y., showing the mobilization of the fleet in 1912 and anchorages used by individual ships in 1918; a map of the North Sea, prepared by the Commander of the Mine Force, U.S. Atlantic Fleet, showing locations of British and American mines, 1918; and a map, identified as a record of the London Headquarters, of the coast of Europe from Gibraltar to Norway annotated to show names of ports not included on the published base maps, to emphasize other ports, and to show mine barrages.

198. U.S. NAVAL SUPPORT FORCE, ANTARCTICA. 1956-57. 15 items.

During Operation Deep Freeze II in the Antarctic an Army-Navy trail party was formed to establish a base at 80° S. 120° W., known as Byrd Station. The records of this party consist of a published report describing the mission and organization of the operation, the planning and logistics involved, and the actual field activities of the party; Hydrographic Office base maps of parts of Antarctica annotated to show the long-range reconnaissance flights of the entire route from Little America to Byrd Station and short-range flights in direct support of ground operations by number and date of each flight; Hydrographic Office base maps of parts of Antarctica annotated by members of the ground operations of the trail party to show observation points made along the course of the trail, the exact trail from Little America to Byrd Station, and the "Fashion Line" between the Ross Ice Shelf and the Rockefeller Plateau; and several sheets of position computations made at Byrd Station.

RECORDS OF THE OFFICE OF THE CHIEF OF NAVAL OPERATIONS. RG 38

The Office of the Chief of Naval Operations, established in 1915, directs the preparation and logistical support of the operating forces of the Navy and the coordination of the bureaus and offices of the Navy Department.

The Naval Oceanographic Office (formerly the Hydrographic Office), which is attached to the Office of the Chief of Naval Operations, is the official mapping agency of the Navy Department and its records constitute a separate record group (see entries 185-192). Aside from the activities of the Naval Oceanographic Office the Office of the Chief of Naval Operations has no large-scale mapping program, although some of its other component units, particularly the Office of Naval Intelligence (ONI), prepare maps to illustrate information they have compiled or for use as working tools. The Naval Oceanographic Office publishes many of the maps compiled by these offices; some may be found in the miscellaneous chart series in Record Group 37 (see entry 188).

For detailed descriptions of the maps in Record Group 38, see The National Archives, *Cartographic Records of the Office of the Chief of Naval Operations*, Preliminary Inventory No. 85 (Washington, 1955).

199. OFFICE OF NAVAL INTELLIGENCE. 1884-1943. 272 items.

The Office of Naval Intelligence was established in 1882 as a part of the Bureau of Navigation. From 1909 to 1915 it was under the supervision of the Aide to Operations in the Secretary's Office; since 1915 it has been a division in the Office of the Chief of Naval Operations. The functions of ONI include the collection and distribution of information, the direction of naval attachés abroad, and the investigation of individuals and organizations suspected of disloyal activities.

The cartographic records of ONI reflect its activities in the collection and distribution of information. Most of these maps were forwarded to the Office by naval attachés abroad. A few records were made within the Office. Among the records are maps of the world annotated to show political boundaries, economic conditions, statistics relating to world trade, mandates, and naval facilities of the United States and other world powers. Maps of foreign countries show information relating to these areas, such as maps illustrating the Sino-Japanese War, maps showing anglicized versions of place names, maps showing naval facilities and communication networks, and maps with information about foreign trade.

Arranged by numbers assigned in the agency. A card catalog lists these records by area.

RECORDS OF THE BUREAU OF NAVAL PERSONNEL. RG 24

The Bureau of Naval Personnel, first established in the Department of the Navy in 1862 as the Bureau of Navigation, originally was concerned with providing the Navy with materials necessary for navigation. In 1889 it was reorganized and given responsibility for the recruiting, training, discipline, and assignment of enlisted men and the appointment and assignment of officers, and it also assumed supervision of the Naval Academy. In 1942 the Bureau was renamed the Bureau of Naval Personnel.

Bureau of Navigation

200. GENERAL RECORDS. 1898-1935. 6 items.

These include manuscript maps illustrating naval activities of the Spanish-American War, three of which show the positions and the courses sailed by the American and Spanish ships off Santiago, Cuba, on July 3, 1898. A fourth shows the track of Admiral Cervera's squadron from Spain to Cuba, April 1-July 3, 1898. There are also two published base maps of the United States overprinted to show U.S. Navy recruiting districts and divisions and their headquarters, 1919 and 1935.

201. NAVAL WAR COLLEGE. 1905-32. 9 items.

Photoprocessed maps consisting of a general map of northeastern Colombia, 1905; strategic charts of the world, 1913, the Atlantic and Pacific Oceans, 1912, and the Pacific Ocean, 1929, showing distances; and a series of bound maps, dated 1932, with tabular data from economic and strategic studies of the world on foreign trade, trade areas, shipping, and the economic vulnerability of the principal maritime nations.

RECORDS OF THE BUREAU OF ORDNANCE. RG 74

The Bureau of Ordnance, established in 1842, is responsible for the design, manufacture, procurement, maintenance, and issue of all armament of the Navy, and for the operation, maintenance, and repair of naval gun factories, ordnance plants, torpedo stations, proving grounds, powder factories, ammunition depots, mine depots, and magazines.

202. GENERAL RECORDS. 1842-1923. 18 items.

Published maps of the United States showing inspection districts and local offices of the Bureau, 1920. Manuscript, processed, and annotated maps of areas along the Potomac River within the District of Columbia showing ownership of lands, about 1842-68. A large-scale manuscript map of the naval magazine at Hingham and Weymouth, Mass., 1905. A processed contour map of the naval nitrates plant at Indian Head, Md., 1918. A manuscript map showing the track of the U.S.S. *Constitution* from Cape Cod to Cape Hatteras and a manuscript map of Buzzard's Bay, Mass., 1876. Blueprint copies of maps of the world, the Atlantic and Pacific Oceans, and the Caribbean Sea, showing the specific density of seawater at 65° F. Arranged in series by subject.

DEPARTMENT OF THE AIR FORCE

RECORDS OF THE ARMY AIR FORCES. RG 18

An Army Air Service was organized in 1918 to consist of the Bureau of Aircraft Production and the Division of Military Aeronautics, successors of the Aviation Section in the Office of the Chief Signal Officer. In 1926 the Service was redesignated the Air Corps. In 1939 the functions of the Air Corps were divided between the Office of the Chief of the Air Corps and General Headquarters, Army Air Forces, and in 1941 the Air Corps was renamed the Army Air Forces. Record Group 18 includes the records of the Army Air Forces and its predecessors to 1947. The records of the United States Air Force for 1947 are in Record Group 341 (see entries 219-221).

The compilation and production of aeronautical charts for air navigation began in 1923 when the Air Section of the Training and War Plans Division of the Army Air Service authorized and furnished specifications for 52 air navigation strip maps. Much of the work was done by other mapping agencies using information supplied by the Air Section. By 1928 38 sheets of the series, showing principal Army air routes in the United States, were completed. In the same year a separate Map Unit was established under the Information Division to procure and disseminate charts and maps for navigational purposes. Use of the strip maps was gradually discontinued after 1930 as the more detailed Coast and Geodetic Survey aeronautical charts were issued. The Information Division of the Air Corps also was responsible for experimental work in aerial surveying and mapping.

In 1939 the Map Unit was redesignated the Map Section; after 1941, when the Air Corps became the Army Air Forces, the Section evolved into the Aeronautical Chart Service, redesignated the Aeronautical Chart and Information Center in 1951. The records of these successors to the Map Section are described in entries 217 and 221.

Aviation Section of the Office of the Chief Signal Officer

203. ENGINEERING DEPARTMENT. 1917-18. 6 items.

Blueprint copies of maps of Love Field, Tex., and vicinity, including maps of Dallas County showing the location of the airfield and roads and a topographic map of the airfield showing facilities; a map of the area around

Brooks Field, Tex., showing property owners and roads; and maps of Rich Field, near Waco, Tex., showing facilities of the field and locations of buildings.

204. BALLOON SCHOOLS. 1918. 1 item.

A blueprint copy of a plan of the U.S. Army Balloon School located at Camp John Wise, near San Antonio, Tex.

Army Air Service

205. GENERAL RECORDS. 1919-24. 7 items.

Published and annotated maps of the United States showing proposed airways; isogonic lines and annual changes for 1915, meteorological stations, and boundaries of aviation forecast zones; the route of the 32-hour transcontinental flight from New York to San Francisco, 1919; and military activities of the Army, the Navy, and the Army Air Service, 1921. Published patrol maps of the Marfa and Eagle Pass Districts, prepared for the 1st Bombing Group, El Paso, Tex. A photoprocessed map showing the 1924 round-the-world flight of the Air Service.

206. INFORMATION GROUP. 1920. 3 items.

Published and photoprocessed maps of the United States showing landing fields and activities of the Air Service. A map of the northeastern United States showing "America's Model Airway" from Washington, D.C., to Dayton, Ohio.

207. TRAINING AND WAR PLANS DIVISION. 1918-25. 6 items.

Published and photoprocessed maps of the United States showing aerial routes flown and reported by the Director of Military Aeronautics, landing fields and proposed airways systems, and proposed model Army airways and routes for the U.S. Mail Service. An experimental air navigation map for the area between Dayton, Ohio, and Wheeling, W. Va. An aerial mosaic of Washington, D.C., compiled by the School of Aerial Photography, Langley Field, Va., in 1918.

208. PHOTOGRAPHIC SECTIONS. 1920-21. 4 items.

Photomaps of Coblenz, Germany, and the Rhine River from Coblenz to Neuwied and of Washington, D.C., made by the Photographic Section at Bolling Field. An aerial mosaic of the military reservation at Camp Bragg, N.C., made by the Photographic Section at Camp Bragg.

209. AIRWAYS SECTION. 1923-25. 10 items.

Unnumbered airstrip maps of parts of the United States.

Army Air Corps

210. GENERAL RECORDS. 1929-32. 6 items.

A map of North America annotated to serve as a master index to airway strip maps. Published and photoprocessed maps of the United States showing the progress of aerial photography flown by the Air Corps, locations capable of accommodating Air Corps squadrons and groups, and airways routes. A photoprocessed, undated map showing the route of an Army Air Corps Pan-American Flight.

211. PHOTOGRAPHIC SECTIONS. 1929. 1 item.

An aerial mosaic of the Gunpowder Neck, Md., area prepared by the Photographic Section at Bolling Field, Washington, D.C.

212. MATERIALS DIVISION. 1922-32. 11 items.

A series of looseleaf project record books containing reports, illustrations, and correspondence on the methods and equipment used in aerial photography for surveying and mapping. These record books were started by the Engineering Division of the Air Service located at McCook (later Wright) Field, Dayton, Ohio, and were continued by the Engineering Section of the Materials Division of the Army Air Corps located at Wright Field.

213. INFORMATION DIVISION. 1923-36. 19 items.

Three photoprocessed index maps of the United States, dated 1926-29, showing the coverage of airstrip maps 1 through 52; and published copies of 16 of the maps from that series.

Army Air Forces

The organizations responsible for the cartographic activities of the Army Air Forces (AAF), which succeeded the Air Corps in 1941, were the Aeronautical Chart Service and its predecessors, the Map Section and the Map-Chart Division. The Map Section procured and distributed maps and charts obtained from various sources, including the U.S. Geological Survey and the Engineer Reproduction Plant (predecessor of the Army Map Service). The Map Section was reorganized in 1942 to become the Map-Chart Division, which was in turn reorganized to form the Aeronautical Chart Service in 1944. The Aeronautical Chart Service was charged with the preparation of specifications for and the compilation, reproduction, maintenance, and distribution of aeronautical charts. Although much of the actual cartographic work was done by other Federal agencies, the Chart Service allotted funds to those agencies and prepared work programs pertaining to the production of air charts needed in the war effort.

Among the new chart series produced were the Western Hemisphere, World Long Range, World Planning, World Weather, Approach Charts of Strategic Areas, and large-scale Target Charts. In addition, the Army Air Forces instituted the most extensive program of aerial photography that had been undertaken until that time. These programs have been continued by its successor, the U.S. Air Force (see entries 219-221).

214. GENERAL RECORDS. 1942-43. 198 items.

A set of photomaps of the "Desert Theater" in the southwestern United States; the French Congo and Abyssinia sheets from a series of maps of Africa at the scale of 1:2,000,000 overprinted to show air facilities; a contour map of Tanaga Island in the Aleutians, prepared for the Army Air Forces by the U.S. Geological Survey from aerial photographs flown by the U.S. Navy; maps of Formosa and part of China near Shanghai showing roads; and a series of topographic maps of China.

215. ASSISTANT CHIEF OF AIR STAFF—INTELLIGENCE. 1942-44. 628 items.

A base map of western Europe. A photoprocessed map of North Africa showing airports, landing grounds, and seaplane bases. Relief maps of parts of Japan and Formosa. Flak maps of Kyushu, Japan. Maps of cities and towns in Manchuria showing road patterns and military targets. Charts of target areas in zones of military activities during World War II overprinted with target grids. Panels of maps and aerial photographs of target areas in North Africa including for each selected area a general locational map, a large-scale map showing military targets, and an aerial photograph. Stargraph direct-plotting charts for celestial navigation.

216. WEATHER DIVISION AND ITS PREDECESSORS. 1942-46. 434 items.

A map of the world showing climatic regions and basic seasonal climatic data for each region. A catalog of weather-plotting charts issued by the AAF in 1945. Maps compiled by the Weather Information Service in 1943 including a base scale and direction-indicating chart, a preliminary climatic atlas of the world, and an atlas illustrating strategic aspects of climate in the Iberian Peninsula.

Among the records of the Climatological Division are weather-plotting charts for several regions of the world showing weather stations and monthly sea surface isotherms, and atlases showing strategic aspects of climate in Italy, southern France, and the Balkans. The records of the Weather Research Center include base plotting charts, some with sea surface isotherms shown, winds-aloft charts, flight charts, and base charts on special projections.

The Air Weather Service cooperated with the Weather Bureau in the compilation of maps illustrating the historical weather of the Northern

Hemisphere. The maps published from October 1945 through September 1947 have the imprint of the Air Weather Service but are maintained with the records of the Weather Bureau as an integral part of the historical series of Northern Hemisphere weather maps (see entry 406).

217. AERONAUTICAL CHART SERVICE. 1939-47. 5,208 items.

Incomplete sets of maps and other publications issued by the Aeronautical Chart Service (ACS). Among the records is a pamphlet on reconnaissance mapping with aerial photographs, an incomplete set of bulletins published monthly by the ACS listing new and obsolete charts, a standard style sheet for an aeronautical chart, and a flow diagram of chart reproduction processes.

A series of index maps and catalogs of index maps to the charts published by the AAF and by other agencies for the AAF. Special maps including strategic air charts of the Northern and Southern Hemispheres; a strategic air planning chart of the Asiatic-Pacific Theater, 1942-45; two series of maps of the Northern Hemisphere showing political boundaries and time zones, physical regions and ocean currents, annual precipitation and other aspects of climate, vegetation, population density, economic activities, transportation routes, isobars and prevailing winds, and monthly climatic zones; a topographic map of the Northern Hemisphere; an aeronautical chart of the world showing airways and estimated distances; a map of the northeastern boundary area of the United States overprinted with information about defense areas; a strategic planning map of the Northern Hemisphere with a gazetteer and list of sources, compiled by the Board on Geographic Names and the Arctic, Desert, and Tropical Branch of the AAF; and a series of azimuthal equidistant charts centered on various points throughout the world.

An incomplete series of World Aeronautical Charts (1:1,000,000) showing terrain, ground transportation facilities, and aeronautical facilities. Related to these are the World Pilotage Charts (1:500,000) and the World Approach Charts (1:250,000) with similar but more detailed information for selected areas of strategic importance. Other series include cloth charts of Japan, Korea, and Southeast Asia; special training charts of areas in the United States; aeronautical planning charts, long-range air navigation charts; charts prepared for use in problems given in extension courses; gnomonic tracking charts on two scales, 1:10,500,000 and 1:4,000,000; and plans of cities in Japan, Manchuria, and China.

218. ARMY AIR FORCE COMMANDS. 1942-45. 188 items.

Incomplete series of maps published under the direction of specific Army Air Force commands. Among the records are charts of islands in the South Pacific and a tactical map of part of Kern County, Calif., compiled under the direction of the 13th Air Force; and target charts, photomaps of target areas, and perspective charts of target areas in Japan and the South Pacific compiled by the A-2 (Intelligence) sections of the 20th Air Force and the 21st Bomber Command.

RECORDS OF HEADQUARTERS UNITED STATES AIR FORCE. RG 341

The U.S. Air Force, which succeeded the Army Air Forces in 1947, requires maps for planning purposes, for air navigation, and for the conduct of tactical operations. The Aeronautical Chart and Information Center (ACIC) is responsible for meeting these requirements. Many standard series of charts and a variety of special maps and charts are produced, including strategic planning charts, navigational charts, and the World Aeronautical Charts, which have been adopted as the standard aeronautical chart series by the International Civil Aviation Organization. The mapping activities of the Aeronautical Chart and Information Center are worldwide in scope, although the preparation of aeronautical charts of the United States is mainly the responsibility of the Coast and Geodetic Survey (see entry 377).

219. GENERAL RECORDS. 1951. 1 item.

A copy of Air Force Manual 96-3, *Aeronautical Charts*, describing the characteristics, purposes, and functions of the principal types of aeronautical charts.

220. AIR WEATHER SERVICE. 1948-57. 3 items.

A copy of Air Weather Service Manual 105-0-1, *Constant Pressure Analysis and Forecasting Manual*, January 1948, prepared for the use of field forecasters as an aid in the preparation of surface and upper-air forecasts. An index catalog to weather-plotting charts, 1957, and a weather-plotting chart of the Western Pacific area and Eastern Asia, 1949.

221. AERONAUTICAL CHART AND INFORMATION CENTER. 1947-63. 4,016 items.

Catalogs of index maps and lists of maps and other publications issued by the ACIC. A series of bulletins issued monthly, describing current charts and charts declared obsolete. Quarterly acquisitions lists from the Map-Chart Library of the ACIC. A circular on the use and preparation of azimuthal equidistant charts.

Incomplete series of aeronautical charts and special maps issued by the ACIC, including a series of maps of the Northern Hemisphere showing political boundaries, time zones, climate, vegetation, population density, economic activities, and transportation routes. A series of maps designed for use at the Air Force Academy and other training schools; jet navigation charts; radar charts; ZD (azimuthal equidistant) charts centered on various points throughout the world; NS (special navigation) charts; and XM (aeronautical planning and training) charts.

Continuations of the World Aeronautical Chart, at 1:1,000,000; the World Pilotage Chart, at 1:500,000; and the World Approach Chart, at 1:250,000 (see also entry 217). A three-volume lunar atlas, 1960-63, containing a history of the atlas project and photographs of the moon and parts of the moon, some overprinted to provide a complete lunar coordinate grid system; and a few charts of the moon and parts of the moon, 1960-61.

JOINT MILITARY AGENCIES

RECORDS OF THE OFFICE OF STRATEGIC SERVICES. RG 226

The Office of Strategic Services (OSS), originally designated the Office of Coordinator of Information, was charged with collecting and analyzing strategic information required by the Joint Chiefs of Staff for military and other operations. It was terminated in 1945.

The cartographic records of the OSS are not described because most of them have not yet been declassified. They consist generally of maps prepared in the Office of Coordinator of Information, maps prepared or gathered by the Division of Map Intelligence and Cartography of the Research and Analysis Branch of the OSS, and maps prepared by or for the use of Dr. J. A. Morrison of the OSS.

DEPARTMENT OF JUSTICE

GENERAL RECORDS OF THE DEPARTMENT OF JUSTICE. RG 60

The Office of the Attorney General was established in 1789. The Attorney General was authorized to represent the United States in all suits before the Supreme Court and to give legal advice to the President and the heads of the executive departments when requested to do so. It was not until 1870, however, that a Department of Justice was established, with the Attorney General at its head.

The cartographic records of the Department were acquired principally from outside sources or were submitted as exhibits in court cases or investigations.

222. DIVISION OF RECORDS. ca. 1900-20. 10 items.

Manuscript and annotated maps and graphs, some identified as having been used as exhibits in court cases. Among these are maps of the United States and of the States of Oklahoma and Kansas showing railroad systems; maps of the United States and parts of the United States showing areas controlled by certain oil companies, refining points, and pipelines identified as common carriers or private carriers; a map of New York Harbor identifying certain port and terminal facilities; a plan of a lock and dam on the Yamhill River, Oreg.; a ground plan of Walter Reed Hospital, Washington, D.C., identifying the buildings by structural type; and graphs apparently comparing the production of oil with that of other commodities from 1890 to 1906.

RECORDS OF THE OFFICE OF ALIEN PROPERTY. RG 131

The first Office of Alien Property was created in 1917 to discover, administer, and dispose of enemy-owned property in the United States and its possessions; it was discontinued in 1934 and its functions were transferred to the Department of Justice. The Second Office was established in 1942 and terminated in 1946. It was succeeded by the Office of Alien Property in the Justice Department, which was abolished in 1966. The cartographic records in Record Group 131 are a series of maps pertaining to properties in the United States owned by a foreign company whose parent firm was German.

223. SEIZED ENEMY PROPERTIES, WORLD WAR II.
      ca. 1927-39. 27 items.

Published and photoprocessed charts and plans of harbors on the Atlantic and gulf coasts of the United States annotated to show port facilities believed used by N. V. Potash Export My., Inc., or N. V. Potash (Kali) Export Maatschappij of Amsterdam, sales agent in the United States and other countries in the Western Hemisphere for the Franco-German potash cartel.

RECORDS OF THE IMMIGRATION AND NATURALIZATION SERVICE. RG 85

The Immigration and Naturalization Service, established in 1891, is responsible for administering laws relating to the admission, registration, and naturalization of aliens, and to exclusion and deportation; for detecting civilian alien enemy internees; for controlling foreign travelers in the United States; and for supervising naturalization work in the courts.

224. ALIEN REGISTRATION DIVISION. 1940. 1 item.

A photoprocessed map of the United States showing the number of aliens in each State and the percentage of aliens included in each State's population.

POST OFFICE DEPARTMENT

RECORDS OF THE POST OFFICE DEPARTMENT. RG 28

The Post Office Department makes maps for its internal use and for dissemination of information about postal facilities. More detailed descriptions of the cartographic records of the Division of Topography (see entry 226) are included in The National Archives, *Records of the Bureaus of the Third and Fourth Assistant Postmasters General, the Bureau of Accounts, and the Bureau of the Chief Inspector of the Post Office Department*, Preliminary Inventory No. 114 (Washington, 1959), and *Records of the Post Office Department*, Preliminary Inventory No. 168 (Washington, 1967).

225. DIVISION OF AIRMAIL SERVICE. 1919-41. 75 items.

Blueprint plans of existing and proposed landing fields to be used by the Airmail Service, and published maps of the United States showing existing and proposed locations of airmail routes and landing fields. Arranged in series by subject.

226. DIVISION OF TOPOGRAPHY AND PREDECESSORS. 1839-1960.
    2,729 items.

The records of this Division include State, county, city, and local center maps showing postal information. There are several series of the post-route State maps. One includes maps of several States, or parts of States, issued from 1867 to 1891. Another series is composed of maps of individual States and dates from 1894 through 1960. The maps in each of these series show post offices, mail delivery routes, frequency of mail service, distances between post offices, and mail-carrying railroads. Those of a later date also show airmail routes. Both groups of maps show county boundaries. Revised editions of these State maps are published from time to time. A number of sheets are missing from this set, however, particularly from those published before 1938. There are also manuscript compilations for many of the State maps. These maps usually have several dates for corrections.

A post-route atlas of the United States and of the individual States and territories compiled under the direction of David Burr in 1839.

A series of published post-route State maps dated 1917 is annotated with information concerning navigable waters, particularly in the east coast States.

Three separate series of published post-route State maps for the period 1935-40 are annotated. One set shows boundaries of congressional districts. A second set emphasizes certain cities and towns, perhaps to indicate the location of first-class post offices. The maps in the third set bear unexplained six-digit numbers, generally along the railroad lines.

Other records include local center maps, county maps, city maps, and a representative sampling of the rural delivery route maps, which are blueprint copies of maps of local areas annotated to show rural mail routes and accompanied by official descriptions giving directions, stops, and mileages for each route. The local center maps are manuscript maps of rural areas showing the delivery routes servicing each area. The county maps are photoprocessed maps of individual counties showing mail routes and post offices. The city maps, which are manuscript, show postal facilities.

Arranged in series by type of map and thereunder alphabetically by name of State, county, city, or area.

DEPARTMENT OF THE INTERIOR

RECORDS OF THE OFFICE OF THE SECRETARY
OF THE INTERIOR. RG 48

The Office of the Secretary of the Interior produces maps only for its own administrative use, although it has general supervision over agencies that have primary mapping and mapmaking functions. The cartographic records of the Office of the Secretary include maps made by offices or divisions that were abolished and whose files were absorbed into a central filing system within the Office. Also included are records transferred to the Office from other departments. For detailed descriptions, see The National Archives, *Cartographic Records of the Office of the Secretary of the Interior*, Preliminary Inventory No. 81 (Washington, 1955).

227. GENERAL RECORDS. 1865-1923. 278 items.

Manuscript, annotated, published, and photoprocessed maps of the United States and parts of the United States showing natural resources, national parks and forests, the status of the public domain, Indian tribal locations and reservations, judicial districts, mining districts and claims, railroads, and reclamation projects. Maps and profiles of railroad lines. Maps and plats of Washington, D.C., showing existing and proposed Government reservations, property owners and the acquisition of properties, and highways. Maps of cities in more than one congressional district, 1903. Plans of Federal reservations, particularly the Hot Springs (Ark.) Reservation. Maps of Alaska showing railroads. Maps and other records relating to the Lower Colorado River Project, 1906-12. A plan of the Lemhi Land and Irrigation Project, Idaho.

Arranged in series by subject.

228. RECORDS OF THE OFFICE OF EXPLORATIONS AND SURVEYS OF THE WAR DEPARTMENT PACIFIC RAILROAD SURVEYS. 1849-58. 337 items.

These records were transferred to the Department of the Interior from the Office of Explorations and Surveys in the War Department in 1865. They include annotated topographic maps and profiles showing the general routes of surveys and explorations to determine the most practical route for a railroad between the Mississippi River and the Pacific Ocean, manuscript topographic maps and profiles of routes or parts of routes of specific surveys, and an incomplete set of published maps and profiles of general and specific surveys. Most of these records were prepared by or under the direction of personnel in charge of the individual surveys or in the Office of Pacific Railroad Explorations and Surveys of the War Department from notes and data gathered on the expeditions. Many were used in, or represent compilations of, maps and profiles in the published 13-volume *Reports of Explorations and Surveys To Ascertain the Most Practicable and Economical Route for a Railroad from the Mississippi River to the Pacific Ocean . . . 1853-1856. . .*(Washington, 1861).

In addition to the routes explored for railroads these maps show geology, drainage, topography, Indian tribal locations, settlements, and roads and trails. There are a few lithographed and manuscript landscape sketches made by artists accompanying the expeditions.

Arranged by principal route of exploration; those records pertaining to all or several of the routes are in a general file.

229. PACIFIC WAGON ROADS OFFICE. 1857. 1 item.

A published map of the western division of the Fort Kearny, South Pass, and Honey Lake Road showing the route surveyed, topography and drainage, and camps and trading posts along the route.

RECORDS OF THE BITUMINOUS COAL DIVISION. RG 222

The major functions of the Bituminous Coal Division, established in 1939, and its predecessor, the second National Bituminous Coal Commission (1937-39), were to determine average production costs for bituminous coal in each production area and to establish minimum and maximum prices based on these costs. These agencies also established marketing regulations; carried on research relating to the conservation, production, distribution, and use of bituminous coal; and assisted in the adoption of a maximum workday and minimum wage limits in the industry. The Division was abolished in 1943.

230. GENERAL RECORDS. ca. 1937-43. 10 items.

A map of the United States annotated to show boundaries of production districts and minimum price areas. A map of the United States annotated to show boundaries of districts, noted in pencil on the back of the map as marketing areas. A map of the United States overprinted to show the number of tons of coal produced by each State, the number used by each State, and the rates of interstate shipments. A map showing railroad lines, coal districts, and coalfields in the northeastern quarter of the United States. A map of part of the United States annotated in colors to differentiate the inner and outer coal districts in Pennsylvania, West Virginia, Virginia, Maryland, and Kentucky and the Hocking district of Ohio, and to show "affected territory" in parts of

Michigan, Ohio, and Indiana. Maps of Kansas, Nebraska, and South Dakota annotated to show towns to which District 15 shipped coal in 1937 and towns that had natural gas available. The map of Kansas is further annotated to show where Colorado and Kansas rates equalize, and the map of Nebraska is annotated to show where Colorado and Production Group 7 rates equalize. A map of Iowa annotated to show towns receiving coal shipments from different groups, and market areas originally proposed by District 15.

RECORDS OF THE FISH AND WILDLIFE SERVICE. RG 22

The Fish and Wildlife Service was established in 1940 through a consolidation of the Bureau of Biological Survey (established in 1885) and the Bureau of Fisheries (established in 1903). The Bureau of Fisheries had been the successor of the U.S. Commission of Fish and Fisheries. The functions of the Fish and Wildlife Service are the conservation of the Nation's wildlife and the maintenance of the welfare of commercial fisheries in the United States.

The Fish and Wildlife Service makes extensive use of maps, charts, and aerial photographs in acquiring lands and in developing and managing the areas under its administration. Both cadastral and topographic surveys are made by the Service to facilitate its activities. The mapping program of the Service involves the preparation of various types and scales, including landownership maps, maps showing boundaries of units administered by the Service, maps used in planning construction projects, and maps pertaining to the distribution of fish and wildlife.

United States Fish and Fisheries Commission

231. DIVISION OF INQUIRY RESPECTING FOOD FISHES. 1888-98.
    115 items.

Maps prepared from investigations of fish life and fur seals in Alaskan waters. Most of these records were prepared from surveys conducted by personnel assigned to the U.S.S. *Albatross*. That ship was assigned to survey waters off the coast of Alaska and the west coast of the United States and to study the fish life. Upon several occasions when it was in Alaskan waters it was assigned to make special investigations of fur seals.

Among the records are published maps of Alaska showing coastal topography and hydrography, locations of salmon canneries, and details of harbors; and published maps of the Bering Sea including an 1893 map showing hydrography and a map showing the distribution and migration of fur seals, about 1897.

A series of published maps of fur-seal rookeries in the Pribilof Islands as surveyed in 1891 by Joseph Stanley-Brown, a special agent of the Department of the Treasury. These maps were specially prepared for use in the fur seal arbitrations before the Paris Tribunal (see entry 46). The task of keeping this information current was assigned to the United States Fish and Fisheries Commission. Later records consist of a series of the Stanley-Brown maps annotated to show the distribution of seals, limits of hauling and breeding grounds, and photographic stations, 1892-97. These observations were made by Stanley-Brown in 1892, by C. H. Townsend yearly from 1893 to 1896, and by Lucas and Clark in 1897. A series of Coast and Geodetic Survey charts of seal rookeries in the Pribilof Islands annotated to show limits of rookeries after the breeding season was over, from observations by C. H. Townsend in 1898. A series of photoprocessed copies of maps by Henry Elliot showing the areas occupied by breeding fur seals, and hauling grounds of nonbreeding seals from 1872 to 1874, annotated to show these areas in 1890. The original maps by Elliot are in Record Group 76 (see entry 46).

Bureau of Fisheries

232. ALASKAN FISHERIES SERVICE. 1908-19. 68 items.

Coast and Geodetic Survey charts of the southern and southeastern coasts of Alaska annotated to show fish traps, fisheries, canneries, and packing plants.

233. ALASKAN FUR SEAL SERVICE. 1904-37. 39 items.

Manuscript and annotated published maps of seal rookeries on St. Paul and St. George Islands in the Pribilof chain showing boundaries of breeding and hauling grounds, the number of seals at the height of season, harem count, and the positions from which photographs were taken.

Biological Survey

234. GENERAL RECORDS. 1891-1939. 24 items.

A published map showing the routes of the Death Valley Expedition, 1891; published maps compiled by C. Hart Merriam including a map of North America showing principal life areas, 1892, and a map of the United States showing principal life zones, 1897; a photoprocessed map of Lower California, 1913; photoprocessed maps of the United States showing Federal wildlife refuges, bird refuges, and game preserves; maps of some of the States showing Federal wildlife refuges, 1934-39; and a map of the Huron Migratory Bird Refuge, Mich., 1937.

Fish and Wildlife Service

235. GENERAL RECORDS. 1939-41. 4 items.

Photoprocessed maps including a map of the United States showing national wildlife refuges; a map of North Dakota showing easement refuges; and maps of the Bosque del Apache Refuge in New Mexico and the Noxubee Refuge in Mississippi.

RECORDS OF THE OFFICE OF GEOGRAPHY. RG 324.

The Office of Geography, under the Assistant Secretary—Mineral Resources, Department of the Interior, provides research and other staff services for the interdepartmental Board on Geographic Names and the Secretary of the Interior in the field of foreign geographic names.

The original United States Board on Geographic Names was established in 1890 to ensure the uniform usage of geographic names by the executive departments of the Federal Government. It has existed since then under a variety of titles, except during the period 1934-43, when it was defunct. The present Board on Geographic Names was established in 1947. In 1958 its records and functions relating to domestic geographic names were transferred to the U.S. Geological Survey.

Record Group 324 is composed chiefly of publications of the Board on Geographic Names and cartographic records compiled by the Division of Geography, predecessor of the Office of Geography, for use in name-decision cases.

Division of Geography

236. CARTOGRAPHIC SECTION. 1943-47. 150 items.

Manuscript, annotated, and published maps compiled in the Cartographic Section of the former Division of Geography, generally from information supplied by, or at the request of, the former United States Board on Geographic Names. These are numbered in sequence, 1-342, although many maps are missing from the series. Most of the first hundred maps in this series pertain to the United States. Among these are several maps of parishes in Louisiana; a map of the crest of the Sierra Nevada south of Mount Whitney; maps of areas in the vicinity of Paunsagunt Plateau, Utah; a group of maps of the Eastern Shore areas in Maryland and Virginia; and a group of maps of the west coast of Florida showing the Keys. A small group of maps of Burma shows relief, rainfall, geological structures, natural regions, and ethnic distributions.

The rest of the maps in this series pertain chiefly to foreign areas, although there are a few of parts of the United States, similiar to those described above. Many of these were prepared for other Government agencies or from information furnished by other agencies. Among these are maps of Norway,

Formosa, and Thailand showing boundaries of political subdivisions; maps prepared from information compiled by the Foreign Metals Division of the Bureau of Mines consisting of base maps of Australia and China, and maps of Australia, China, Manchuria, New Caledonia, and Japan showing important metallic ore deposits and the locations of metallurgical plants; a panel of maps of countries in the Middle East showing petroleum facilities prepared for the Petroleum Administration for War; a series of maps of Alaska showing railroads and steamship routes, prepared for the House Committee on Territories; and several maps of the world showing the coverage of place-name surveys, the status of directions and guides issued by the Board on Geographic Names, and proposed work programs for the Board in 1945.

A few of the maps are not numbered. Among these are maps of provinces in Bulgaria showing names appearing on maps prepared by the Geographic Section, General Staff of the British Army, and recommendations by the Board on Geographic Names; a map of Tibet showing geographic names; a photoprocessed map of the Soviet Union indexing the sheet coverage of the "Great Soviet Atlas ll"; a sketch of the Continental Divide in Colorado; and a map of Cape May, N.J., and vicinity.

An important function of the Cartographic Section during World War ll was the addition of correct names to maps compiled by other Government agencies. The latter submitted blueline prints of maps scheduled for publication; the Section then added the approved names. These prints were then returned to the agency requesting the information; after the agency finished with these annotated prints they were returned to the Division of Geography. A representative sampling of blueline prints of maps compiled by the Army Map Service with the annotations by the Cartographic Section of the Division of Geography has been retained as a permanent record to show the technique of this activity.

Board on Geographic Names

237. GENERAL RECORDS. 1890-1964. 218 items.

Two copies, at different scales, of a map of the United States annotated to show mountain areas and related nomenclature adopted by the United States Geographic Board on February 6, 1907.

Catalogs of publications issued by the Board and its predecessors, editions of 1949, 1951, and 1953.

Printed reports and supplements to reports issued by the Board, 1890-1964, relating to decisions on place names; and special publications of the Board consisting of directions for the treatment of geographic names in specific areas, guides to geographic names, and special-decision lists. Gazetteers 1, 2, and 14 listing place names and their geographic coordinates for British East Africa; Madagascar, Reunion, and the Comoro Islands; and Antarctica.

Arranged in series by kind of publication and thereunder by publication number or date, when applicable.

RECORDS OF THE GEOLOGICAL SURVEY. RG 57.

The Geological Survey was established in 1879 in the Department of the Interior to conduct investigations and publish reports on the mineral and water resources of the United States, to make topographic maps, to classify public lands, and to supervise mineral leasing operations on public and Indian lands and naval petroleum reserves. Four agencies that were engaged in similar work preceded the Geological Survey and were absorbed by it wholly or in part. Two of these agencies, the United States Geological and Geographical Survey of the Territories (the Hayden Survey), 1867-79, and the United States Geographical and Geological Survey of the Rocky Mountain Region (the Powell Survey), 1869-79, operated under the supervision of the Department of the Interior; therefore their records are now filed with those of the Geological Survey. Most of the records of the other two surveys, the United States Geographical Surveys West of the One Hundredth Meridian (the Wheeler Survey), 1869-79, and the United States Geological Exploration of the Fortieth Parallel (the King Survey), 1867-80, are among the records of the Office of the Chief of Engineers (see entries 112 and 113) under whose jurisdiction they operated.

The Geological Survey has long functioned as a principal mapping agency of the Federal Government. Surveys, investigations, and studies relating to topography, geology, minerals, water resources, and conservation constitute the major work of the technical divisions of the Survey.

Topographic maps are a product of field and photogrammetric surveys and office compilations. The quadrangle series, planned eventually to cover the entire United States, may be considered the Nation's basic map coverage. The surveying and mapping operations are conducted chiefly through regional offices, but the central office in Washington standardizes and edits all work. Special topographic and planimetric maps and indexes are published to fill specific needs in connection with USGS work or that of other Federal agencies.

Investigations of the geology and the minerals and mineral fuel resources of the United States result in a number of map series, including maps showing surface geology, planned utimately to cover the entire country, and maps showing special geologic, stratigraphic, or petrographic features. As a result of special surveys, reports and maps are published relating to particular mineral and mineral fuel deposits important to the national economy.

Water investigations are made through a large number of field offices. Data is collected for other agencies of the Government with the cooperation of the States and municipalities concerned. Hydrologic studies are conducted in two principal fields—water quality and surface- and ground-water availability.

Maps also are produced for operational use in the classification of Federal lands regarding mineral and water resources, and for the administration of leased mines. Other maps are compiled to accompany particular investigations to determine dam sites and water-storage potentials, and location and extent of mineral deposits on Federal lands.

In addition to performing the basic tasks of exploring, mapping, and appraising our natural resources, the Geological Survey conducts fundamental research in many of the earth sciences.

Predecessor Agencies

238. UNITED STATES GEOLOGICAL AND GEOGRAPHICAL SURVEY OF THE TERRITORIES. 1869-81. 73 items.

Published maps and a few manuscript and proof copies compiled from the surveys made under the direction of F. V. Hayden in parts of the Idaho, Montana, Utah, Colorado, and Wyoming Territories. Among the records are general maps showing the areas surveyed; topographic and drainage maps; maps showing primary triangulation; maps showing arable land, grasslands, forested areas, geology, and coal deposits; maps showing ancient ruins; panoramic views of selected areas; and diagrams showing geologic sections of certain parts of the areas surveyed. The maps of Colorado cover parts of adjacent territories and are bound in atlas form. There are two editions of the atlas, one dated 1877 and the other, 1881. The maps of the other territories are loose. Among them are maps from surveys of the Yellowstone Park area including geologic and topographic maps of the entire area and special maps of geyser basins.

239. UNITED STATES GEOGRAPHICAL AND GEOLOGICAL SURVEY OF THE ROCKY MOUNTAIN REGION. 1875-79. 20 items.

Maps compiled from surveys made under the direction of John Wesley Powell. Among these are published maps of Utah Territory showing topography, irrigable areas, and timberlands. A few manuscript maps of Utah showing topography and drainage features. A portfolio of published maps of the Black Hills area including a geologic map, a topographic map, and a perspective view of the area. A portfolio of published maps and related records of the geological survey of the Uinta Mountains, Utah, including a topographic map, a geologic map, diagrams showing geological structure and displacement, and stereograms of the displacement.

Geological Survey

240. GENERAL RECORDS. 1914-55. 11 items.

Published maps of the United States showing physiographic regions and the distribution of representative quadrangles appearing in sets of selected maps, editions of 1919, 1941, and 1946. An administrative planning map of the United States showing the areas covered by the 15-minute quadrangles.

Maps of Virginia and Colorado showing the status of aerial photography flown by the Geological Survey to 1952. A photoprocessed map of part of southwestern Louisiana indexing the area covered by aerial photography and showing the relationship of the film to topographic quadrangles based on the film, 1934.

An undated map of the United States showing coalfields.

Publications relating to mapping activities of the Geological Survey, including circulars with information about mapping in Alaska; instructions on topographic mapping with a description of the Twinplex stereoplotting instrument; notes on State plane coordinate systems and their relation to polyconic quadrangle maps; a manual for the preparation of illustrations for reports; a reprint of a Texas reclamation bulletin on the factors for interconversion of latitudes and departures in feet, and differences in latitude and longitude in seconds for latitudes 25° to 50°; and a description of a set of 50 atlas sheets showing physiographic features of interest to engineers.

Maps of the United States showing the progress of topographic surveying and triangulation by the Geological Survey and the Coast and Geodetic Survey, and the astronomical stations of each, 1888; and the progress of topographic and geologic surveys by quadrangles, 1917.

241. OFFICE OF THE DIRECTOR. 1881-1941. 1,443 items.

Maps from the USGS library consisting of published post-route maps of Mississippi, Louisiana, Missouri, and Arkansas, dated 1839, annotated to show population in each county or parish by race and status (free Negro or slave), and information about crop yields and numbers of livestock. The dates and authority for these annotations are not given. They are believed to have been compiled from statistics of the Bureau of the Census during the Civil War. Another record is a manuscript map of part of Florida south of Mosquito Inlet showing positions and communication lines established by the Army in its operations against the Seminole Indians, 1856.

Records of the Illustrations Section consist of incomplete sets of published maps and related cross sections, graphs, and diagrams, appearing in annual reports, professional papers, bulletins, monographs, and water supply papers. Among these are maps pertaining to local areas in the United States and Alaska showing details of geology and topography. A number of these maps relate to coal lands and other mineral areas. Others are land-classification maps and maps of forest areas showing burned-out areas, types of trees, density of woods, and related information. There are maps of the United States showing the status of known geology, coalfields, national parks and forests, and other general information. Some published maps prepared as illustrations for these publications may also be found in the cartographic records of the House of Representatives (Record Group 233).

Other records of this Section include manuscript compilations prepared for inclusion in the professional papers, monographs, bulletins, and water supply papers. At 5-year intervals the Geological Survey compiles a comprehensive list of its publications with a subject, area, and author index. This list serves as a finding aid to these manuscript and published maps. Some manuscript maps prepared for inclusion in the water supply papers are among the maps of river surveys described in entry 242.

Arranged in series by origin; the records of the Illustrations Section are arranged in two sets, manuscript and published, both of which are arranged by the kind of publication in which they were included and thereunder by publication number.

242. TOPOGRAPHIC DIVISION. 1879-1966. 55,000 items.

Published maps prepared by the Map Information Office, including maps of the United States and its territories showing the status of topographic mapping, by quadrangles, the status of aerial mapping and the agencies responsible for coverage of specific areas, the status of horizontal and vertical control and the agencies responsible, and the coverage of aerial mosaics and the agencies holding the films. Some of the maps showing the status of topographic mapping include appraisals of the mapping and indications of areas inadequately mapped. These maps are revised when changes are necessary, generally on a yearly basis. A published bibliography of USGS maps covering Civil War battlefield areas is included.

General records of the Topographic Division, including publications relating to methods of surveying and mapping, a glossary of names for topographic forms, a chart of symbols used on topographic maps, a chart showing standard forms of type for use on maps, and a model for a quadrangle report showing the method of recording information necessary for a published quadrangle. Index maps of the United States and of individual States showing the availability of published quadrangle sheets and the agency of origin for each sheet. Special maps published by the USGS are listed. These index maps are published periodically as new maps are completed. There is also a series of maps of each State showing names of the quadrangles established by the Geological Survey and other agencies.

The Topographic Division is responsible for the systematic mapping of the United States and its territories and possessions, and for special topographic maps. The basic topographic survey is by quadrangles, which are areas bounded by specific parallels and meridians. The areas covered by quadrangles vary in size from 7 1/2 minutes to 1 full degree of latitude and longitude. These standarized maps show in great detail not only topography but also a wide variety of cultural features. Other agencies are responsible for surveys by quadrangles in areas of interest to them. Among these agencies are the Corps of Engineers and its subordinate units and the Department of Agriculture and its subordinates. The Geological Survey cooperates with these agencies in making the surveys and in some instances publishes the maps compiled by them. It reprints many of those prepared by the Corps of Engineers for civilian use.

The manuscript records of the Topographic Division include series of maps of the United States showing drainage and culture and base maps of States showing drainage and topography. Original drawings from the topographic surveys and resurveys of quadrangles, national parks, forests, forest reserves, mining districts and areas, battlefields, military reservations and monuments, rivers, lakes, reservoir and dam sites, farm projects, urban areas, and other special areas. These drawings show details of topography, drainage, culture, and boundaries. Manuscript quadrangles covering California surveyed in cooperation with the State of California. Shaded relief maps of States, national parks and monuments, and cities. Original planetable control sheets showing triangulation stations. Original plats of the Cunningham coal and claims in Alaska showing topography and drainage.

Arranged in series by type of map or map coverage. Within series the maps are generally arranged by State or name of sheet. The planetable control sheets are arranged by numbers assigned in the agency. A card index lists most of the original topographic drawings, regardless of series, alphabetically by name of sheet. These are also located on State index maps.

Published maps covering the United States and its territories and possessions. Numerous editions and revisions are missing from these series, particularly for the period before 1950. Many of these maps are the published versions of the manuscript maps described above. Among the records are a map of North America showing drainage and political boundaries; maps of the United States, some with insets of the territories and possessions, including base and outline maps at varying scales showing drainage and political boundaries; maps showing topography and topographic regions; and maps of individual States including base maps showing drainage and political boundaries and maps showing topography, urbanized areas, highways, population, and Federal and State lands. Maps of national parks, forests and monuments, battlefields, reservoir and dam sites, mining areas and districts, rivers and lakes, military reservations, monuments, metropolitan areas, and topographic quadrangles. Special maps include a portfolio of maps, with descriptive text, relating to the physical geography of Texas; a portfolio of maps illustrating physiographic features found in the United States, prepared for the topographic atlas of the United States prepared for the International Map of the World; reconnaissance shaded relief maps of Alaska; and a few planimetric quadrangles of parts of the United States.

Arranged in series by kind of map or area and thereunder by sheet name. The State index maps described earlier in this entry indicate the areas covered by the quadrangles and special maps published by the USGS, the Tennessee Valley Authority, and the Office of the Chief of Engineers.

243. GEOLOGIC DIVISION. 1879-1966. 4,500 items.

Manuscript and annotated maps including maps prepared by or under the direction of Arnold Hague showing geology and related information about areas in the northwestern United States, primarily in the Yellowstone Park area. Maps of mining districts, chiefly at Leadville, Colo., showing mine shafts, mine depths, and geologic structure. Manuscript and annotated maps used in the preparation of Geologic Folio No. 217, Ray Quadrangle, Ariz. Map and graphs, including film negatives of maps, prepared during a strategic mineral investigation of the Bauxite, Ark., area showing geologic structure, ore grades, mines, drill holes, and potential drill holes. Among this latter series are planetable sheets and diagrams of ore bodies.

Arranged in series by subject.

Published series including geologic folios of selected areas in the United States with descriptive text, maps showing general geology, economic geology, and topography, and structural diagrams. General geological maps of North America and the United States. State maps showing the geological map coverage by the Federal and State governments and by private individuals. Geological quadrangles including cross sections of geological formations, with descriptive text. Special maps of States, parts of States, military reservations, and other select areas showing surface formations. Miscellaneous photogeologic maps of selected areas prepared in cooperation with the Atomic Energy Commission. Maps of the United States, groups of States, individual States, and parts of States showing coalfields, oilfields, and gasfields. Maps prepared from investigations of these fields in the United States and in foreign areas showing geology, topography, and ownership and development of the fields, with related descriptive text and geological cross sections. Aeromagnetic and geological maps from geophysical investigations of selected areas. Maps of the Tennessee and Missouri River Basins showing mineral resources and development of the rivers.

Arranged in series by kind of map. The maps are listed in the 5-year cumulative list of publications issued by the Geological Survey and in the monthly and semiannual supplemental lists.

244. WATER RESOURCES DIVISION. 1911-66. 215 items.

Published maps of the United States showing district boundaries and field offices of the Division, and areas covered by annual reports on surface water supplies. A review accompanied by a map relating to streamflow and ground water in the United States, 1954. A photoprocessed map of the San Luis Valley, Colo., showing water-table contours. Published *Hydrologic Investigations Atlases* for selected areas in the United States, showing the availability of ground water, relation of depth of ground water to river levels, average precipitation and runoff, and availability of ground water for domestic use. Among these atlases is a detailed study of the hydrology of the San Bernardino and the eastern San Gabriel Mountains, Calif., with maps and graphs showing topography, geology, drainage, climate, precipitation, and runoff. Published hydrologic investigations relating to ground-water availability, floods, hydrogeology, and hydrochemistry, 1961-66.

Published maps of West Virginia and Pennsylvania overprinted to show stations and transmission lines used in public power service in 1920 and 1921. Lists, keyed to numbers on the map, identify the power companies.

245. CONSERVATION DIVISION. 1930. 24 items.

Published maps and related publications with information about land classification in Colorado and Wyoming and the Great Plains. These maps show farm and grazing lands by type; drainage; and physiographic regions. A publication showing the utilization of water resources in the Snake River Basin.
Arranged in series by subject.

246. HYDROGRAPHIC BRANCH. 1900 and 1903. 19 items.

Manuscript maps from a survey of a canal line through the Uinta Indian Reservation, Utah, 1900; and a blueline map of Caddo County, Oklahoma Territory, showing school and Indian lands reserved and existing and proposed bridges, 1903.

247. DIVISION OF WEST INDIAN SURVEYS. 1919-22. 26 items.

A published outline map of Hispaniola, showing its division into 30-minute quadrangles and giving the name of each quadrangle, prepared for use in reporting the progress of topographic surveys of the island. A published outline map of the Republic of Haiti and outline sheets of the quadrangles. Published topographic sheets of the Dominican Republic. Manuscript sheets of the Banao area, Dominican Republic.

248. FIELD OFFICES. 1927 and 1940. 2 items.

A blueprint map of Georgia, compiled in the Atlanta field office, showing recording and nonrecording riverflow measurement gages operated by the Geological Survey in cooperation with other Federal agencies and with the Georgia Division of Mines, Mining, and Geology, 1940.

A photoprocessed map of Wisconsin, compiled in the Madison field office, showing mean annual precipitation, 1892-1926.

Aerial Photographs

249. GENERAL RECORDS. 1938-48. 12,800 items.

Negatives from photography flown in numerous project areas across the country for the use of the Topographic Division in making topographic maps. Accompanied by index negatives and prints. Scales vary.

RECORDS OF THE BUREAU OF INDIAN AFFAIIRS. RG 75

The Bureau of Indian Affairs, established in the War Department in 1824, was transferred in 1849 to the Department of the Interior.

Most of the maps in Record Group 75 were prepared by or for the Bureau for use in performing its functions relating to the surveying and allotment of Indian lands, and the supervision of land management, conservation, irrigation, and road-construction projects in the reservations. A few of the maps were acquired from other sources for reference of administrative purposes or for use as exhibits.

For a detailed listing of the cartographic records in Record Group 75, see The National Archives, List of Cartographic Records of the Bureau of Indian Affairs, Special List No. 13 (Washington, 1954).

250. GENERAL RECORDS. 1878-1944. 164 items.

Published maps of the United States and that part of the United States west of the Mississippi River showing the distribution and approximate area of Indian reservations, the locations of Indian agencies, the Bureau's district boundaries and headquarters, and hospitals, schools, and irrigation projects operated by the Bureau. Some of the earlier maps also show the number of Indians in each reservation. A published map of Alaska showing facilities operated by the Bureau, such as hospitals, headquarters for field nurses and physicians, reindeer stations, and radio stations. Published maps showing jurisdiction of Indian agencies in South Dakota, Kansas, and Nebraska.

Manuscript and published maps of individual Indian reservations showing boundaries, place names, drainage features, roads and railroads, schools, churches, swamplands, agency reserves, other reserved lands, and withdrawn lands.

A published volume with descriptive text and illustrations relating to instructions for preparing maps and plans and to the symbols to be used on maps prepared by the Bureau.

Arranged in series by subject or type of record.

251. CENTRAL MAP FILES. 1800-1939. 16,656 items.

Manuscript, published, annotated, and photoprocessed maps of the United States and parts of the United States, including Alaska, containing a wide variety of information about Indians and Indian lands. Included are general maps showing routes of explorations, Indian tribal lands, Indian land cessions and purchases of lands from Indians, existing and proposed reservations, changes in reservations, townships and townsites in Indian lands and reservations, military forts and reservations in Indian lands, roads and railroads, land grants to railroads through Indian lands, and private land claims and grants.

Maps and plats of Indian reservations or parts of reservations showing topography, drainage features, vegetation, boundary lines, and changes in

boundaries; areas selected for withdrawal from the reservations and additions to
the reservations; irrigated lands and lands subject to irrigation; rights-of-way for
railroads, canals, ditches, electric transmission lines, highways, gas pipelines, and
telephone and telegraph lines; reservoir and dam sites; cultivated and unculti-
vated lands; allotments to individuals; church, school, and agency reserves;
mining claims; timberlands and grazing and mineral lands; and settlements.

Special maps and related records including plats of townsites in Indian
reservations, plans of military reservations, plans of railroad station grounds,
plans of irrigation and reclamation projects, ground and building plans of Indian
schools and reserves and military forts, and plans of power development
projects.

Most of these maps were prepared in the Bureau of Indian Affairs. Others
were sent in by special agents in the field. In many instances maps of other
Government agencies, such as the General Land Office, the Bureau of
Topographical Engineers, and the Geological Survey were used by the Bureau
and placed in the files. Some of the maps were acquired from other sources and
certified or approved for official use. Arranged numerically by file number
assigned in the agency. A card index lists the maps in three ways: by area or
State and thereunder by tribe, Indian reservation, military reservation, or other
administrative unit; by subject; and by map number. Four old map registers
maintained by the Bureau before 1921 contain much information about
individual maps that is not included on the cards.

252. IRRIGATION DIVISION. 1872-1943. 1,998 items.

This Division is responsible for planning and supervising the construction and
maintenance work carried on in irrigation districts on Indian lands. It was
formally established in the Bureau in 1925, although activities relating to
irrigation in Indian lands had been the concern of special officers in the Bureau
earlier. Many of the projects supervised by the Division were begun by the U.S.
Reclamation Service (later the Bureau of Reclamation); the records of those
projects were transferred to the Bureau of Indian Affairs. The Irrigation Division
of the Bureau also cooperated with the Bureau of Reclamation on many of the
projects.

Among the records of this Division are manuscript, annotated, published,
and photoprocessed maps of Indian reservations and parts of reservations.
Included are general topographic and outline maps and maps showing allotments, irrigable and nonirrigable lands, locations of proposed and existing
irrigation projects, cultivated areas, canals and ditches, pumping stations, wells,
dams, and land classification. There are also a few maps of the United States
showing the projects supervised by the Bureau of Indian Affairs. Other records
include plans of canals, dams, reservoirs, and other irrigation facilities installed
on the reservations or on the projects located on the reservations.

Arranged alphabetically by name of State and thereunder by name of Indian
reservation or irrigation project.

253. FORESTRY BRANCH. 1920-44. 43 items.

Published maps of the United States showing Indian reservations, and districts and offices of the Forestry Branch. Published maps of Indian reservations showing drainage, boundaries, roads, trails, railroads, communications lines, powerlines, wells and springs, reservoirs and dams, ranger and fireguard stations, lookout stations, and reserved lands. Many of these maps are identified by "Fire Control Maps." Arranged in series by subject.

254. REALTY BRANCH. 1846-1937. 5,730 items.

Manuscript, annotated, and photoprocessed plats of townships in Indian reservations or of lands formerly in Indian reservations. Most of the records are photoprocessed plats from the General Land Office. A few supplemental plats were prepared in the Indian Office. Some of the plats are the usual township plat as described in entries 256 and 261 under the General Land Office. Others have corrections made in the Bureau of Indian Affairs. A number have notations relating to the disposition of lands within the reservations, such as withdrawals, allotments, and claims. Bound in volumes and arranged sequentially by volume number. Indexes locate the volume and page for a given reservation.

A published map of the Walker River Indian Reservation, Nev., showing lines of public survey, old boundaries, areas reserved for grazing, and the line of reclamation withdrawals, 1937.

255. FIELD OFFICES. 1935. 1 item.

A published map showing the Ute Mountain Jurisdiction of the Consolidated Ute Reservation in Colorado and New Mexico. Much information is included about drainage features, boundaries, reservoirs, roads and trails, wells, communications lines, buildings, and patented and entered lands.

RECORDS OF THE BUREAU OF LAND MANAGEMENT. RG 49

The Offices of the Secretary of the Treasury and the Register of the Treasury were responsible for the disposition of the public domain from the time of the establishment of the Federal Government until 1812. In 1812 the General Land Office was established as a Bureau within the Treasury Department to superintend and execute all transactions involving public lands except the work of surveying and mapping. For many years the surveys were made under contracts secured by Surveyors General, who were independent officers from the first appointment in 1796 until 1836, when they were placed in the General Land Office. In 1849 the General Land Office was transferred to the Department of the Interior. The functions of the Office were to supervise the survey, management, and disposition of the public domain and generally to execute all laws relating to public lands. In 1946 the General Land Office was consolidated with the Grazing Service of the Department of the Interior to form the Bureau of Land Management.

The General Land Office was one of the earliest mapping agencies of the Federal Government, and its activities relating to mapping fall into three broad categories: precise land identification, land status and survey progress, and the maintenance of records for purposes of legal reference and map compilation. The first involves the platting of townships from data obtained from the field surveys along with the reproduction of the plats for official and public use; the second, the compilation of maps showing information concerning the extent of surveys and other data useful in the management of the public domain; and the third, the retention and maintenance of maps and plats prepared through the operations of the office as well as those submitted in accordance with law in the course of seeking right-of-way grants through public lands.

The Bureau of Land Management continues to maintain the official engineering and drafting service for the survey, resurvey, and mapping necessary to the identification and description of the remaining public lands.

Most of the records described in the following entries are from the files of the General Land Office. Only a few cartographic records of the Bureau of Land Management have been transferred to the National Archives.

General Land Office

256. RECORDS RELATING TO MAPPING ACTIVITIES. 1909-46. 18 items.

Textual publications consisting of an historical description of the public land system; regulations governing surveys of homestead entries within national forests; specifications for describing tracts of land for use in Executive orders and proclamations; general rules for restoration of lost or obliterated corners and subdivisions of sections; a table giving corrections for chaining on slopes; and a chronological list of the publications containing instructions for surveying public lands from 1815 to 1947.

Published maps of the United States showing principal meridians, baselines, and areas governed thereby; a published map of the Western States showing land districts and district land offices; a sample township plat showing its size, the style of lettering, and the general character of topographic data included; maps of the United States annotated to show authorized surveys and surveys to be executed in fiscal years 1943 and 1944, and the program for fiscal year 1947, the latter showing the extent of the Missouri River Project and revested lands in Oregon and California; and maps of Alaska annotated to show mapping priorities for 1942-46, proposed work for fiscal years 1943 and 1944, and lands occupied by Indian reservations, military and lighthouse reserves, national parks, farms, and homestead sites.

Arranged in series by subject.

257. GENERAL RECORDS. 1816-1946. 811 items.

An incomplete set of published maps of the United States, 1873-1941, and individual States and territories, 1876-1944, compiled from the official records of the General Land Office. These maps show the extent of the public land surveys, private land claims and grants, Indian and military reservations, national parks and forests, railroads and railroad land-grant limits, and the location of land offices, offices of the surveyors general, and cities and towns. The maps of States and territories also show boundaries and county seats. Beginning with 1896 the maps of the United States show the land purchases, cessions, and annexations in the growth of the continental United States. There is also a set of maps of the Western States showing activities of the agencies of the Department of the Interior. Arranged by area and thereunder by date of edition.

Incomplete sets of special maps published by the offices of the surveyors general in the early 1800's and the General Land Office from 1836 to 1946, including base and outline maps of the United States; maps showing the routes of principal explorations in the United States; maps of the United States and of individual States and territories showing the progress of public land surveys for specific years; maps and plats of Indian lands and reservations, some showing lands opened to entry; plats of national parks, forest reserves and national forests, abandoned military reservations, and oilfields and gasfields; maps of boundary surveys of forest reserves and national forests, national parks, and Indian reservations; and maps of States and territories showing lands designated by the Secretary of the Interior under the provisions of the Enlarged Homestead Acts. Other maps pertain to special studies or surveys of local areas, such as the study of the unsurveyed public lands in Monroe County, Fla.; surveys of the site of the Franklin D. Roosevelt Library and residence, Hyde Park, N.Y.; surveys of the villa sites at Flathead Lake, Mont.; studies of the ecology of Ferry Lake, La.; and surveys of coalfields in Alaska. Arranged alphabetically by name of State or territory and thereunder by map number.

An incomplete set of published maps pertaining to surveys of a few State boundaries and a series of maps prepared as a result of investigations along the Red River concerning the Oklahoma-Texas boundary dispute. Arranged numerically by assigned map number.

These published maps have been described individually in The National Archives, *List of Cartographic Records of the General Land Office*, Special List No. 19 (Washington, 1964).

258. DIVISION B (PATENTS). ca. 1886-96. 1,072 items.

Manuscript and annotated plats of townships and parts of townships in California, Colorado, Oregon, Idaho, Montana, New Mexico, Wyoming, and South Dakota showing mines and mining claims and in some instances patent numbers and dates, survey numbers, and document numbers. Some of the plats, particularly those for California, also show boundaries of returned mineral lands. Most of the plats are undated, although the Colorado plats, which are manuscript tracings, have claim approval certifications and dates. Dates for most of the patents are from the period 1872-94. Arranged alphabetically by name of State and thereunder by township and range under the governing meridian.

259. DIVISION E (SURVEYS). 1785-1946. 29,889 items.

Manuscript and annotated maps (1790-1946) unofficially referred to as the "Old Map File," which includes maps of the United States and of individual States and territories showing their development and the disposal of public lands. Among these records are maps of States and territories or parts thereof showing unsurveyed public lands; the progress of public surveys; railroad land-grant limits and county and land district boundaries; private land claims, grants, and purchases; Indian reservations and claims; military reservations; forest reserves and national parks and forests; grazing districts, mineral lands, mining districts, and mining claims and leases; reclamation projects; settlements; roads and railroads; and other detailed information pertaining to local areas. There are also plats of active and abandoned military reservations, Indian reservations, forest reserves, national parks and forests, and maps of boundary surveys of some of the reserves. Most of these maps are from surveys made by deputy surveyors under contract. Many are certified or approved by the Surveyor General of a State or territory as conformable to field notes of the survey or as exhibited on the original plats on file in his office. Some of the maps were prepared to accompany the annual reports of the Surveyors General or the Commissioner of the General Land Office. Many were compiled in the General Land Office from the original surveys on file. There are some maps published by the General Land Office or by other agencies and annotated in the General Land Office. Arranged alphabetically by State and thereunder numerically by assigned number. These maps are described individually in Special List No. 19, cited in entry 257.

Manuscript and annotated maps and plats of the survey of the boundaries of public land States or territories and Indian land boundaries that later become State boundaries. Some of the maps pertain to original boundary surveys. Others pertain to resurveys, often made in response to a dispute between two or more States over the location of a boundary line or as the result of an error in the original survey. Included are some composite maps showing lines run by two or more surveyors. Among the records are some landscape sketches showing boundary monuments, a few plans of boundary monuments, and several diagrams showing the connections between State boundaries and the township surveys along both sides of a State boundary. Two groups of maps relate to the Texas-Oklahoma boundary dispute along the Red River. There are a few maps of the boundaries of the United States with the British possessions, Texas, and Mexico. Arranged numerically by assigned map number.

A series of field notes and related textual records identified as the "Old Case F File." Most of these are bound in volumes, and many include maps. Most of the field notes relate to maps of State, territorial, and Indian land boundaries described in the previous paragraph. Some of the notes relate to specific maps in the "Old Map File" mentioned above, to special published maps described in entry 257, and to maps in other record groups. The notes of State and territorial boundary surveyors often include astronomical observations, instructions, and reports. There are also field notes of Indian land cessions and reservations; national parks; mineral lands and timberlands and leases in Michigan Territory; a naval ammunition depot and air station, and abandoned military reservations in New Jersey; and the U.S. Marine Corps Reservation at Quantico, Va. Some of the notes relating to Indian lands are from surveys of nonpublic-land States, particularly North Carolina and New York. Arranged numerically by assigned number.

Manuscript plats and diagrams of Indian lands and boundaries, consisting of a volume of Indian grants and reserves in Indiana, Michigan, and Ohio, 1807-49; a volume of diagrams, dated 1864, showing tracts of the Kansas Half-Breed lands in connection with the public land surveys; a volume of plats, dated 1857-65, of the Sac and Fox and Wyandotte lands in Kansas and the Omaha lands in Nebraska also showing connections with the public land surveys; and two volumes of plats of "Indian Reservation Exteriors" including boundary lines of Indian reservations in several States and exterior lines of townships within some of the reservations, particularly in the Indian territory, 1856-92.

Manuscript, annotated, published, and photoprocessed plats of townsites, city parks, cemeteries, and Government properties located in the public-land States. The information shown on these plats includes the exact location of the site in relation to the lines of public land surveys and, for the townsites, public lands reserved within the sites, street layouts, lot numbers, railroad lands, and in a few instances names of landowners. Many of the plats were certified by boards of townsite trustees who were given responsibility under the supervision of the Commissioner of the General Land Office for the subdivision of sites and the sale of town lots. Most of the early plats were certified by a Surveyor General. The later plats were certified by the Commissioner of the General Land Office and approved by the Secretary of the Interior. The published and processed plats are arranged in a series as a published set. The manuscript and annotated plats form their own series. Within each series the plats are arranged alphabetically by name of site. A card catalog lists the plats alphabetically by name of site and also alphabetically under State. There are a few bound volumes of field notes of townsite surveys arranged in a separate series.

A bound volume of plats of townships in Alabama, Florida, Louisiana, and Mississippi showing sections reserved for the Navy's timber requirements. Tree species are identified.

Lithographed township plats of scattered areas in south-central and southern California annotated apparently to show certain selections or withdrawals of public lands. One plat has on the reverse a note reading "California Oil Land Plats." A series of plats showing the status of lands within Naval Petroleum Reserves Nos. 1 and 2 in California, including an index map showing the location of the reserves and the area withdrawal to July 9, 1914. These plats show railroad, mineral, and other patented and pending lands, State selections, desert land entries, and oil wells within the reserves. Another small group of plats of this area bears annotations showing oil in certain sections on July 10, 1908. Arranged by subject and thereunder by township and range numbers.

Township diagrams annotated to show withdrawals of public lands in Colorado, Montana, and New Mexico. These status diagrams were annotated for the use of the Committee on Conservation and Administration of the Public Domain, 1930-31. The withdrawals shown include forest reserves, Indian reservations, parks and monuments, first- and second-form reclamation areas, stock driveways, coal and oil lands, oil and phosphate reserves, reservoir sites, game and bird reserves, land reserved under the Carey Act, lands reserved under State acts, and lands withdrawn for survey or resurvey. Arranged alphabetically by name of State and thereunder by principal meridian and township and range.

Manuscript and annotated lithographed plats of private land claims in the States of Arizona, California, Colorado, Florida, and New Mexico, and a few claims in Louisiana, Illinois, and Missouri. These private land claims originated in grants or other land concessions from governments possessing sovereignty over territory that later became a part of the United States. These claims were surveyed by deputy surveyors under contracts. Most of them were approved by a surveyor general. The plats show boundaries of the claims and their relationship to the adjacent public land surveys. Bound in volumes and arranged alphabetically by State. Indexes locate individual claims by name for California, New Mexico, and Florida.

Manuscript and annotated lithographed plats of the survey and resurvey of baselines and meridians, standard parallels and guide meridians, and the exterior boundaries of townships in most of the public-land States. Some show township lines for parts of States and others show only the boundaries of lines of one township. Some of the diagrams or plats contain much detail, including vegetation, drainage, roads and trails, private land claims, and potential land use. Other diagrams show only the survey lines and a few adjacent terrain features used as reference points. Most of these plats were examined and approved by the surveyor general in the State or territory represented. Bound in volumes and arranged alphabetically by State and thereunder numerically by volume number. Index maps or diagrams serve as finding aids to all the States except Ohio and Louisiana.

Manuscript plats of the original township surveys in Illinois, Indiana, Iowa, Kansas, Missouri, and Ohio. Included are plats and field notes of the survey of the old Seven Ranges in Ohio, the first of the public land surveys, 1785-87. There are a few miscellaneous manuscript and annotated plats for Michigan, Minnesota, and Nebraska, and a few published plats for other States. With the exception of the survey of the Seven Ranges most of the plats represent surveys made by deputy surveyors under the supervision of a surveyor general. Three plats were prepared from the survey field notes for each township. The plats were approved by the surveyor general supervising the surveys within a certain district, and the original was filed in his office, later to be turned over to the State. The second plat was sent to the local office having jurisdiction over the township, and the third was sent to the headquarters office in Washington. In addition to showing the township and section lines, these plats also show drainage, roads and trails, Indian villages, boundaries or private land claims and grants, boundary lines of Indian cessions and reservations, swamplands, and forested areas. Acreage is indicated for fractional sections. Descriptive information about the soils and corner section posts is sometimes given on the reverse of the plats. Frequently there is more than one plat for a given township. In some instances there are resurvey plats of a later date. In other instances there are plats covering resurveys of fractional townships where a discrepancy may have occurred in the original survey. Also there may be fractional plats covering parts of a township surveyed at different dates. Arranged by name of State and thereunder, with the exception of the Ohio plats, numerically by township and range number under the governing meridian. The plats and field notes for the old Seven Ranges in Ohio are arranged by township and range number and the other Ohio plats are bound in volumes. An index map locates those plats for Ohio that are bound in volumes.

Manuscript plats and diagrams prepared by U.S. surveyors and cadastral engineers to accompany reports of special field examinations, investigations, and surveys, 1917-45. These records generally represent surveys of areas omitted in the original township surveys, such as islands in rivers and new lands created by river or coastal changes. The plats include information about the exact locations of these areas in relation to previous public land surveys, former meander lines of rivers, former coastlines, and in some instances swamp areas. The group survey number is usually shown on the plats. Among the records are a few plats compiled from resurveys of boundaries of Indian and military reservations. Arranged alphabetically by State.

Manuscript copies of field notes from township surveys in Illinois, Indiana, Iowa, Kansas, Missouri, and Ohio. These notes were copied from and compared with the original field notes and approved by the surveyor general for the State or territory represented. The manuscript plats for these States relate directly to these field notes. In addition to a detailed description on running the township and section lines, the notes include much descriptive information about topography, natural vegetation, and potential uses of the land. Bound in volumes and arranged by State and thereunder by volume number. Index maps for each State locate the numbered volumes for each township.

260. DIVISION F (LAND GRANTS, RAILROADS, RIGHTS-OF-WAY, AND RECLAMATION). 1851-1939. 10,776 items.

Published General Land Office State maps annotated to show railroad land-grant limits, and manuscript and annotated maps showing the limits of land grants to States and corporations for specific railroads and wagon roads, arranged alphabetically by State.

Manuscript and annotated maps and diagrams showing rights-of-way through public lands for railroads, military and other roads, highways, canals, irrigation ditches, transmission lines, sites of reservoirs and quarries, and other rights-of-way. These maps show the precise location of the lines and sites in relation to the section and township lines in surveyed areas or to prominent land features in unsurveyed areas. Among the railroad maps are maps of proposed lines, located lines, and lines of constructed roads; plans of railroad station grounds are included. Most of the maps are manuscript on tracing cloth prepared by the individual companies and forwarded for the approval of the Secretary of the Interior.

The railroad maps are arranged by bundle or tube number. The military and wagon road maps are filed with the railroad maps. Some of the canal, reservoir, irrigation ditch, and other right-of-way maps are arranged by State and thereunder alphabetically by name (usually that of the company, individual, or association requesting the right-of-way). The canceled or relinquished right-of-way maps are arranged alphabetically in numbered bundles and filed by former tube number. Finding aids include card indexes and lists.

Manuscript, annotated, and processed maps and plans of proposed canals, reservoirs, and reclamation systems for areas in Western States to be segregated and reclaimed under the Carey Act of August 18, 1894, and amendments of 1896 and 1901; and manuscript maps of irrigation districts in several of the Western States submitted in accordance with provisions of the Smith Act of August 11, 1916.

Records relating to the revested Oregon and California Railroad Co. lands in Washington and Oregon and to the reconveyed Coos Bay Wagon Road lands in Oregon about 1903-39. Among these records are a map showing the status of lands in the grant to the Oregon and California Railroad Co. in Oregon on June 1, 1912, annotated to show selected and unselected primary lands; maps showing both the Oregon and California Railroad and the Coos Bay Wagon Road lands as of June 30, 1938; and photoprocessed and published township plats of the area annotated to show sections and parts of sections involved in the revestment of unsold lands within the grants. The plats are arranged numerically by township and range numbers.

261.   DIVISION K (INDIAN LANDS).   1904-31.   1,240 items.

Township plats and diagrams of lands in the following Indian reservations: Fort Peck and Flathead in Montana; Devils Lake and Fort Berthold in North Dakota; Standing Rock in North and South Dakota; Cheyenne River, Rosebud, and Pine Ridge in South Dakota; and Colville in Washington. Most of these plats are annotated to show the classification and status of lands offered for settlement. One set of plats for the Fort Peck lands shows the total acreage appraised in 1928.

Manuscript and annotated maps and diagrams and a few statistical tables relating to lands within former Indian reservations and agencies, including the Cheyenne River Agency in South Dakota, the Otoe and Missouri in Kansas and Nebraska, the Fort Peck in Montana, and early cessions and reserves in Michigan.

Township plats of lands in the Moqui and Navajo Indian Reservations in Arizona and New Mexico, annotated to show the area or estimated area of surveyed or unsurveyed odd-numbered sections within the limits of the land grant to the Atlantic and Pacific Railroad, 1904-10.

Arranged by State and thereunder by name of reservation or tribe.

262. DIVISION N (MINERAL LANDS). 1872-1908. 45,367 items.

Manuscript plats of mineral claims in Alabama, Alaska, Arizona, Arkansas, California, Colorado, Idaho, Montana, Nevada, New Mexico, Oregon, South Dakota, Utah, Washington, and Wyoming. Most of the plats are arranged by mineral survey number, although some of the California plats are arranged by township and range number and a few by county. The mineral survey numbers also relate to textual records among the General Land Office mineral patent records.

263. LAND CLASSIFICATION DIVISION. 1938-46. 1,335 items.

Manuscript, annotated, and photoprocessed maps showing land classification and use in the Western United States and Alaska. Among these are maps of the United States and of individual States and parts of States showing lands withdrawn from public settlement, type of withdrawals and dates of proclamations authorizing the withdrawals, and maps showing vacant and unappropriated lands. A series of Grazing Service maps for Arizona, Region 9, annotated to show boundaries of grazing allotments with the names of individuals or companies leasing the areas. Manuscript outline maps of several States showing county boundaries and township and range lines. A series of counties in the Western States, except Arizona, annotated to show Federally owned lands. Most of the county maps used as base maps were prepared by State highway departments or commissions and by the National Resources Planning Board. Some were made by the General Land Office in cooperation with the Works Projects Administration. The project for inventorying Federally owned lands was begun under the direction of the National Resources Committee in 1939 and transferred to the General Land Office in 1940. Related maps are in Record Group 187, Records of the National Resources Planning Board.

The maps are arranged in series by subject and thereunder by area.

264. GENERAL LAND OFFICE FIELD OFFICES. ca. 1795-1930.
22,367 items.

Manuscript and annotated lithographed plats of townships in Alabama, Illinois, Indiana, Iowa, Kansas, Mississippi, Missouri, Wisconsin, and parts of Ohio, Indian Territory, and Washington. Most of these plats are duplicates of the original township plats (see entry 259) which were sent to the local land offices for use in recording the initial disposal of the public lands. Some of these plats show different types of land-entry numbers and in some instances names of entrymen. They also show disposal of lands to railroad and canal companies and lands reserved for Federal or State use. There are also manuscript township plats of parts of Oregon showing the donation claims and the names of the claimants.

These plats were sent to the headquarters office in Washington, D.C., when the local land offices were closed. Bound in volumes and arranged by State. An index map for each State locates the township plats by volume.

A map of the Republic of Mexico showing adjacent parts of Southern United States published from official surveys of the Mexican Government under the direction of Pedro Garcia Conde in 1845; some unidentified annotations appear on the map. It is reported to have been received from the District Cadastral Engineer's Office, Glendale, Calif.

Miscellaneous manuscript maps and plats of military reservations in Wyoming Territory and of existing or proposed wood and hay reservations for some of the posts, 1869-86, prepared by members of the Corps of Engineers, U.S. Army, and acquired by the Land Office at Cheyenne, Wyo. These drawings show the boundaries of the reservations and topographic and cultural features in adjacent areas. One map from this Office, but separate from this group, is a General Land Office map of Wyoming Territory, 1876, with annotations relating to the public land surveys.

Grazing Service

265. GENERAL RECORDS. 1934-45. 197 items.

A published map of the Western States showing established and proposed grazing districts under the Taylor Grazing Act and separate diagrams of grazing districts established by order of the Secretary of the Interior during 1935-40.

Photoprocessed maps and diagrams of grazing districts and parts of grazing districts in Arizona, Colorado, and New Mexico showing the status of lands within each district, such as vacant lands, State lands, patented lands, railroad lands, lands in national parks and forests, Indian allotments and withdrawals, and reclamation and other withdrawals or disposals of lands, 1938-40. Photoprocessed maps of the Lost River Grazing District in Idaho, Region 5, annotated to show the status of lands within separate divisions. A photoprocessed map of the Elk Grazing District in Nevada, 1941.

Bureau of Land Management

266. GENERAL RECORDS. 1947-54. 46 items.

A published map of the United States including territories and insular possessions showing the extent of public surveys, national parks and forests, Indian reservations, national wildlife refuges, and reclamation projects, 1953; published maps of Arizona, 1953, and Wyoming, 1947, showing essentially the same information. These maps are a continuation of the published record set of U.S. and State maps described in entry 259. A published atlas of Alaska showing Federal land withdrawals and reservations by type and controlling Government agency; included is a checklist giving the authority and dates for the individual withdrawals, 1952. A series of detailed maps of the Louisiana coast prepared by the Coast and Geodetic Survey for the Bureau of Land Management and the State of Louisiana aerial photographs made in 1954 and 1957.

267. DIVISION OF CADASTRAL ENGINEERING. 1947-66. 210 items.

Two manuscript plats and typed copies of field notes of the dependent resurvey of tracts of Cherokee Indian School lands in Swain County, N.C., approved June 21, 1951.

Manuscript plats and type copies of field notes of islands in Illinois and Missouri and of parts of a few townships in Missouri and Kansas. The plats are filed with the Headquarters Office plats of the General Land Office described under entry 259. The field notes are filed with the bound volumes of General Land Office field notes described in the same entry.

RECORDS OF THE BUREAU OF MINES. RG 70

The functions of the Bureau of Mines, established in 1910, include the inspection of mines, mills, and smelters; the testing of fuels for Government use; the issue of licenses controlling the production and use of nonmilitary explosives; the operation of experimental and other plants for the production of helium and synthetic liquid fuels; the collection of information about mineral resources, including production, consumption, and employment figures; the study of accidents in mines; and the conduct of research in a variety of subjects, such as methods of mining, improvement of mining conditions, and production of minerals for defense and industry.

268. GENERAL RECORDS. 1908-44. 234 items.

Published, manuscript, and annotated maps and map-graphs of the United States showing safety districts and related facilities of the Bureau, about 1918, the average annual value of mineral products by State, 1923-32, the distribution of bituminous coal and lignite deposits, 1944, and the value of metallic products by State, county, and mining district. Photoprocessed maps and plans of the experimental mine and explosive experiment station, Pittsburgh, Pa. Photoprocessed maps and plans illustrating a report on the disaster at the Speculator Mine, North Butte, Mont., 1917. Maps of States annotated to show coal areas, oil shale classified lands, and naval oil shale reserves. Township plats annotated to show areas in Colorado and Utah covered by naval oil shale reserves and oil shale classified lands. State maps annotated to show the numbers of men employed in the coal industry and the amounts of coal mined. Published relief maps and cross sections of the Salt Creek and Teapot areas, Wyo. Manuscript maps and related records of the Seminole Oil Pool, Okla., including contour maps, cross sections, graphs on oil production, and general geologic sections.

Maps annotated to show the geologic structure of the holdings of the Utah Copper Co. Maps of Alaska annotated to show the proposed reorganization of service districts of the Bureau of Mines. Miscellaneous items, including a topographic map of the anthracite coalfields in Pennsylvania; a plan showing the progress of test borings in Lake Michigan at Milwaukee, Wis.; manuscript tracings of cross sections of mines; plans of the Bates Mine, Mich., showing ore bodies at different levels; and a map showing patented mining claims in the Joshua Tree National Forest. Arranged in series by subject.

269. PETROLEUM DIVISION. 1919-29. 3 items.

A photoprocessed map of the world showing sources of supply and marketing affiliations of the Royal Dutch Shell combination, 1919. A map of the world annotated to show the distribution and relative magnitude of oil reserves, oil production, and prospective oilfields. A published map of the United States showing natural-gas pipelines and plants, and carbon black plants, 1929.

270. COMMON METALS DIVISION. 1928. 1 item.

A published map-graph of the United States with insets of Alaska and the Philippine Islands showing, by State and by district yielding over $100,000, the value of production of gold, silver, copper, lead, zinc, and iron ore.

271. COAL ECONOMICS DIVISION. 1929. 3 items.

Published map-graphs of the United States showing information about bituminous coal, such as interstate movement, the total production by State, and the distribution of Pocahontas-Tug River coal.

RECORDS OF THE NATIONAL BITUMINOUS COAL COMMISSION, 1935-36. RG 150

The major function of the first National Bituminous Coal Commission, established in 1935 and abolished in 1937, was to determine average production costs for bituminous coal in each of nine areas and to establish minimum prices based on these costs. For the continuation of certain functions previously exercised by the bituminous coal code authorities of the National Recovery Administration, the Commission was empowered to establish marketing regulations; to conduct research related to the production, use, conservation, and distribution of bituminous coal; to guarantee rights of collective bargaining to miners; and to provide for the adoption of maximum-hour and minimum-wage limits in the bituminous coal industry.

272. GENERAL RECORDS. 1935-36. 60 items.

A photoprocessed map of the United States showing minimum price areas and the schedule of districts established by the Bituminous Coal Conservation Act of 1935. Maps of the United States annotated to show centers of production of petroleum asphalt, rock asphalt, gilsonite, wurtzilite, and ozocerite; asphalt-carrying railroads; cities known to have used rock asphalt for pavement; and main ports for the shipment of asphalt. A panel of maps of individual States showing coal districts, the type of coal mined in each district, and railroads serving the districts. A map of the area served by the Baltimore and Ohio Railroad showing coalfields and the types of coal mined in the fields. Maps of parts of West Virginia showing coal districts and railroads serving the districts.

A series of maps of States annotated apparently to show gas and oil pipelines by size and producing centers of oil and gas. There is also a group of manuscript overlays for the State maps showing only the pipelines and production centers. A map of the Los Angeles Basin oilfields annotated with a table naming each field and giving the date of discovery and peak amount produced by each field to 1927. A cross section of an oilfield showing the water intake; water, gas, and oil deposits; and wells.

A graph showing the volume of bituminous coal sales, 1870-1930. A table showing the amount of bituminous coal produced in the various fields, 1920-32. Graphs showing the amounts of electric power produced and consumed and the relative growth of power equipment utilization and energy consumption during the period 1839-1939.

RECORDS OF THE NATIONAL PARK SERVICE. RG 79

The National Park Service was established in 1916 in the Department of the Interior. It was directed to promote and regulate the use of national parks, monuments, and other reservations for purposes of recreation and conservation. Before the establishment of the Service, park administration was under the direct supervision of the Secretary of the Interior.

General Records

The records described under this heading cannot be attributed to any specific office or division of the National Park Service. Maps of the early military parks and battlefields were prepared by national park commissions under the direction of the Secretary of War before the jurisdiction of these areas was transferred to the National Park Service in the Department of the Interior. The earlier maps of national parks accompanied reports to the Secretary of the Interior, and the later published and photoprocessed maps were issued by the National Park Service without reference to a specific office or division.

273. MAPS OF BATTLEFIELDS, NATIONAL MILITARY PARKS, AND
CAMPAIGN AREAS. 1896-1921. 11 items.

Published and photoprocessed copies of maps of the battlefield of
Gettysburg drawn from original surveys made by engineers of the Gettysburg
National Park Commission in 1903 and 1916, a perspective view of the
Gettysburg National Military Park from a drawing made in 1919, a photoprocessed copy of the multisheet topographic map of the Gettysburg battlefield
compiled under the direction of G. K. Warren of the Corps of Engineers, and two
blueprints of maps of the country between Fredericksburg, Va., and Harrisburg,
Pa., one showing the route of the Army of Northern Virginia (Confederate)
during the Gettysburg campaign and the other the route of the Army of the
Potomac (Union); a photoprocessed map of the battlefield of Shiloh, Tenn.,
showing troop positions on the first day of battle (April 6, 1862) and a
published map showing troop positions on the second day of battle (April 7),
compiled for the Shiloh National Military Park Commission in 1900; and a
published military map showing the theater of operations in the Tullahoma,
Chickamauga, and Chattanooga campaigns, prepared by the Chickamauga and
Chattanooga National Park Commission, 1896-1901, from a map compiled in
1874 by the Corps of Engineers.

274. MAPS ACCOMPANYING REPORTS OF SUPERINTENDENTS OF
NATIONAL PARKS TO THE SECRETARY OF THE INTERIOR.
1905-8. 2 items.

Published maps of the Yellowstone National Park, 1905, and the Sequoia
and General Grant National Parks and the Sierra Forest Reserve, 1908, showing
existing and proposed roads and trails.

275. MAPS OF THE UNITED STATES SHOWING AREAS ADMINISTERED
BY THE NATIONAL PARK SERVICE AND OTHER RECREATIONAL
AREAS. 1933-48. 8 items.

Published maps of the United States showing national parks and other areas
administered by the National Park Service, and various other types of
recreational areas under the control of Federal or State governments. On the
reverse of each map is a list of the individual areas by agency of supervision.

276. MAPS OF NATIONAL PARKS AND NATIONAL MONUMENTS.
1931-40. 64 items.

Two incomplete sets of published and photoprocessed maps of national
parks and national monuments. Arranged alphabetically by name of park or
monument.

277. MAPS SHOWING CONSERVATION WORK IN COOPERATION WITH STATE PARKS. 1934-35. 2 items.

A manuscript map showing proposed park developments under several project numbers in the Proctor-Piper State Forest, Vt., 1934; and a blueprint of the proposed recreational project plans in the Baxter State Park, Maine, in the summer of 1935.

278. PARK, PARKWAY, AND RECREATIONAL AREA STUDY MAPS. 1937-39. 16 items.

Photoprocessed State park, parkway, and recreational area study maps of North Carolina, Mississippi, Louisiana, and Tennessee prepared under the direction of the National Park Service State supervisor in cooperation with the State authorities; and a photostat of a map of the United States showing the status of State cooperation and completion of preliminary reports on the study as of September 30, 1939.

279. MAP SHOWING EXISTING AND POTENTIAL RECREATIONAL LANDS IN IOWA. 1940. 1 item.

A photoprocessed map of Iowa showing State, county, and city parks, parkways, and monuments.

280. ROAD, ROUTE, AND HIGHWAY MAPS. 1919-44. 4 items.

A published map showing the route of an automobile tour from Reno, Nev., to San Diego, Calif.; a photoprocessed map of part of the Red Lodge-Cook City highway, an approach road to the Yellowstone National Park; and photoprocessed maps prepared in cooperation with the Alaska Highway Land Planning Survey to show roads and highways in Alaska and proposed accommodations along the routes.

281. COLORADO RIVER BASIN RECREATIONAL SURVEY. 1943-46. 15 items.

General maps of the Colorado River Basin showing routes of ground and air travel, geological provinces, life zones, remnants of prehistoric cultures, reservoir sites, and public recreational areas; maps of individual recreation areas in the region; and maps of the Colorado River region of Utah showing population distribution, the status of lands, and areas suggested for recreational use.

The Chesapeake and Ohio Canal Company and Its Predecessor, the Potomac Company

The Potomac Company, chartered by the Assemblies of Maryland and Virginia in 1784, was organized in 1785 for the purpose of improving the navigation of the Potomac River by deepening the channel and cutting canals around the falls. Because of financial difficulties it was dissolved in 1828 and its property was transferred to the Chesapeake and Ohio Canal Company.

282. MAPS OF WASHINGTON, D.C. ca. 1791-1852. 3 items.

Numbered Coast and Geodetic Survey reproductions of three early maps of Washington: L'Enfant's plan, 1791 (No. 3035a); Ellicott's plan, 1792 (No. 3035); and an undated map engraved by W. J. Stone, Washington, D.C. (No. 3036).

283. MAPS AND PLANS RELATING TO THE CHESAPEAKE AND OHIO CANAL. 1826-1937. 116 items.

A published map of the country between Washington, D.C., and Pittsburgh, Pa., showing the proposed and located routes of the canal, adjacent topography, and property to be acquired by the company; survey plats of the canal; plans of proposed improvements to the canal; right-of-way maps and profiles of railroads paralleling or serving the canal; and plans of locks and other canal facilities.

Arranged numerically by assigned map number. A list identifies each map. A few maps are restricted and may be examined only with the permission of the National Park Service.

Other maps pertaining to the canal are filed with the numbered C & O Canal series in the records of the National Capital Parks (see entry 284).

National Capital Parks

That part of the former Office of Public Buildings and Public Parks that operated and maintained the park system of the National Capital was established under the National Park Service in a separate field office, the National Capital Parks. The records of the National Capital Parks include those of the Office of Public Buildings and Public Parks, and its predecessor, the Office of Public Buildings and Grounds; those of committees and commissions serving the District; those established by National Capital Parks since its establishment; and some that were prepared by other units of the National Park Service.

284. NUMBERED FILE. 1797-1958. 7,650 items.

Manuscript, annotated published, and photoprocessed maps, plans, and drawings pertaining to the National Capital Parks system.

Maps of Washington, D.C., including published and photoprocessed copies of such early maps as the Dermott ("tin case") map and Ellicott's plan; photoprocessed maps annotated to show triangulation stations, traverse stations, and benchmarks; annotated published maps of the permanent system of highways in the District, 1908-33; manuscript and published maps of the city showing public reservations under the control of the National Capital Parks or its predecessors, 1884-1947; and manuscript and published maps of the National Capital Parks system in the District and in nearby areas in Maryland and Virginia, 1948-53.

Maps and plans of individual parks, parkways, recreational areas, and grounds around public buildings, including plans showing walks and driveways, lighting systems, water and sewage connections, and landscape development.

Sketches, plans, and construction drawings of memorials and monuments in Washington; drawings and plans relating to the White House and the Capitol grounds, including some relating to the 1927-28 reconstruction of the White House.

Other records include maps of areas along the Chesapeake and Ohio Canal and the Potomac River, including maps of Roosevelt Island and Columbia Island; maps of Arlington National Cemetery and vicinity; and maps and plans of old forts in or near the District of Columbia.

Most of these records were prepared by the National Capital Parks or its predecessors, the Office of Public Buildings and Grounds, and the Office of Public Buildings and Public Parks of the National Capital. Others came from other branches of the National Park Service, from temporary commissions, or from private architectural or construction firms. The fort plans are from the Fortifications File of the Office of the Chief of Engineers.

Arranged numerically by a subject system assigned in the agency. Accompanied by a list of the records by file number and a card catalog that lists subjects alphabetically.

285. MASTER AND PROGRESS PLANS FOR WASHINGTON, D.C. 1936-37. 90 items.

Manuscript and annotated photoprocessed plans of parks and reservations in the District, including plans of the central area around the Mall, of the Rock Creek Park and Zoological Park areas, and of minor parks and reservations, showing alterations to be made in roads and walks and in buildings and other structures. These plans, compiled in the Branch of Plans and Designs of the National Park Service, are arranged in sets of numbered sheets.

286. DISTRICT OF COLUMBIA RECREATION SYSTEM PLAN. 1930-41. 89 items.

Manuscript, annotated, and photoprocessed maps of the District of Columbia consisting of outline maps of individual sections of the District showing streets and blocks, and maps of existing and proposed recreation centers. The latter show all public recreation facilities available in each section, including playgrounds, parks, school grounds and properties, museums, libraries, and social agencies. Included also are maps showing the results of the survey of traffic injuries to children under 15 years of age in the District during the period 1931-38.

Most of these records were prepared as part of the District of Columbia Work Projects Administration recreation projects sponsored by the President's

District of Columbia Recreation Committee, representing the National Park and Planning Commission, the Board of D.C. Commissioners, the Board of Education for the District of Columbia, and the National Capital Parks. Arranged in sets by recreational sections and centers.

287. ROCK CREEK POLLUTION STUDIES. 1935. 66 items.

Manuscript maps, diagrams, and tables prepared to accompany the *Report on Measures for Elimination of Pollution of Rock Creek and Its Tributaries in Washington*, prepared for the Eastern Division, Branch of Engineering, National Park Service. Included are a map showing sewerlines within the Rock Creek drainage basin, a map of the drainage areas within the District showing areas served by combined or separate systems, rainfall frequency-intensity charts, hydrographs showing runoff, a list of rainstorms producing excessive runoff during the period 1925-34, plans of diversion by relief sewers, and maps, plans, and profiles of proposed tunnel lines and outlets.

Aerial Photographs

288. GENERAL RECORDS. 1937. 61 items.

Large-scale photographic prints (in 61 sheets) from aerial photographs covering a strip of Northwest Washington bounded approximately by 14th and 35th Streets; accompanied by a graphic index prepared in the Cartographic Branch. The aerial photographs were prepared by the Todd Mapping Service of Washington.

289. ARLINGTON MEMORIAL BRIDGE. 1923-42. 640 items.

Manuscript, annotated, published, and photoprocessed maps, plans. and drawings pertaining to the Arlington Memorial Bridge. Among these are maps showing its location and approaches, and the pedestals designed for statues on the bridge. The Arlington Memorial Bridge Commission prepared most of the records, although some were furnished by private architectural firms.

Most of the records are arranged in an alpha-numeric system assigned by the Commission. A typescript list and a card catalog serve as finding aids.

RECORDS OF THE BUREAU OF RECLAMATION. RG 115

The Bureau of Reclamation, established in 1902 as the Reclamation Service, builds and operates dams and hydroelectric powerplants and distributes the power produced by those plants. Its other responsibilities include the construction and operation of irrigation works in the Western States, flood control, river regulation, the improvement of navigation, and the development and administration of recreational facilities in connection with Bureau reservoirs and other projects.

When the Irrigation Division was established in the Bureau of Indian Affairs in 1925 it inherited the functions and records pertaining to irrigation projects located on Indian lands that had been administered by the Bureau of Reclamation. Many maps prepared by the Bureau of Reclamation before 1925 may be found among the records of the Irrigation Division of the Bureau of Indian Affairs (see entry 252).

Reclamation Service

290. GENERAL RECORDS. 1905-7. 7 items.

Published maps, including a map of the United States showing reclamation projects and gauging stations and rivers surveyed by the U.S. Geological Survey; a topographic and hydrographic map of the Uinta Indian Reservation, Utah; and topographic maps of the Yuma Project in Arizona and California, the Salt River Project in California, and the Klamath Project in California and Oregon.

Arranged in series by type of map.

Bureau of Reclamation

291. GENERAL RECORDS. 1904-51. 408 items.

Published and photoprocessed maps, consisting of maps of the United States showing average precipitation; maps of the Western United States showing existing and proposed reclamation activities, boundaries of the Bureau's administrative regions, powerplants and transmission lines, aqueducts and reservoirs, and reclamation dams; maps of several of the Western States showing irrigation, hydroelectric development, and reclamation projects; maps of river basins showing land classification, Federal and private irrigation projects, areas irrigated and potentially irrigable, canals, plans for future development, and conservation areas; and maps of individual reclamation projects showing the canals and the areas irrigated, and plans of dams built on the projects.

Arranged in series by subject or type of map.

292. COMMISSIONER'S OFFICE. 1907-63. 1,357 items.

Before public lands on reclamation projects can be opened for entry or settlement, a plat which legally describes the farm units must be approved and filed with the Bureau of Land Management. These records consist of published and photoprocessed plats of townships located in Federal irrigation projects showing farm units and areas for which water-right applications may be made. They also show private lands, reserved lands, canals and laterals, areas approved for irrigation and the dates of approval, and the acreage of irrigated areas within each farm unit or area of private lands.

Arranged alphabetically by name of project.

RECORDS OF THE OFFICE OF TERRITORIES. RG 126

The Office of Territories, established in 1950, is the successor of the Division of Territories and Island Possessions, which had been established in 1934 to supervise those activities relating to the territories of the United States that had been a function of the Secretary of the Interior since 1873. The Division, acting through the governors of the territories and the High Commissioner of the Philippines, was responsible for the administrative supervision and coordination of Federal activities in Alaska, Hawaii, Puerto Rico, the Virgin Islands, and the Philippine Islands. The Bureau of Insular Affairs administered Puerto Rico unitl 1934 and the Philippine Islands until 1939. The Division of Territories also supervised the Alaska Railroad and the Alaska Road Commission and administered the U.S. Antarctic Service through an executive committee composed of representatives of several agencies.

Office of the Secretary of the Interior

293. TERRITORIAL FILES. 1923-27. 90 items.

Maps relating to Alaska including published maps of the territory accompanying the annual reports of the Governor showing Army, Navy, other Government and commercial radio stations, offices of the Governor and the Surveyor General, lines of the Alaska Railroad, judicial districts, lines of communications, and national forests and reservations, 1923-27; maps of Alaska prepared by or for the Alaska Road Commission showing wagon roads, sled roads, pack trails, railroads, and telegraph and telephone lines; maps by the Alaska Railroad showing the progress of construction of certain railroad lines; a land survey map of the Bering River Coal Field; and maps and plans of other coalfields, particularly the Chickaloon Mine, showing progress of the complete work on the mine facilities and topography with cross sections of coalbeds and a plan of a coal storage cleaning plant.

Topographic maps of the Hawaiian Islands and of individual islands in the group prepared from Hawaiian Government and Hawaiian Territory Surveys, 1878-1906. Some of the maps are annotated or overprinted to show crown and government lands, homestead settlement tracts, grazing lands, forest lands and reserves, and cultivated areas. A short series of maps showing information about properties in Honolulu, one of which has a note indicating that the maps were referred to by the Governor of Hawaii in a letter to General Macomb and were transferred to the Secretary of the Interior, July 14, 1911.

Arranged by geographical area.

Division of Territories and Island Possessions,
U.S. Antarctic Service

294. GENERAL RECORDS. 1939-42. 30 items.

Manuscript and annotated maps and charts of Antarctica and parts of Antarctica prepared during and after the Antarctic expedition of 1939-41. Included are a general map of the continent showing place names, the route of the Ellsworth expedition of 1935, and the fringe of the continent; a basic communications plan for the U.S. Antarctic Service showing local and long-range communications lines and facilities and emergency communications system plans; and maps of parts of the continent in the vicinity of East Base, located in Palmer Land, and West Base, located at Little America III. The latter group includes maps showing sledge routes and the trails of different parties, flight tracks and often the areas covered by photographs made during the flights, shorelines and the limits of shelf ice, crevasses, pressure ridges, place names, triangulation and other control points, caches and campsites, radio stations and towers, and harbor soundings. Detailed descriptions of these maps are in The National Archives, *Records of the United States Antarctic Service*, Preliminary Inventory No. 90 (Washington, 1955).

295. AERIAL PHOTOGRAPHS. 1940. 12,000 items.

Oblique photographs of parts of Antarctica, shot from handheld cameras, including one set of negatives and one incomplete set each of prints and duplicate negatives. Flight line indexes are available in the Cartographic Branch. The flights are indexed as follows: West Base Flights A, AA, AL, C, E, EL, F, G, H, K, L, LG, M, RI, W, and X; and East Base flights of March 5, May 20, September 21, September 28, November 4, November 12, December 22, December 28, and December 30. Scales vary.

DEPARTMENT OF AGRICULTURE

RECORDS OF THE OFFICE OF THE SECRETARY OF AGRICULTURE. RG 16

The Secretary of Agriculture is responsible for administering the affairs of the Department as a whole and for coordinating the work of the various bureaus and services that perform the major functions of the Department.

296. GENERAL RECORDS. 1914-40. 120 items.

Published and photoprocessed maps and atlases of the United States including an atlas showing the field activities of the individual bureaus within the Department, 1914; a map showing areas covered by the major land-management activities of agencies in the Department and in other Government departments, 1930; and a map showing areas authorized for flood-control examinations and surveys, 1936-37.

An atlas showing kelp groves along the Pacific coasts of the United States, southern Alaska, and Lower California. Published and annotated maps of the Columbia River Basin showing its drainage features. Photoprocessed maps of the metropolitan areas of Philadelphia, Pa., and Los Angeles, Calif.

Arranged in series by subject.

297. COMMITTEES OPERATING UNDER THE DEPARTMENT OF AGRICULTURE. 1941-45. 470 items.

A series of published and annotated maps and atlases with related graphs, tables, and textual descriptions prepared by local postwar planning committees for the Southwest Inter-Mountain region, the California-Nevada region, the Appalachian region, and the Southeast region, and an *Atlas of Agriculture of the Northern Great Plains* prepared by the Northern Great Plains Council. These maps show soil types, crop distribution, natural vegetation, climate, distribution of livestock, distribution and characteristics of population, industrial potentials and development, transportation facilities, marketing areas, topography, drainage, irrigation development and facilities, and settlement patterns. There is also a set of photoprocessed maps showing the boundaries of the Pacific Northwest Committee for Post War Programs.

A series of published maps from the Mississippi Backwater Areas Study, Yazoo Segment, a joint investigation by several agencies in the Department of Agriculture. The maps, prepared by the participating agencies, show distribution of population, separate taxing areas, land use, frequency of floods, organized drainage districts, landownership and tenure, forest conditions, and soils.

298. DIVISION OF PUBLICATIONS. 1914-40. 1,440 items.

A copy of the *Atlas of American Agriculture* published in 1936 and separate copies of parts of the atlas published from 1918 to 1924. The maps and textual descriptions in these atlases contain information relating to relief, soils, climate, and natural vegetation. A record copy of *The Distribution of Important Forest Trees of the United States* (1938), with maps of the United States and parts thereof showing the distribution of individual species of trees; textual information is included. Publications with graphic summaries of agriculture in the United States from census returns of 1921 and 1931, farm tenure for 1936, physical features and land utilization for 1937, and farm taxation for 1937.

A copy of the *Geography of the World's Agriculture* (1917), with maps of the world and related textual information on climate, precipitation, soils, crops, livestock, and vegetation. Manuscript and published maps of the world and other graphic illustrations, apparently used for the 1941 *Yearbook of American Agriculture*, showing climate, vegetation, soils, and precipitation. An outline map of Connecticut, 1914.

Sets of published maps of the United States showing State, territorial, and county boundaries decennially from 1840 to 1940. One set shows only the boundaries; the other includes names of the counties.

A publication entitled *Slotted Templet Method for Controlling Maps From Aerial Photographs* (1940).

Arranged in series by subject.

299. OFFICE OF THE STATISTICIAN. 1889. 16 items.

A published atlas entitled *Album of Agricultural Statistics of the United States* with maps of the United States showing by State percentages of farmlands and nonfarmlands, farmland types, crop acreages and yields, values of livestock, percentages of rural population, values of farmlands, and farm tenure.

300. OFFICE OF LAND USE COORDINATION. 1939-44. 31 items.

Published maps of the Western United States showing the extent, planning, and operations of the water facilities program. Published maps of the United States overprinted to show the extent of aerial photography conducted by the Department of Agriculture. Arranged in series by subject.

301. OFFICE OF PLANT AND OPERATIONS. 1944-47. 4 items.

Maps of the United States overprinted to show the extent of aerial photography compiled by the Department of Agriculture. This series is a continuation of the series described in entry 300 as the Office of Land Use Coordination, which was abolished in 1944. Arranged chronologically.

RECORDS OF THE BUREAU OF AGRICULTURAL ECONOMICS. RG 83

The Bureau of Agricultural Economics was established in the Department of Agriculture in 1922 through the consolidation of the Bureau of Markets and Crop Estimates with the Office of Farm Management and Farm Economics. The new Bureau continued and expanded the activities that had been carried on by its predecessors since about 1900. These were research and regulatory work in marketing, the compilation and dissemination of crop and livestock statistics, and the investigation of the management and operation of individual farms. The Bureau later became responsible for research in agricultural finance, land use, community organization, and related subjects. In 1953 the Bureau was abolished and its functions were transferred to other agricultural agencies, chiefly the Agricultural Research Service.

Bureau of Crop Estimates

302. GENERAL RECORDS. n.d. 1 item.

A manuscript map of the United States showing planting dates for spring wheat.

Office of Farm Management

303. GENERAL. 1910-20. 40 items.

Manuscript and published maps of the United States showing State boundaries, major cities, and drainage and topography, about 1915-20; Part LV, Section 1 (Rural Population), of the *Atlas of American Agriculture*, 1919; a photoprocessed map of the world showing the international trade in wheat, about 1915; and undated photoprocessed maps of Austria-Hungary and the Balkan countries showing agricultural data.

304. SECTION OF AGRICULTURAL GEOGRAPHY. ca. 1915. 19 items.

A published map of the United States showing irrigated areas, compiled from the 1910 census; and annotated maps of the United States showing climatic data of importance to agriculture.

Bureau of Agricultural Economics

305. GENERAL RECORDS. ca. 1920-50. 497 items.

A published map of the United States showing field activities of the Bureau of Agricultural Economics, 1941; undated manuscript world maps showing population density and agricultural regions; an annotated map of the United

States showing average annual precipitation, about 1941; published maps of the United States showing existing and proposed land use, 1933-50; an undated published map of the United States showing native vegetation; a published map of the United States showing rural cultural regions, 1940; published maps showing farming regions in the United States, 1938-49; published maps and related graphs showing agricultural economic data pertaining to the United States and parts of the United States, about 1930; a map of the United States annotated to show lands purchased by the War and Navy Departments, 1944; a published map of the United States showing estimated population changes, by county, during 1940-43; an undated photoprocessed map of the United States showing areas of poor farmland; and base and outline maps of the United States and parts of the United States, some showing political subdivisions, 1920-40.

Published maps showing minor civil divisions in parts of the United States, 1940; undated published State maps showing crop reporting districts; undated annotated State maps showing irrigation projects; an annotated map showing per capita nonrepayable Federal expenditures, by county, in the western half of the United States, about 1939; a processed map index to land adjustment areas in the Southern States, 1942; published maps of the United States and parts of the United States showing population changes, 1940-43; published maps illustrating a study of migration from Pennsylvania to other States during the period 1870-1930; an undated published map of the Appalachian area showing unidentified areas; a published map showing seasonal range sheep movements in parts of the West, 1938-39; undated maps of parts of Montana annotated to show lands granted to the Northern Pacific Railroad; undated annotated maps from investigations of grazing lands in the Santa Fe Railroad land grant in Arizona; an undated photoprocessed map of the San Jacinto watershed in Texas showing landownership and size of holdings; undated maps of the Southern and Central Pacific Railroad land-grant areas in California annotated to show leased lands; undated manuscript maps of Kentucky, one showing physiographic regions and one showing transportation routes serving the Bluegrass region; a manuscript map of Michigan showing State-owned and State tax lands, 1934; and manuscript and published maps of Nevada showing potentially irrigable areas, 1944.

Published maps of North Dakota, one showing a precipitation effectiveness index, and one showing the average wheat yield, 1931; undated published graphs showing climatic conditions in the Harney Basin of Oregon and at Havre, Mont., as indicated by annual tree ring growth; a published map of Wisconsin showing population by ethnic stocks, 1940; and an undated manuscript topographic map of western Maryland.

306. DIVISION OF LAND ECONOMICS. 1925-50. 1,563 items.

Among the general records of the Division are manuscript world maps illustrating activities of the U.S. Department of Agriculture, about 1925; manuscript and photoprocessed statistical maps of the United States relating to rural population for the period 1790-1935; photoprocessed maps of the United States showing changes in farm population, by county, for the period 1930-35; manuscript maps of the Southeastern United States showing the distribution of the slave population during the period 1750-1840; manuscript and photoprocessed maps of the United States showing types, sizes, and numbers of farms for the period 1860-1950; manuscript and photoprocessed maps of the United States showing improved lands and the amount of land in farms during the period 1850-1935; photoprocessed maps of the United States compiled from farm economic studies for the years 1920-38; photoprocessed maps of the United States compiled from studies of farm employment, 1929-37; a photoprocessed map of the United States showing number of workers engaged in manufacturing, 1930; manuscript and photoprocessed maps of the United States illustrating studies of farm operators, 1910-35; photoprocessed maps of the United States showing the distribution of loans and grants made by the Department of Agriculture to farmers, 1930-39, a photoprocessed map of the United States showing the locations of production credit associations, 1937; undated photoprocessed maps of the United States showing rural areas in need of improvement; manuscript and photoprocessed maps of the United States showing the distribution of farms with modern facilities, 1918-30; photoprocessed maps of the United States showing types of roads serving farms, 1930; photoprocessed maps of the United States showing cropland acreages and areas of crop failure, 1934; photoprocessed maps of the United States compiled from cropland protection studies, 1929-34; manuscript and photoprocessed maps relating to the sale and distribution of farm products, 1918-36; an undated photoprocessed map of the United States showing the average fall precipitation; photoprocessed maps of the United States showing farm drainage projects, 1930; a photoprocessed map of the United States showing the increase in acreage of irrigated land during 1919-29; a photoprocessed map of the United States showing the amount of woodland pasture on farms, 1929; photoprocessed maps of the Eastern United States showing changes in the amount of agricultural land in originally forested counties, 1929-34; a photoprocessed map of the United States showing the distribution of unoccupied farm dwellings, 1935; an undated photoprocessed map of the southern Appalachians showing counties involved in an unidentified study; manuscript and photoprocessed maps of the United States showing the areal distribution of various types of crops during the period 1839-1935; manuscript and photoprocessed maps of the United States showing the distribution of livestock, poultry, and bees, 1850-1935; and manuscript and photoprocessed maps of the United States showing the distribution of goods produced by livestock, poultry, and bees, 1839-1935.

Photoprocessed maps of the United States showing wood and nursery products produced on farms, 1929; manuscript maps of the United States compiled from studies of truck farming, about 1898; photoprocessed maps of the United States showing farms not reporting livestock by kind, 1935; photoprocessed maps of Alabama compiled from farm economic studies, 1929-34; a published map of the world showing average amounts of cotton produced, 1926-31; undated manuscript maps and a chart showing the distribution of certain types of draft animals in the world, 1840-1925; an undated manuscript map of Russia showing agricultural regions; undated manuscript maps of South America showing the distribution of rainfall, crops, and livestock; manuscript maps of Chile showing the distribution of crops and livestock, 1923; manuscript maps of Argentina, Chile, and Uruguay showing farm economic conditions and the distribution of crops and livestock, 1908-16; and photoprocessed maps showing agricultural problem areas in Arkansas, Louisiana, Mississippi, and Texas, 1937-38.

Among the records of the Water Utilization Section are published maps of the Western United States showing major water supply areas, about 1943; a map of the Southwestern United States annotated to show the status of water planning operations, 1939; and published maps and graphs relating to various aspects of irrigation and water management in the United States, 1940-42.

307. DIVISION OF LAND UTILIZATION. 1930-47. 1,226 items.

Among the general records of the Division are published maps of the United States showing land-utilization projects, 1938; published maps of the United States showing the status of the county land-use programs, 1939-41; maps of the Southeastern United States annotated to show the status of county land-classification activities, 1938; manuscript and published State and county land-classification maps, 1938-40; and miscellaneous manuscript, published, and annotated maps of parts of various States relating to crops, soils, land use, and other natural and cultural features of agricultural areas, about 1930-41.

Among the Berkeley, Calif., office files of the Land Use Planning Section are manuscript and photoprocessed maps and graphs showing land adjustment areas and flood-control projects for 1940, population and crop acreages for the period 1880-1960, and changes in the number of tenant farms during the period 1930-35; a map of the Western United States showing per capita nonrepayable Federal expenditures during the period 1933-39; maps and charts showing the status of planning activities in the United States, about 1940; an undated photoprocessed map showing prohibited and restricted military areas; manuscript and published maps showing irrigated and nonirrigated lands, 1930-39; an annotated map of the United States showing potential recreation sites, about 1930; manuscript charts from economic studies of Western States, about 1945; published maps showing the distribution of Japanese-Americans in the Pacific Coast States, 1940; a map of the upper Colorado River Basin, 1938; manuscript charts and a map relating to studies of farm real estate in the Western States, about 1945; graphs showing the distribution of heads of families by State and occupation, about 1939; published maps and graphs from studies of migration to the Pacific coast, 1930-39; undated miscellaneous published maps and graphs pertaining to the Pacific Northwest and the Pacific Southwest; manuscript and annotated maps relating to agriculture and grazing in Arizona, 1935-43; undated Arizona county maps annotated to show unidentified returns by school district;

Arizona county maps showing information about soils and irrigation, 1929-41; and maps showing project areas, drainage basins, and watersheds in Arizona, 1936-41.

Manuscript and published maps showing a wide range of climatic and agricultural information pertaining to California, 1935-42; manuscript and photoprocessed charts showing statewide economic conditions in California, 1930-47; maps relating to projects in the Central Valley of California, 1940-44; maps relating to the Madera Irrigation District, 1939; maps of the Sacramento Valley, 1939-42; maps and charts relating to the San Joaquin Valley, 1935-42; maps and charts relating to the Imperial Valley, 1936-39; maps relating to agriculture in southern California, about 1940; maps of San Diego County, about 1939; maps of Santa Cruz County, 1936-40; maps of Yuba County, 1939; and undated miscellaneous maps of other California counties and cities and of various watersheds, river basins, and project areas.

Undated general State and county maps of Idaho and maps pertaining to farming, irrigation, and grazing in Idaho; a map of Montana showing project areas and land use, about 1936; an undated annotated map of the Flathead Indian Reservation, Mont., showing landownership and use and proposed use; miscellaneous undated maps of Nevada; maps showing agricultural problem areas and projects in New Mexico, 1930-36; miscellaneous maps of Oregon, 1935-43; maps of local areas in Oregon showing existing and potential irrigation, 1937-38; maps and charts relating to Benton County, Oreg., 1939-40; maps and a chart relating to Josephine County, 1939-40; undated maps and charts relating to Coos County; and miscellaneous maps relating to Oregon, 1935-39.

Maps of Utah relating chiefly to drainage and irrigation, about 1942; maps of local areas in Utah, about 1942; maps showing dry farmlands in Utah, about 1939; and undated maps of local areas in Utah; undated maps of Washington and local areas of Washington relating cheifly to land use and ownership; undated maps and other records relating to the Columbia Basin Project; and other miscellaneous maps of parts of Washington.

The records of the Tobacco Section include a published map of the Eastern United States showing tobacco-growing districts by type, 1932.

308. DIVISION OF FARM POPULATION AND RURAL WELFARE.
n.d. 2 items.

Published maps from surveys of isolated agricultural areas in Lincoln and Benton counties, Oreg.

RECORDS OF THE BUREAU OF AGRICULTURAL ENGINEERING. RG 8

Irrigation and agricultural drainage investigations were begun in 1898 and 1902, respectively, by the Office of Experiment Stations in the Department of Agriculture. These functions, and the pertinent records, were transferred in 1915 with other agricultural engineering activities of the Department to the Office of

Public Roads and Rural Engineering, which in 1918 became the Bureau of Public Roads. In 1920 a Division of Agricultural Engineering was set up in the Bureau to perform this work; in 1931 the Division was given bureau status. In 1939 most of the functions of the Bureau were combined with those of the Bureau of Chemistry and Soils to form the Bureau of Agricultural Chemistry and Engineering.

In 1939 the drainage and irrigation activities were transferred to the Soil Conservation Service. Shortly before, the Bureau of Agricultural Engineering had transferred to the National Archives its inactive map records (described in entries 309-311). The records of current activities were retained and transferred to the Soil Conservation Service with the transfer of the related functions.

The Bureau prepared maps chiefly for use as aids in planning drainage, irrigation, and farm development investigations. These maps were prepared from surveys made by agricultural engineers assigned to projects in the field.

Although described separately below, the drainage investigations records of the three predecessors of the Bureau of Agricultural Engineering are maintained in two consolidated series; one contains general records not pertaining to a single or a specific State, and the other, arranged alphabetically by State, includes the records for projects that are located in specific States.

Office of Experiment Stations

309. DRAINAGE AND IRRIGATION INVESTIGATIONS. 1901-15.
    557 items.

Manuscript maps including a map of the United States showing drainage investigation projects, 1907-11; a map of the Netherlands showing reclaimed marshlands; a map of lower (northern) Egypt showing drainage features; and a map of eastern Arkansas and northern Louisiana showing natural drainage investigations. Other records consist of plans of engineering equipment used in drainage investigations and a description of topographic symbols.

Manuscript maps, profiles, and cross sections from surveys of individual farms throughout the United States showing proposed and constructed drainage systems, water levels, methods of draining fields, salt and alkali content of soils and water, and proposed and constructed irrigation systems. There are also maps of watersheds and proposed drainage districts; a plan of the Cheyenne, Wyo., experimental farm; and special maps showing typical everglades areas in Florida.

Arranged by State where applicable. There is a general category for those maps or plans not pertaining to an individual State.

Office of Public Roads and Rural Engineering

310. DRAINAGE AND IRRIGATION INVESTIGATIONS. 1915-18. 600 items.

Manuscript maps of farms throughout the United States showing proposed and constructed drainage and irrigation systems with related cross sections and profiles. General maps of watersheds and proposed drainage systems. A map showing flood-control measures on the Salamonie River in Indiana, and a map showing improvements on the Little Sioux River in Iowa. A diagram showing salt content of ground water in Arizona.

Arranged by State where applicable. There is a general category for those maps or plans not pertaining to an individual State.

Bureau of Public Roads

311. DIVISION OF AGRICULTURAL ENGINEERING. 1918-31. 700 items.

A manuscript map of the United States showing airmail and radio service facilities of the Post Office Department. A manuscript map of the United States showing the distribution of the origin and use of picric acid by carload shipments, 1921-22. A manuscript map of the southeastern Atlantic coastal plain showing counties.

Manuscript maps of individual farms throughout the United States showing proposed drainage and irrigation systems, including related cross sections and profiles. General manuscript maps of watersheds and proposed drainage districts. Published maps of California showing agricultural and irrigated areas, canals, irrigation district boundaries, and hydroelectric plants. Maps of orange groves in Florida showing the physical condition of individual trees.

Manuscript and photoprocessed maps of individual farms prepared from the farm development investigations in the States of Georgia, Minnesota, Michigan, Mississippi, North Carolina, Ohio, and Virginia. These maps show, for the cooperating farms, farm layouts, soils, crops raised and crop acreage, buildings, and roads.

Published maps and cross sections prepared to illustrate a study of the drainage basin of the Red River of the North.

Arranged in series by subject. Most of the records pertaining to the drainage investigations and the farm development investigations are arranged by State.

Bureau of Agricultural Engineering

312. FARM DEVELOPMENT INVESTIGATIONS. 1931-39. 300 items.

A continuation of the series described in entry 311, as well as a few photoprocessed maps annotated to show the annual increase in improvements to each farm. Arranged by State.

RECORDS OF THE AGRICULTURAL MARKETING SERVICE. RG 136

The Agricultural Marketing Service, established in 1953, was given those functions of the former Production and Marketing Administration that related to marketing. The functions of the Service are divided into two broad categories: marketing research and marketing services.

Production and Marketing Administration

313. GRAIN BRANCH. 1951-52. 16 items.

Published maps of the United States showing by county and sometimes by State loan purchase agreement rates for individual grain crops in 1951 and price support rates in 1952.

RECORDS OF THE AGRICULTURAL RESEARCH SERVICE. RG 310

The Agricultural Research Service, established in 1953, superseded the Agricultural Research Administration which had been established in 1942 to consolidate most of the physical, biological, chemical, and engineering research in the Department of Agriculture.

Agricultural Research Administration

314. AGRICULTURAL RESEARCH CENTER AND ITS PREDECESSORS. 1941-47. 2 items.

Published maps of the Agricultural Research Center, formerly the Beltsville Research Center, Beltsville, Md., showing the assignment of lands to the various offices of the Department of Agriculture. Roads and property lines also are shown.

RECORDS OF THE BUREAU OF ANIMAL INDUSTRY. RG 17

The primary functions of the Bureau of Animal Industry, established in 1884 and abolished in 1958, were the administration of numerous statutes and regulations enacted to protect the public from the harmful effects of diseased meat products, the eradication of animal diseases, and the improvement of the Nation's livestock. The Bureau operated through an extensive field service supervised by several headquarters divisions, each responsible for certain activities of the agency.

315. GENERAL RECORDS. n.d. 1 item.

A 1932 base map of the United States with later annotations apparently made in the central office, showing animal experiment stations discontinued, retained, and transferred. The stations are further classified as Federal stations, State stations operating with Federal cooperation, field headquarters, and field laboratories. The map also shows what appear to be regional or district boundaries.

RECORDS OF THE AGRICULTURAL STABILIZATION AND CONSERVATION SERVICE. RG 145

The Agricultural Stablization and Conservation Service (ASCS) was established in 1961 to succeed the Commodity Stabilization Service. The latter agency had been created in 1953 to succeed the Production and Marketing Administration, which in turn had inherited its functions from the Agricultural Adjustment Agency (established in 1933 as the Agricultural Adjustment Administration).

The ASCS is responsible for programs relating to acreage allotments and farm marketing quotas, price supports, foreign supply and purchase, stabilization of sugar production and marketing, the International Wheat Agreement, and defense food activities.

The cartographic records of the ASCS consist chiefly of aerial photographs; one of the agency's major functions is to authorize and direct the procurement of aerial photographs to be used in compliance checks in the farm acreage allotment programs. As a result of this function a large body of aerial photographs covering most of the United States has been accumulated over a period of about three decades.

Agricultural Adjustment Administration

316. GENERAL RECORDS. n.d. 10 items.

Processed maps of several groups of States showing the classification of counties according to gross income per rural farm inhabitant and the proportion of rural farm population to the total population in each county in 1929. Related graphs show the numbers of school-age children in agricultural counties and the total number in each State from 1920 to 1935.

317. OFFICE OF THE ADMINISTRATOR. 1937. 1 item.

A photoprocessed map of the United States showing for selected regions the average number of days per month "with clouds 0.1 or less" during the period 1900-36. A table gives for each numbered region on the map the average number of cloudy days per month.

318. PLANNING DIVISION. n.d. 1 item.

A published map of the United States showing generalized agricultural regions.

319. PROGRAM PLANNING DIVISION. 1931-37. 163 items.

Records of the Land Policy Section consisting of base maps of the Western United States annotated to show the location of lands offered for sale by private individuals and the location of land purchase projects; and maps of parts of Vermont relating to the transfer of submarginal farmlands to forest areas. The Vermont maps include manuscript and annotated maps, many apparently prepared in the field, of counties and farm areas showing landownership and lands appraised or proposed for purchase, improvement plans, road surveys, and maps of lakes and State forest lands.

A map of the Western United States, compiled by the Production Planning Section, annotated to show the three major wheat-growing regions.

320. NORTH CENTRAL DIVISION. 1937. 1 item.

A photoprocessed map of the North Central States showing areas covered by aerial surveys flown by the Corn-Hog Control Association in 1935 and the AAA in 1936, and surveys to be flown in 1937.

321. SOUTHERN DIVISION. 1937. 1 item.

A photoprocessed map of the Southern States showing areas covered by aerial survey contracts.

322. WESTERN DIVISION. 1937-41. 10 items.

A base map of the Western United States annotated to show areas covered by aerial survey contracts in 1937. Photoprocessed maps of individual Western States showing areas open to bid for aerial survey contracts in 1941.

Production and Marketing Administration

323. TOBACCO BRANCH. 1952. 1 item.

A published map of the Eastern United States with an inset of Puerto Rico showing tobacco-growing districts and the types and acreages of tobacco grown in each district.

Aerial Photographs

324. GENERAL RECORDS. 1935-42. 51,900 items.

Photography covering most of the agricultural areas in the United States, secured by predecessors of the Agricultural Stabilization and Conservation

Service, particularly the AAA. Included are 17,000 rolls of film negatives, 9,000 cut film negatives, 14,000 index negatives, and 11,900 index prints. Photographed at the scale of 1:20,000.

RECORDS OF THE BUREAU OF ENTOMOLOGY AND PLANT QUARANTINE. RG 7

This Bureau, established in 1934 with antecedents dating back to 1854, cooperated with the States in the study and control of insects and in planning programs to prevent the spread of plant diseases.

Bureau of Plant Quarantine and Its Predecessors

325. GENERAL RECORDS. 1931. 1 item.

A published base map of parts of Maricopa, Pinal, and Pima Counties, Ariz., showing townships and their subdivisions, roads, railroads, canals, and schools.

326. MEDITERRANEAN FRUIT FLY ERADICATION CAMPAIGN. 1930-33. 1,528 items.

Published, annotated, and manuscript maps and related statistical tables dealing primarily with the Mediterranean Fruit Fly Eradication Campaign in Florida, 1930-33. Among these records are dot maps of Florida showing the number and location of fruit fly infestations within each county and maps of counties and townships showing the locations of infested citrus groves, land types, vegetation, names of property owners, buildings, packing houses, and roads. This program was begun under the Plant Quarantine and Control Administration and completed under the Bureau of Plant Quarantine. The maps were compiled and drawn by draftsmen attached to the eradication campaign organization and were approved by district inspectors. The State and county maps are arranged separately. The county maps are arranged alphabetially by name of county.

Bureau of Entomology and Plant Quarantine

327. GENERAL RECORDS. 1950. 1 item.

A published map of the Northeastern United States showing counties and principal drainage features.

328. DIVISION OF DISEASE AND INSECT CONTROL. 1930-47. 110 items.

Manuscript and published outline maps of the United States and regions of the United States showing the areas and degrees of infestation and the status of efforts to control or eradicate the European corn borer, the barberry, Dutch elm disease, the dog fly, the citrus canker, the Mexican fruit fly, the Japanese beetle, the gypsy moth, the potato tuber worm, phony peach disease, peach mosaic disease, the pink bollworm, white pine blister rust, the white-fringed beetle, and the sweet potato weevil. Other maps show the status of projects, among these the uses of rotenone and pyrethrum to control diseases. Related tables and graphs accompany these maps, which were compiled and published in the central office from information obtained from field personnel and cooperating State agencies. Arranged alphabetically by name of insect or disease.

RECORDS OF THE OFFICE OF EXPERIMENT STATIONS. RG 164

The Office of Experiment Stations was established in 1888 to disseminate scientific information among the agricultural experiment stations and to publicize the results of agricultural experiments. It administered the funds provided by Congress for the support of the research in agriculture and rural life that was carried on by the experiment stations and it coordinated research activities. The Office was abolished in 1953.

329. STATE AGRICULTURAL EXPERIMENT STATIONS. 1937. 5 items.

Published maps of Maryland showing principal soil types and the relative productivity of Maryland soils. These undated maps were prepared by the Maryland Agricultural Experiment Station with the cooperation of the Maryland Departments of Agronomy and Agricultural Economics, and the U.S. Department of Agriculture.

Published maps of West Virginia, prepared by the West Virginia Agricultural Experiment Station in 1937, showing general land classification, soil types, and average degrees of slope.

Maps prepared by the Nevada Agricultural Experiment Station, consisting of a map of northeastern Nevada showing average annual precipitation, the 11 major range areas, natural vegetation, soils, extent of erosion, and proposed seasonal range division.

330. DRAINAGE INVESTIGATIONS. 1908-14. 10 items.

Maps published from drainage investigations conducted by the Office. Included are maps of the California Mesa in California and the Chadburn Project in North Carolina showing drainage facilities; maps and profiles of the Cypress Creek Drainage District in Arkansas including a general map of the area, a map showing watersheds, a map showing overflow areas, and profiles of proposed drainage districts; maps of Jefferson County, Tex., including a general map showing drainage facilities and a map showing proposed drainage districts; and profiles of proposed flood-control ditches in the Big Black River Valley of Mississippi.

Other maps prepared from drainage investigations conducted by the Office are in Record Group 8, Records of the Bureau of Agricultural Engineering, and in Record Group 114, Records of the Soil Conservation Service.

RECORDS OF THE FARMER COOPERATIVE SERVICE. RG 314

The Farmer Cooperative Service was established in 1953 to carry on the work formerly conducted by the Cooperative Research and Service Division of the Farm Credit Administration. It conducts service activities and research on problems of management, financing, organization policies, merchandising, quality, costs, efficiency, and membership encountered by agricultural cooperatives. The Service also works closely with cooperatives to help farmers improve their business operations.

Farm Credit Administration

331. COOPERATIVE AND RESEARCH DIVISION. 1948-51. 4 items.

The photoprocessed map of the United States showing cooperatives visited by Lacey F. Rickey in connection with feed research and service, and a list of the cooperatives keyed to the numbers on the map, 1949. Published maps of the United States showing local purchasing and marketing cooperatives and retail branches of regional cooperatives handling farm supplies, 1948 and 1951.

RECORDS OF THE FARMERS HOME ADMINISTRATION. RG 96

The Resettlement Administration was established in 1935 to supervise rural relief and rehabilitation activities. In 1937 it was renamed the Farm Security Administration, replaced in 1946 by the Farmers Home Administration whose functions are to make farm ownership and operation loans, water-facility loans, and special livestock loans and to insure farm mortgage loans.

Resettlement Administration

332. GENERAL RECORDS. 1935. 1 item.

A photoprocessed map of the United States showing areas in which farm problems appeared to warrant encouragement of a change from crop farming to other types of agriculture or other land uses.

333. SPECIAL SKILLS DIVISION. 1936. 1 item.

A published pictorial map of the United States showing the Administration's regional boundaries and locations of projects.

334. LAND UTILIZATION DIVISION. 1936. 21 items.

Published maps consisting of a map of the United States showing land utilization purchase areas; maps of California, prepared by the Land Use Planning Section, showing the boundaries of Indian reservations with a table showing for each reservation the manner of land acquisition, landownership status, agriculture values, grazing values, and value of commercial timber; maps of California showing watersheds, dates of early and late frosts, population changes in nonurban lands, lands suitable for denser agricultural settlement, erosion, active irrigation districts, lengths of growing seasons, average precipitation, and annual temperatures; maps of the San Joaquin and Sacramento River Valleys in California showing reclamation facilities and reclamation, drainage, levee, and protection districts, and the American River flood-control district; base maps of Santa Cruz County, Calif., and of the State of Arizona; a map of western Nevada showing drainage basins and irrigated or irrigable areas; a revised problem area map of Mississippi; and a roadmap of Region III (Ohio, Indiana, Illinois, Iowa, and Missouri) and a map of the region showing projects.

Arranged in series by subject.

Farm Security Administration

335. GENERAL RECORDS. 1940. 1 item.

A photoprocessed map of the United States showing the location of homestead projects by type of development.

336. LAND USE PLANNING SECTION. 1937. 1 item.

A published map of Region XI, the Pacific Northwest, showing major land-use problem areas.

RECORDS OF THE FEDERAL EXTENSION SERVICE. RG 33

The Federal Extension Service, established in 1923, is responsible for coordinating the extension activities of the Department of Agriculture with those of the State agricultural colleges, for aiding farmers in carrying out new farming and home enterprises, for making known the results of agricultural research, and for taking charge of pertinent displays and exhibits at fairs and expositions.

337. FARM LABOR PROGRAM. 1947. 1 item.

A published map of the United States showing the results of a preliminary survey of major crop areas requiring imported agricultural labor.

RECORDS OF THE FOREIGN AGRICULTURAL SERVICE. RG 166

The primary responsibility of the Foreign Agricultural Service, established in 1930, and known from 1939 to 1953 as the Office of Foreign Agricultural Relations, is to develop foreign markets for the surplus production of U.S. farms.

Office of Foreign Agricultural Relations

338. GENERAL RECORDS. 1945, 1948. 2 items.

A copy of a 1945 publication entitled *Agricultural Geography of the Philippine Islands—A Graphic Summary*, compiled in the Office from information furnished by other Federal agencies, agencies of the Philippine Government, and private sources. Included are maps of the Islands showing relief, climate, vegetation, political subdivisions, population distribution, types of farm regions, the distribution of major food crops and commercial crops, and the distribution of livestock. There are two maps of the world illustrating the value of Philippine exports to and imports from the United States.

A copy of a 1948 publication entitled *Agricultural Geography of Europe and the Near East*, issued as Department of Agriculture Miscellaneous Publication No. 665, compiled in the Office primarily from information released by agencies of various European and Near Eastern governments. The maps illustrating this publication are base maps of Europe and the Near East overprinted with information about political boundaries, relief, climate, soils, population, length of growing season, agricultural workers, land use, percentage of arable lands, crop acreages and yields, numbers and kinds of livestock, and international trade in foodstuffs.

RECORDS OF THE FOREST SERVICE. RG 95

The Forest Service, established in the Department of Agriculture in 1881 as the Division of Forestry, produces numerous maps for operational, administrative, and informational purposes. Although the Service depends on Geological Survey topographic quadrangles for its basic cartographic needs, the Division of Engineering produces topographic maps for all areas in national forests that have not been surveyed by the Geological Survey. The Division also produces large-scale planimetric maps of national forests for use as base maps, and other miscellaneous maps of national forests and adjacent areas. Other divisions of the Forest Service also prepare maps to illustrate the information compiled in their work programs.

For detailed descriptions of the cartographic records in Record Group 95, see The National Archives, *Cartographic Records of the Forest Service*, Preliminary Inventory No. 167 (Washington, 1967).

339. GENERAL RECORDS. 1890-1961. 3,073 items.

Records of the Forest Service not identified by specific unit of origin, including an annotated map of the United States showing the field organization of the Forest Service and the principal cooperating agencies, about 1939; published maps of the United States and parts of the United States showing national forests, purchase areas, and shelterbelt areas, and Forest Service districts, regions, regional headquarters, and forest products laboratories, 1908-55; Presidential proclamations, Executive orders, and maps relating to the establishment of and changes in forest reserves and national forests, published during the period 1891-1935; annotated maps of national forests showing withdrawals as authorized by Executive orders, 1914-22; manuscript and published maps of the United States showing the comparative areas of national forests, 1937, and areas recommended for addition to or elimination from national forests, 1935 and 1942.

Undated maps and graphs showing the existing use and ownership of forest lands in the United States and the land use recommended by the Forest Service; a bound volume of statistical maps, charts, and tables relating to the operation and maintenance of national forests, 1919; manuscript maps showing forest reserve selections in Minnesota, 1903; maps of various national forests annotated to show changes and recommended changes, 1908-37; published maps of parts of the Western United States showing wilderness areas, 1928-61; an undated photoprocessed map of the United States showing critical watershed, erosion, and submarginal areas in national forests; and an undated published map of the United States showing the influence of forests on watershed protection.

Manuscript, annotated, and published maps of North America and parts of the United States showing land classification, 1908-49; photoprocessed copies of annotated Post Office maps showing quadrangle names and triangulation stations, 1911; undated annotated maps of the North Central and Northwestern United States showing the development of Territorial and State boundaries; manuscript isogonic maps of the United States and Canada, 1950-51; a panel of four manuscript maps of the Eastern United States, dated 1922, showing railroads in operation in 1840, 1850, and 1860, and the canals and principal canalized rivers in use in 1915 and those abandoned earlier; manuscript and published State maps showing national forests, 1930-39; annotated maps showing existing and proposed boundaries of various national parks and monuments, 1911-39; published topographic quadrangles showing the area of conflict between the proposed boundary of the Great Smoky Mountains National Park and the Cherokee National Forest, 1940; a manuscript map of the United States showing the acreage of State-owned forests and parks, 1930; published and annotated maps of the United States and individual States showing forest regions and the distribution of major tree species, 1910-48; annotated, published, and photoprocessed maps showing information about commercial timber, 1915-27; manuscript, annotated, and published maps and graphs relating to world forest regions and wood production, 1909-44; manuscript maps of the world, of individual continents, and of the United States showing papermills, pulpmills, and board mills, 1915-37; and a manuscript map of the United States showing, by States, coniferous trees suitable for planting on farms, 1924.

A manuscript map of Wisconsin and one of Minnesota showing timber-using industries, 1915; undated published maps of Texas showing biotic regions and the distribution of tree species; manuscript and annotated maps of the United States showing data from economic studies of rural and forest lands, 1929-35; undated diagrams relating to farm and community development in various States; manuscript maps and related records pertaining to economic studies of the Great Lakes States, 1940; manuscript maps and a graph pertaining to studies of land use in Dorchester Township, N.H., 1934; a manuscript map of the Chippewa National Forest, Minn., showing recommended land use, 1935; manuscript and published maps from studies of the Missouri River Basin, 1948-49; manuscript and published maps of the Rio Grande Valley, 1930; a map of the Columbia River Basin showing a proposed land-management program, 1934; an annotated map showing landownership in the Challis, Salmon, and Sawtooth National Forests of Idaho, 1951; published maps relating to the construction and operation of a road at Hungry Horse Reservoir, Mont., about 1949; manuscript soil and vegetation maps relating to local areas in Massachusetts and Michigan, respectively, 1940; manuscript maps from studies made at the Wagon Wheel Gap Experiment Station, Colo., 1927; a manuscript map of the Northern United States showing a transcontinental route between Portland, Maine, and Portland, Oreg., 1931; photoprocessed copies of right-of-way maps for reservoirs and transportation and communications lines crossing national forest lands, 1890-1913; a manuscript map showing the routes of the Northern Pacific Railroad and the limits of its land grants, 1940; and annotated maps showing land-grant limits and patented unsold lands of the Northern Pacific Railroad lying within national forests, 1930.

A manuscript map of Puerto Rico showing Federal land-management activities, 1949; maps pertaining to forest studies in the Philippines, 1904-9; published maps and graphs relating to waterpower resources in southeastern Alaska, 1914-25; a photoprocessed map of Tongass National Forest, Alaska, showing aerial photoreconnaissance flight lines, 1927; an undated manuscript map of Sakhalin Island and the Ussuri region of Siberia showing mineral resources; published and annotated maps showing proposed organizational changes in the Forest Service's Region 1, 1930; an annotated map of Region 2 showing proposed timber and watershed additions, about 1932; a published map of Region 3 showing principal prime sawtimber areas, 1913; an annotated map of Region 6 showing proposed changes in the boundary with Region 1, 1930; an undated published map showing CCC camps in Region 6; and an undated processed map of the United States showing the population distribution of Region 9.

340. OFFICE OF THE CHIEF. 1934-43. 39 items.

Until 1935 the head of the Forest Service was known as the Forester; since then he has been designated Chief. The records described in this entry include maps prepared during the administration of Dr. Ferdinand A. Silcox for his use and maps from several headquarters units attached to his office.

Included are manuscript maps, graphs, and tables prepared for an address given by Dr. Silcox on April 24, 1934, relating to forest, watershed, and wildlife problems in the United States; maps from the Division of Fiscal Control relating to defense against forest fires in the national forests, 1941-42; maps from the Division of Operation relating to potential guayule production in California, 1942-43; and annotated maps from studies of forest lands in New England made by the Northeastern Timber Salvage Administration following the hurricane of September 1938.

341. DIVISION OF ENGINEERING AND ITS PREDECESSORS. 1907-62.
    3,206 items.

An 18-page report on conventional signs and symbols used by different nations in map preparation, 1908; a published map of the United States showing the status of topographic mapping in national forest areas, 1949; specimen maps and instructions for the preparation of Forest Service maps, 1907-35; published maps of Forest Service regions, 1911-40; an undated published map of the Ashland Forest Reserve, Oreg., and of the Pike's Peak Forest Reserve, Colo.; a set of large-scale standard published maps of national forests, game refuges, and other reservations showing a wide variety of physical and cultural features, 1911-60; published maps of ranger districts within national forests, 1939-47; published maps of national forest purchase units, 1935-36; published topographic quadrangles covering miscellaneous areas in and near national forests, 1937-40, and a set of published quadrangles covering the Prescott National Forest, Ariz., 1947; and miscellaneous undated maps of Puerto Rico.

A general large-scale published map of the State of Washington, 1933; a general published map of the Black Hills area in South Dakota and Wyoming, 1927; photoprocessed copies of maps of national forests and parts of national forests annotated to show transportation systems and plans, 1962; a photoprocessed grazing reconnaissance map of Pryor Mountain Division, Beartooth National Forest, Mont., 1917; a published map and a chart relating to mapping activities in Region 3, 1912-13; photomaps of the Angeles National Forest, 1939; a published map of California showing powerplants and water storage developments, 1930; published maps of trails in Oregon and Washington, 1935-38; an undated photorelief map of the headwaters of the Stehekin River, Chelan National Forest, Wash.; published maps of parts of the Olympic National Forest, Wash., showing information about elks, 1937-38; manuscript, annotated, and published maps of the United States and parts of the United States showing information relating to fire-control activities, 1931-40; a letter and maps relating to the defense of forest lands in California, 1940; manuscript maps pertaining to studies of forest fires in Minnesota and Michigan, 1925-27; published maps showing road systems and proposed road projects in national forests, 1917; maps of Forest Service regions and national forests showing enclosing areas without roads, about 1926; and project files containing manuscript, photoprocessed, and published maps, graphs, and charts, most of which are used to illustrate publications, exhibits, or talks, 1910-59.

342. DIVISION OF TIMBER MANAGEMENT AND ITS PREDECESSORS. 1913-40. 1,101 items.

Published maps of authorized timber sale areas in national forests, annotated with information about tree species, ground cover, and topography and accompanied by textual descriptions, 1913-16; maps of national forests annotated to show areas of intensive timber surveys and cutover areas, 1915-27; an undated published map showing locations of proposed timber sales areas in the Malheur National Forest, Oreg.; an annotated timber settlement map of part of Mount Baker National Forest, Wash., 1937; undated published maps of national forests in Region 1 showing timber access roads; a map of the Bridger National Forest, Wyo., annotated to show road information, 1940; and an undated published map of the Mississippi River delta annotated to show timber areas.

343. DIVISION OF RANGE MANAGEMENT AND ITS PREDECESSORS. 1915-45. 574 items.

An undated annotated map of the Western United States showing existing and proposed grazing districts; annotated maps of Region 4, of California and of individual national forests annotated to show proposed transfers of national forest lands to the Grazing Service, 1945; published and annotated maps relating to the establishment of grazing districts in national forest areas, 1940; undated maps of sheep problem areas in the Southwest; manuscript, annotated, and published maps of experimental ranges and pastures in parts of the West and the Southwest, 1918-36; manuscript, annotated, and published maps of goat ranges in New Mexico, 1915-18; manuscript and annotated maps accompanying reports on the appraisal of rangelands in national forest regions and national forests, 1922-27; manuscript and annotated maps prepared for a report to the National Resources Planning Board, 1934; manuscript maps showing seasonal use and grazing capacities of western rangelands, 1936; undated manuscript maps of western areas showing the extent of range depletion; manuscript maps of Western States showing general classes of land, 1935; maps of several Western States and Forest Service regions annotated to show land values and potential uses, 1940; undated landownership maps of Western States; manuscript maps showing the extent of soil erosion in the Western United States, 1934-35; manuscript and published maps and graphs relating to livestock production in the West, 1914-35; graphs showing the relationship between rainfall and forage production, 1940; and reports and maps relating to rodent and predator control in Forest Service Regions 1 and 2, 1929.

Manuscript exhibit items accompanying a report on the condition of grazing lands within the limits of the Atlantic and Pacific Railroad in Arizona and New Mexico, 1918-19; an undated published grazing reconnaissance map of part of the Madison National Forest, Mont.; published ground-cover maps of the Fish Lake National Forest, Utah, from a poisonous plant reconnaisance, 1916; maps and a report relating to the range management plan for the Uinta National Forest, Utah, 1928; processed and annotated maps relating to land use in Arizona by the Campbell-Francis Sheep Co., 1938; manuscript, annotated, and processed rangeland maps of Forest Service Regions 1 through 6, 1918-35; manuscript and annotated maps of the United States showing shelterbelt project areas, 1935; and miscellaneous undated, unidentified maps.

344. DIVISION OF RECREATION AND LANDS AND ITS PREDECESSORS. 1906-42. 321 items.

Detailed reports, with maps and photographs, on land classification and boundaries of national forests and intensive surveys of special areas and project areas within several of the forests, 1908-42; maps of national forests annotated to show lands withdrawn for ranger stations, 1906-18; and maps and reports showing recreational sites and facilities within national forests, 1917-30.

345. NATIONAL FOREST PLANNING AND ESTABLISHMENT DIVISION AND ITS PREDECESSORS. 1910-52. 871 items.

Annotated State maps showing activities of the public land-management agencies, about 1934; maps of States and parts of States annotated to show areas suitable for national forests, 1923; annotated and published maps of the United States showing forest and wild lands and statistical information relating to agriculture in the forest areas, 1935-41; annotated and published maps of the United States showing population density in 1930 and estimated population pressure on resources by 1936, by county; maps, graphs, and charts pertaining to the acquisition of lands for national forests, 1937-41; statistical tables listing data about forests and their use, about 1930; a manuscript map showing the status of forest lands east of the Great Plains, 1930; maps, reports, and photographs from the 1930 public domain report pertaining to the different types of existing and potential land use and to proposed additions to the public lands; published and annotated maps of the United States and of individual States showing existing and recommended uses of forest lands, 1934; annotated maps of national forests showing vacant public lands, 1934; annotated maps of the United States and of individual States showing numbers of families obtaining support from a national forest, 1934; annotated maps showing forest lands in the Columbia River Basin, 1934; an undated map of the Tennessee Valley; maps of the Great Lakes States annotated to show various aspects of agriculture and forest management, 1934 and 1940; annotated and published maps of grazing districts in Arizona, about 1936; maps pertaining to studies of revested forest lands of the Oregon and California Railroad, 1935-52; reports and accompanying maps relating to proposed national parks to be established in national forest areas, 1936; and maps of the United States annotated to show various aspects of rural occupancy, 1937.

Annotated maps of the United States relating to studies of wild lands, 1937; maps of the area encompassed by the Great Basin and the Snake and Colorado River Basins annotated to show various recreation and conservation projects, 1934-36; undated maps of national forests in Washington annotated with information about vacant public lands; maps of national forests in Washington and Oregon annotated to show the holdings of private and corporate landowners, about 1919; annotated and processed maps and photographs showing changes in national forests and purchase units, 1925-47; annotated maps pertaining to the administration of the Wenatchee National Forest, Wash., about 1947; maps and lists relating to national forest exchange lands in New Mexico, 1932; annotated maps pertaining to boundary studies of the Cochetopa National Forest, Colo., 1910 and 1921; a report on the economic development of the Jackson Hole region of Wyoming, 1933; an undated manuscript map showing the Federal purchase area in Polk County, Tex.; manuscript, annotated, and photoprocessed plats of townships in the Grand River purchase unit of Iowa, 1938; maps of national forest lands lying east of the Continental Divide, about 1934; tabular data relating to the ownership of natural forest areas, 1934; and published statistical maps showing information about forest land resources and uses, 1942.

346. DIVISION OF FOREST PRODUCTS. 1909-35. 5 items.

Published maps of the United States showing the production and consumption of lumber and lumber products, 1909-11; a published map of Canada showing by province the production of lumber, 1912; and a manuscript map of the world showing by major forest area the production of paper and lumber, 1935.

347. DIVISION OF RANGE RESEARCH. 1935-50. 121 items.

An undated annotated map of the United States showing the status of range research; general maps of the Western United States showing forest lands and rangelands and the field organization of the Division of Range Research, 1936; manuscript, annotated, and published maps from a special grazing survey of Roosevelt National Forest, Colo., 1950; and maps and related records pertaining to county range surveys, 1935-38.

348. DIVISION OF SILVICS. 1897-1932. 33 items.

Maps of Latin America showing forest resources, 1897-1923; published maps illustrating dendrologic investigations in North and South America,

1907-13; and photoprocessed maps from insect-control surveys in national forests, 1917-18.

349. FOREST AND RANGE EXPERIMENT STATIONS. 1924-50. 217 items.

A published map of the United States showing the operational regions of the Forest Service experiment stations, 1930; and published maps of research areas under the jurisdiction of the Allegheny, Appalachian, California. Central States, Intermountain, Lake States, Northeastern, Pacific Northwest, Rocky Mountain, Northern Rocky Mountain, Southeastern, Southern, and Southwestern Forest and Range Experiment Stations. Included are general maps of the Forest Service regions and maps showing distributions of tree species, topography, landownership, roads, soil types, and building sites.

350. STATE AND PRIVATE FORESTRY DIVISIONS. 1934. 5 items.

Manuscript maps relating to special studies of forests in Washington and Oregon, conducted in cooperation with State agencies and private forest owners, 1934.

351. CIVILIAN CONSERVATION CORPS PROJECTS. 1933 and 1938. 2 items.

A photoprocessed map of the United States showing sites of emergency construction work in national forests, 1933; and an annotated map of the United States showing occupied and vacant CCC camps, 1938.

RECORDS OF THE BUREAU OF PLANT INDUSTRY, SOILS, AND AGRICULTURAL ENGINEERING. RG 54

The Bureau of Plant Industry, Soils, and Agricultural Engineering was established in the Department of Agriculture in 1943 as a successor of the Bureau of Plant Industry, which had been established in 1901 to coordinate the plant research activities of a large number of autonomous offices and divisions in the Department of Agriculture. In 1954 the functions of the Bureau of Plant Industry, Soils, and Agricultural Engineering were transferred to the Soil Conservation Service.

352. DIVISION OF SOIL SURVEY AND ITS PREDECESSORS. 1900-53. 1,600 items.

Maps of the United States and large regions of the United States showing the distribution of soil groups; maps showing the alkali content of soils in certain areas of the West; maps showing the depth of underground water in areas of the West; land-classification maps of part of Washington showing existing and potential land use; maps of Ohio showing surface geology and glaciology; a map of the Cotton Belt showing soil regions; and maps of counties and parts of counties showing in great detail the distribution of soil types. The county soil map series have been continued by the Soil Conservation Service (see entry 363).

RECORDS OF THE RURAL ELECTRIFICATION ADMINISTRATION. RG 221

The chief function of the Rural Electrification Administration (REA), established in 1935, is to make self-liquidating low-interest loans to individual farmers, to cooperatives, and to public bodies for the purpose of financing the construction and operation of electric generating plants and transmission lines, the wiring of rural properties, and the acquisition and installation of electrical and plumbing appliances and equipment. Since 1949 it has made loans for the purpose of extending and improving rural telephone service. Most of the cartographic records of the REA were prepared during the period 1939-52 by the Mapping Services Section.

353. GENERAL RECORDS. 1950, 1951. 2 items.

Publications describing uniform standards for the preparation of maps to be submitted to the REA by applicants for loans for the construction of electrical or telephone facilities. Each publication is accompanied by sample maps, a sheet showing symbols to be used, and tables for the construction of polyconic projections.

354. MAPPING SERVICES SECTION. 1939-52. 1,283 items.

Published and photoprocessed maps including maps of individual States showing the status of REA projects, annually and semiannually, 1939-51; maps of the United States showing by State the percentage of farms with telephones, the distribution of rural telephone borrowers, and the percentage of farms receiving central station electrical service; maps of areas served by electrical associations borrowing from the REA; maps of individual States showing the numbers and boundaries of electrical systems; maps of individual States showing REA-financed electrical facilities and others, including transmission lines, distribution lines, stations, plants, and the names of REA-financed concerns and others owning the facilities; and maps of individual States showing proposed and existing transmission lines, proposed and existing generating plants, and ownership of facilities. Arranged in series by subject of map.

RECORDS OF THE SOIL CONSERVATION SERVICE. RG 114

The Soil Conservation Service (SCS), originally designated the Soil Erosion Service, was established in 1933 in the Department of the Interior. Although it has been charged with a variety of agricultural conservation responsibilities since its transfer to the Department of Agriculture in 1935 the agency's chief function has been to assist farmers and ranchers in locally organized, farmer-directed soil conservation districts, through its planning technicians and soil and water conservation experts who live and work in the districts.

In performing its functions, the SCS carries on a significant cartographic program which includes compiling soil maps for the National Cooperative Soil Survey, furnishing aerial photographs and drafting and reproduction services for farm and ranch planning, compiling large-scale topographic maps for special purposes, supplying engineering drafting services for watershed and flood-prevention planning, and furnishing cartographic assistance for irrigation and drainage work.

Record Group 114 includes the records of two SCS predecessors, the Soil Erosion Service and the Resettlement Administration.

Soil Erosion Service

355. SOIL EROSION SURVEY. 1934-35. 2,500 items.

Manuscript, annotated, and published maps, including maps of the United States showing drainage basins, soil erosion, and soil-erosion projects; maps of individual soil-erosion project areas; maps of the Chancellorsville, Ga., Homestead Community; a map of the Rio Grande watershed showing acquisitions of lands for Indians; maps of States, counties, and local areas showing the extent of soil erosion and the control methods proposed for each area.

Resettlement Administration

356. GENERAL RECORDS. 1937. 3 items.

An annotated map of the United States showing title-examining offices and maps of the Southwest annotated to show existing and proposed resettlement projects.

357. RURAL RESETTLEMENT DIVISION. ca. 1936. 57 items.

Manuscript maps showing project areas in New York and Pennsylvania.

358. RURAL LAND PLANNING AND DEVELOPMENT DIVISION. 1935. 5 items.

Manuscript and annotated maps of land-use project areas in Vermont.

359. LAND UTILIZATION DIVISION—LAND USE PLANNING SECTION. ca. 1936. 3 items.

Maps of local areas in Texas showing water resources and proposed development.

Soil Conservation Service

360. GENERAL RECORDS. 1934-54. 324 items.

Published maps of the United States showing SCS regional boundaries and headquarters, 1936-53; the extent of soil and soil conservation surveys, 1947-53; basic land resource areas, 1943-44; the extent of soil erosion, 1936-54; soil groups and drainage basins, 1950-51; climate and plant-growth regions, 1937; SCS demonstration projects, 1938; the financial status of SCS agricultural projects, 1936; acreages of wheat, corn, and flax; and soil conservation districts, 1938-54.

Maps of SCS regions showing activities of the agency, 1939-54; undated manuscript maps of the Southwest showing field operations of several agricultural programs; maps and photographs used in Dr. W. C. Lowdermilk's survey of land use in the Old World, 1941; published and photoprocessed general maps of the various SCS regions, 1935-53; published maps of the Vouraikos watershed in Greece, 1946; and miscellaneous published and photoprocessed maps of local areas in the United States relating to agriculture and soil conservation, 1934-54.

361. CARTOGRAPHIC DIVISION. 1938-46. 60 items.

Published color plates used in the preparation of a land-use-capability map of the Coosa River watershed in Georgia, 1945; aerial photomosaics of parts of southern California, 1946; a published topographic map of the soil conservation tract at Beltsville, Md., 1938; and a published topographic map of the engine research laboratory at Cleveland, Ohio, 1941.

362. TECHNICAL COOPERATION–BUREAU OF INDIAN AFFAIRS.
1936-39. 450 items.

Published maps of the Western United States showing soils and erosion, land classification, woodlands, ground-water depths, and other features.

363. SOIL SURVEY. 1944-62. 430 items.

Published maps of counties and other geographic areas showing the distribution of soil types, 1955-62; published soil-survey reports, accompanied by maps or published aerial photographs showing details of soil types by county or other geographical area; and miscellaneous manuscript and annotated maps of the United States and parts of the United States showing soil conservation districts, physiographic regions, irrigated areas, land-utilization projects, and other features, 1944-49.

364. CONSERVATION SURVEYS DIVISION. 1930-54. 2,172 items.

Published and photoprocessed erosion reconnaissance maps of various States and SCS regions, 1935-48; a map of SCS Region 10 showing the status of conservation surveys through 1938; undated published State maps showing land-resource areas; published maps of the United States and of various States, regions, and local areas showing soil-conservation problem areas, 1939-54; undated maps of part of the Northeastern United States showing time priorities for soil- and water-conservation work; published maps from conservation surveys of project areas in several different States, 1937; published maps showing erosion, present land use, and land-use capabilities in various States, 1936-37; published photomaps from conservation surveys of Baldwin and Tift Counties, Ga., and Essex County, Va., 1938-46; published maps of various Western States showing land-use capabilities, 1950-51; published maps and graphs illustrating a study of conservation irrigation in relation to conservation districts in the United States, 1947; published maps of various States and SCS regions and districts, 1942-60; manuscript, photoprocessed, and published maps of the Fort Hays, Kans., soil-erosion project, 1930-37; a manuscript map and related records from the sand-dune project at Dalhart, Tex., 1936-39; annotated maps of the Buford-Trenton Project in North Dakota, about 1953; manuscript planetable sheets from surveys of farms in Nebraska, 1926-39; manuscript and annotated soil maps of part-time farms in several Southwestern States, 1936; miscellaneous soil and land-use maps of farms in various parts of the United States, 1936-39; maps and photographs showing soils, erosion, and land use in the southern Great Plains, 1936-39; soil and alkali maps of project areas in Utah and New Mexico, 1936; a map of SCS Region 2 showing soil types, 1936; maps of Regions 2 and 4 showing cotton production, 1949; a map of Arkansas showing critical areas of specialized crops, 1942; annotated maps of Dawson Co., Mont., showing landownership and land use, about 1939; undated published maps from the Northeastern Nevada Cooperative Land Use Study; a nomograph for computing the rate of soil decline, 1946; a map of the U.S. Naval Radio Station, Cheltenham, Md., showing fields and classes of land, 1950; and a map and a table relating to soil types and soil erosion in Puerto Rico, 1936.

365. WATER CONSERVATION AND DISPOSAL PRACTICES DIVISION.
     1929-55. 4,246 items.

Among the records of the Sedimentation Section are a published map of the United States showing the adequacy of reservoir sedimentation survey data, 1950; manuscript planetable and cross-section sheets and field notebooks from sedimentation surveys of lakes, streams, and reservoirs in many parts of the United States, 1936-47; manuscript field notebooks from surveys of sedimentation in stream channels and valley lands, 1935-40; a published map of California showing the San Joaquin and Sacramento drainage basins, 1947; and manuscript and annotated maps and construction drawings relating to the Rocky Creek and Statesville Bedload Experiment Stations in North Carolina, 1936-37.

Among the records of the Hydrologic Section are maps showing the boundaries of major drainage basins in the United States, 1937-49; maps showing drainage problem areas in SCS Regions 1 and 2, 1949-55; maps showing the status of watershed and drainage-basin projects in the United States, 1943-54; an aerial mosaic overprinted to show a subwatershed work plan, 1949; maps from studies of rainfall in SCS Region 8, 1936-52; general maps of the United States and parts of the United States showing projects and activities of the SCS and the U.S. Geological Survey, 1937-39; maps of various regions and States showing soils, erosion, topography and geology, agricultural lands, ground-water supplies, irrigation, streamflow, rainfall and runoff, and drainage projects, 1929-47; tables containing data from rainfall and runoff studies conducted at several erosion experiment stations in Texas, Oklahoma, Wisconsin, Kansas, Washington, Ohio, and Missouri, 1931-41; blueprint plans of engineering equipment apparently used in SCS projects, 1937-38; maps of a hypothetical subwatershed, 1953; maps of watershed and drainage project areas in many parts of the United States, 1936-52; base maps of pilot watersheds in SCS Region 2, 1953; a map of the United States showing the areas of responsibility for flood-control activities, 1936-53; an undated chart showing typical regional organizations for flood-control work; State maps annotated to show locations of recording and staff gages, 1939; lists of stream discharge measurement stations in various States, 1939; a published base map for a special survey of the March 1938 flood in southern California; maps pertaining to the spring floods of 1943 in parts of the Central United States; undated published maps of watersheds in the United States showing drainage features and county and State boundaries; detailed maps of watersheds showing a wide range of physical and cultural features, particularly those pertaining to agriculture, soil erosion, and flood control, 1936-55; and an undated manuscript map showing the alluvial plain in the vicinity of Oxford, Miss.

366. CLIMATOLOGICAL AND PHYSIOGRAPHIC DIVISION. 1934-42.
    168,161 items.

A map of the United States showing 1930 Weather Bureau stations and climatological sections, 1934; an undated map of the United States showing tentative SCS research regions, 1936; an undated map of the United States showing soil conservation project areas; files of climatologist C. Warren Thornthwaite, including maps showing climatic regions, temperatures and precipitation, and various aspects of agriculture over the entire world and in Italy, Mexico, and parts of the United States, 1900-39; compilation maps from studies of precipitation and temperature patterns in the United States for the period 1898-1940; manuscript maps showing climatic data accumulated at the Kingfisher Project and the Guthrie Experimental Farm, both in Oklahoma, the Muskingum Project in Ohio, and the Upper Ohio and Susquehanna drainage basin project in Pennsylvania, 1936-40; manuscript maps of the Great Plains showing precipitation and agricultural data, 1939-41; maps of Oklahoma showing climatic regions, natural vegetation, crops, Indian tribes, explorers' routes, and dates of land openings, 1939-41; undated precipitation maps of southern Missouri and northern Arkansas; maps of the Atlantic coast piedmont showing physiographic regions, precipitation, and erosion, 1938-39; rainfall maps of the Lenoree River drainage basin, S.C., 1939-40; maps of the Spartanburg (S.C.) Project Area, 1936-39; undated maps of the Polacca Wash, Ariz.; maps and graphs relating to climate and vegetation in the Southwest, 1936-42; and a group of maps of Ohio and Oklahoma showing weather conditions at 6-hour intervals, 1936-38.

367. ENGINEERING DIVISION. ca. 1915-40. 4,641 items.

Undated maps of the United States illustrating the advantages of drainage and irrigation works; maps of the United States showing values of lands on which loans were closed during 1933-34; a map of the Western United States showing the snow course network for irrigation and water-supply forecasting, 1936; undated maps of river basins showing areas of arable farmland suggested for retirement; maps of the Big Four Drainage District, Ill., 1937; maps of the Grand Prairie rice region of Arkansas, about 1934; numbered files of maps, plans, and construction drawings relating to specific drainage projects and facilities, including a card catalog listing subjects and areas, 1915-40; and miscellaneous unnumbered maps, profiles, and construction drawings relating to specific drainage projects, 1920-35.

368. LAND UTILIZATION DIVISION. 1930-52. 3,263 items.

Maps of the United States and parts of the United States showing land-utilization projects, 1936-52; maps of the United States showing the status of title clearance for lands purchased by the Federal Government, 1936-37; maps of the United States showing the extent of game, forestry, and recreational development in project areas, 1936-37; State maps showing recreation sites in land-utilization project areas, about 1938; maps showing land-utilization problem areas in various States, 1935-38; maps of proposed land-utilization projects, 1937-41; maps showing Indian land purchase projects, 1934-37; specimen maps for land-utilization projects, 1938; undated project files containing maps showing land classification and ownership, locations of recreation areas, and the boundaries of individual projects; maps showing projects rejected, about 1935; maps from studies of land-utilization units in the Great Plains, 1937; undated maps showing climatic provinces in the Colorado and Rio Grande Basins of Colorado and in the Great Basin of Utah according to the Thornthwaite system; maps of the Pacific Northwest showing resettlement areas and land-utilization problem areas, 1937; undated maps of California showing various aspects of climate, settlement, grazing, and agriculture; manuscript land classification and soil maps of parts of Idaho, 1936-38; maps of Montana and Nevada, 1936; maps of the Hereford Irrigation Area, Tex., 1937; a land-use classification map of Gray's Harbor, Wash., 1936; and maps of Wisconsin showing population and public forest areas.

369. PROJECT PLANNING DIVISION. 1936-52. 102 items.

Maps from land and water inventories of Fresno and Stanislaus Counties, Calif., 1950-52; a topographic map of part of the California migrants' camp near Coachella; and a topographic map of the Price River Community Project, Utah, 1936.

370. LAND ACQUISITION DIVISION. 1935-38. 1,250 items.

Maps showing lands being acquired for SCS projects.

371. AERIAL PHOTOGRAPHS. 1933-39. 21,000 items.

Photography covering widespread areas of the United States. Included are 2,500 film rolls, 16,00 cut-film negatives, and 2,500 index negatives and prints. Scales vary from 1:15,840 to 1:31,680.

DEPARTMENT OF COMMERCE

GENERAL RECORDS OF THE DEPARTMENT OF COMMERCE. RG 40

The Department of Commerce was established in 1903 as the Department of Commerce and Labor. It was given its present designation in 1913 when a separate Department of Labor was created. The Department's functions are to promote the growth of American business and commerce, to foster the development of the merchant marine, to assist in the economic development of communities and regions with lagging economies, to improve and extend scientific, engineering, and commercial standards, to advance knowledge of the oceans, the earth, and the atmosphere, and to administer the Nation's patent and trademark systems. Most of these activities are conducted by the Department's subordinate bureaus, whose records constitute separate record groups.

Business and Defense Services Administration
Office of Area Development

372. INDUSTRIAL LOCATION DIVISION. 1957. 1 item.

A published map of the United States showing urban target areas for purposes of the National Industrial Dispersion Program. These target areas are defined as urban areas with a residential population of 200,000, or 16,000 residents employed in defense-related industries concentrated within a 2-mile radius of the installation.

RECORDS OF THE BUREAU OF THE CENSUS. RG 29

The Bureau of the Census was not established as a permanent agency of the Government until 1902, although decennial censuses of the population of the United States had been taken since 1790. Later censuses have included housing, agriculture, manufactures, minerals, industries, governmental units, and the retail, wholesale, and service trades. Maps are produced at virtually all stages of the Bureau's work, including the planning, collecting, and publishing of statistical data.

For detailed descriptions of the cartographic records in Record Group 29, see The National Archives, *Cartographic Records of the Bureau of the Census*, Preliminary Inventory No. 103 (Washington, 1957).

373. GENERAL RECORDS. 1860-1957. 1,647 items.

Textual publications relating to the mapping activities of the Bureau, including a monograph summarizing the investigations made to select a suitable method for remeasuring the areas of the United States by State, county, and minor civil division for the census of 1940; and a census tract manual, dated 1947, with supplements for 1950 and 1952 describing the nature and use of census tracts, the procedure for defining census areas, and the definition and establishment of census tracts.

Published maps of the United States showing regional boundaries and offices, field offices, and population sampling units for the Bureau, 1953-57.

Published maps and atlases with information compiled by the Bureau. Among these are maps of States and parts of States giving the density of population by county or administrative district. This information is given frequently by race or, in the case of pre-Civil War maps of the Southern States, by whites, freedmen, and slaves.

Editions of the *Statistical Atlas of the United States* for the years 1870, 1900, 1914, and 1924 with maps and related charts giving information about weather and climate, topography, geological structures, distribution of major forest trees, the territorial status of the country, the density of foreign-born population and their distribution in the United States by country of birth, illiteracy, religious groups, employment and occupations, student population, distribution of wealth, per capita public indebtedness and taxation, amount and sources of Government revenue, growth of the public debt, amount and nature of Government expenditures, range of cultivation of principal crops, relative population figures by sex, birthrate, proportion of death by certain diseases, insanity and idiocy, migration of population, centers of manufacturing, wages, and value of manufactured products.

Special maps and atlases, including a map of Alaska, 1882; maps of Indian reservations in New York, 1890; a map showing navigable rivers in the United States, 1890; atlases relating to the growth in population and area of metropolitan districts, 1900-40; a map showing types of farming areas in the United States, 1930; maps showing the density of population in the United States; maps showing drainage basins and irrigation areas, 1939-50; maps showing the distribution of livestock production, 1942; maps showing the economic areas of States and cities; and maps showing the birth registration status for 1922 and 1923 and the death registration status for 1920 and 1927.

An atlas showing selected industries reported in the 1937 census of manufactures, with locations of manufacturing establishments, wage earners, and value added by manufactures.

Arranged in series by kind of maps and thereunder chronologically by date of census.

374. GEOGRAPHY DIVISION. 1850-1952. 54,500 items.

The records of the Office of the Chief of this Division consist of training manuals with information on how to read maps and aerial photographs; and a publication entitled *Areas of the United States, 1940*, that contains descriptions of the land and water areas for the individual States, counties, minor civil divisions, incorporated areas, and territories and island possessions with maps of the States, territories, and island possessions showing minor civil divisions.

The cartographic records of the Drafting, Map Files, and Reproduction Section of the Operations Branch consist of base and outline maps of the world, the Western Hemisphere, and the United States; and manuscript, annotated, and photoprocessed maps, graphs, and tables containing information compiled for and from the decennial census and others, 1920-52. These were used as illustrative devices or as working tools in undertaking a census.

Among the records in the latter group are maps summarizing religious surveys, vital statistics, and census activities in the territories and island possessions; studies of trade, business, industries, manufactures, sales, wholesale and retail trade, agriculture, hospitals, the hotel and amusement businesses, employment, wages, and population; and drainage projects, alluvial lands, and drought areas. There are maps showing supervisors' districts, metropolitan areas, and congested production areas. There are map records of the Boston conference on sales and trade, 1937; of a special study on retail buying habits in Morrow County, Ohio; and of a real property survey of the District of Columbia. Another series of maps shows local governmental units, per capita aid to local governments, and per capita property tax collection.

Other records of the Section consist of base maps of the United States annotated to show statistical information from the 1950 Census of Agriculture; manuscript maps of certain cities showing the areas covered in the special tabulations on urbanized areas, 1950; panels of maps showing the growth of population in the United States from 1790 to 1950; and published maps of the United States showing statistical information about agriculture from the 1954 Census of Agriculture. The latter series was prepared for inclusion in the *National Atlas of the United States.*

There are also published outline maps of the United States and manuscript and published outline maps of the individual States showing county boundaries, 1920-52; and published maps of States showing county and minor civil division boundaries, 1930-50.

The records of the Cartographic Analysis Section in the Operations Branch include the "Office Copy Maps" showing enumeration districts in each county, 1880-1940, and a set of bound volumes containing written descriptions of the boundaries for that period.

The enumeration district maps generally are large-scale maps of cities, counties, and other small political units, either published or photoprocessed, with annotations in color to show boundaries and numbers of the enumeration districts, wards, minor civil divisions, and townships. These maps are prepared in advance of each decennial census as the boundaries and numbers of the districts are reestablished in preparation for the new census. The maps prepared for a given census are kept in the Bureau for use in the preparation of the maps for the next census. When the new maps are prepared, those of the preceding census are transferred to the National Archives.

The enumeration district descriptions are typewritten verbal descriptions of the enumeration district boundaries; they are in bound volumes. Some of the descriptions also include the names, addresses, and rates of pay for enumerators; special instructions to enumerators; and population, number of dwellings, and number of farms in each district.

Other records of this subsection include a series of maps of Indian reservations annotated to show boundaries of supervisors' districts.

Arranged in series by unit of origin within the Geography Division and thereunder by kind of map. There is an appendix listing the enumeration district maps in Preliminary Inventory No. 103.

375. INTERNATIONAL STATISTICS PROGRAMS OFFICE. 1940-56. 293 items.

This Office is responsible for working with the International Cooperation Administration in the Department of State on census projects and problems in foreign countries. Personnel from the Bureau of the Census lend technical assistance to foreign countries undertaking censuses. They also conduct training programs for census technicians from foreign countries in census geography and graphic presentation of statistical data.

The records of this Office consist of manuscript maps and other graphic illustrations showing information about population distribution and vital statistics in the Latin American countries, including some of the nations in the West Indies. These records were prepared in the 1940-45 period, although some of the information dates from 1900. Published maps of Central America and the Greater Antilles prepared for the census atlas project consist of general maps showing landforms, climatic regions, natural vegetation, and roads and railroads, and maps of the individual countries showing population distribution for rural and urban areas, 1950-56. There is also a relief map of Central America and a map of Puerto Rico showing the density of urban and rural population, 1956.

RECORDS OF THE COAST AND GEODETIC SURVEY. RG 23

A survey of the coast of the United States was authorized by Congress in 1807 but it was not until 1816 that an organization, known as the Survey of the Coast, was established. The activities of the Survey soon ceased for lack of appropriations but the Survey was reestablished in 1832. In 1871 it was authorized to undertake geodetic operations on a nationwide scale, and in 1878 it was renamed the Coast and Geodetic Survey (C&GS). In 1965 the Survey became a part of the newly organized Environmental Science Services Administration (ESSA). The records created by the Survey since that time are in the National Archives with the records of ESSA, in Record Group 370.

The Coast and Geodetic Survey is responsible for hydrographic and topographic surveys of coastal waters and adjacent land areas of the United States and its possessions; surveys of inland waters (except the Great Lakes); geodetic control surveys; compilation of data for nautical and aeronautical charts; tide and current observations; and geomagnetic, seismological, gravitational, and other geophysical measurements and investigations. Among these activities the first four are fundamentally cartographic, and to some extent all involve mapping. These responsibilities are carried out by the scientific and technical divisions of the Survey.

Until the establishment of the Republic of the Philippines in 1946 the Coast and Geodetic Survey was responsible for the nautical charts covering the Philippine Islands. The charts were compiled and published in the Philippines; copies were forwarded to the Washington headquarters, where they were incorporated with the existing set of numbered charts. With the establishment of the Republic, the Hydrographic Office of the U.S. Navy became responsible for the continuation of the nautical chart series covering the Philippines that was originated by the Coast and Geodetic Survey.

376. GENERAL RECORDS. 1850-1955. 619 items.

Maps of the United States showing coastal areas assigned to various Federal agencies and commercial concerns for standard topographic mapping in the National Defense Program; the status of mapping of frontier areas and areas to be mapped under a 1933 mapping project; and civil airways and air mileages.

Publications relating to maps and mapping activities of the C&GS, including a description of aeronautical chart symbols, 1948; descriptions of charts issued; descriptions of map projections; descriptions of special mapping projects, with maps included; texts, with charts included, on the magnetic declination in the United States, 1902-25, and Alaska, 1920; a report on the need for better surveys and charts of Alaska, 1918; reports on geodetic survey operations in the United States, 1903 and 1924-26; a description of Arctic tides, 1911; reports on the triangulation of parts of the United States, 1914-15; a description of the magnetic ranges of San Francisco Bay, Calif., 1920; a report on the magnetic survey and seismographic observations of the vicinity of the Paricutín Volcano, Michoacán State, Mexico, 1943; a definition of geodetic and other survey terms, 1945; notes with related charts on the U.S. coast by A. D. Bache, 1861; and gazetteers for coastal areas of Washington, Oregon, California, Alaska, and the Philippines.

Index maps of the United States and parts thereof outlining the coverage by date of topographic and hydrographic surveys made by the C&GS. Index maps of each State showing triangulation and first- and second-order leveling. Maps of coastal areas showing the nautical chart coverage, by chart number, over the period 1837-1946.

An atlas of the Philippine Islands compiled in the Philippines under the supervision of Rev. José Algue, S.J., director of the Manila Observatory from surveys conducted by the Jesuit Fathers, 1899. These maps were published by the Coast and Geodetic Survey in 1900. Included are maps of the whole archipelago showing political subdivisions, ethnography, volcanoes, ocean depths, meteorological and seismographic stations, and the distribution of earthquakes. The remaining maps are relief maps of the individual islands.

A 10-sheet planimetric map of Liberia published by the C&GS from SHORAN-controlled mosaics of aerial photographs by the Aero Service Corporation, Philadelphia, Pa., 1953.

Manuscript and annotated maps and nautical charts identified as the papers of Henry L. Whiting of the Coast and Geodetic Survey. Included are maps from surveys of harbors, rivers, and coastlines, primarily in Massachusetts, and maps and sketches showing samples of map presentation. There are also maps showing progress of surveys along certain coastal areas, maps from boundary surveys of West Point, N.Y., maps showing limits of charts prepared by the Survey, a few unidentified manuscript maps, and a few pages of field notes.

Arranged in series by subject or type of map.

Office of Cartography

377. AERONAUTICAL DIVISION. 1926-65. 31,000 items.

A set of published charts prepared for use in aerial navigation in determining aircraft position and direction, the most direct aerial routes, approaches to airfields, the locations of ground-to-air radio transmitters and the patterns of radio beams, and magnetic declination. The charts show two basic types of information: physical and cultural features that can be used as visual aids to aerial navigators, including vertical relief, shorelines, drainage features, roads and railroads, cities and towns, and prominent landmarks; and aeronautical information, including airports, lights, radio ranges, radio stations, auxiliary fields, and dangers to aircraft, such as high-tension lines. The scales of the charts vary according to the use for which the individual series are designed.

Among the records are Sectional Charts of the United States, their apparent forerunners, called Regional Charts, and World Aeronautical Charts covering the United States, Mexico, Canada, and Alaska. These three series are general aeronautical charts designed for contact (visual) navigation. Flight charts and their apparent forerunners, the Airways Route Charts, are strip charts covering corridors 100 miles wide along the principal air routes in the United States and Alaska. Local Charts give details of metropolitan areas. Instrument Approach Charts show approaches to airports; Landing Charts on the reverse side show details of the airport facilities. Other series include Instrument Landing System Charts covering air terminals having instrument landing system installations; Radio Facility Charts giving details of radio information to facilitate the planning and execution of cross-country flights, and Danger Area Charts showing boundaries areas dangerous to aircraft and describing the types of dangers existing in the areas.

Also among these records are Direction Finding Charts designed to facilitate the plotting of radio bearings; Planning Charts designed for planning aircraft routes; Aircraft Position Charts covering the North Atlantic Ocean, Western Europe, Northwest Africa, and the Caribbean Sea, designed for long-range air navigation by U.S. commercial carriers; Route Charts showing air routes; Magnetic Charts of parts of the world showing lines of equal magnetic declination and equal annual change; Jet Navigation Charts of North America; Sectional Aeronautical Charts overprinted with air defense grids; and special aeronautical maps of the United States showing air routes and of the world showing great-circle routes.

Ten plastic relief maps, two plaster molds, one aluminum mold, and descriptive texts relating to the process of making plastic relief maps are included as representative samples of that technique.

A set of published catalogs, with index maps that also serve as a finding aid, is included.

Arranged in series by chart name and thereunder by identification assigned in the C&GS.

378. NAUTICAL DIVISION. 1839-1965. 17,000 items.

A set of the published numbered charts issued by the Coast and Geodetic Survey, designed to include copies of all editions and corrections. The current procedure is to add any changes or corrections to the plate of a chart and print new charts incorporating these corrections. The dates for the new printings are given on the charts. New editions are prepared when the corrections become too voluminous or when changes in format occur. Many of the older editions, however, dated before 1925, bear hand corrections and editorial changes which bring the charts up to a later date than the date of edition publication.

Most of these charts are the nautical charts of the coasts of the United States and its territories and island possessions. There are four types of nautical charts, drawn at varying scales: Sailing Charts, on the smallest scale, covering large ocean areas and designed for fixing ships' positions; General Charts of ocean-coastal areas on small scales designed for offshore coastwise navigation; Coast Charts showing coastal areas, including navigable rivers and bays, on a larger scale designed for inshore coastwise navigation; and large-scale Harbor Charts designed for entering and maneuvering within harbors. There are also other charts covering the intracoastal waterways of the Atlantic and gulf coasts.

These charts show soundings, bottom contours, underwater obstacles, aids to navigation, and character of the sea bottom. They also show details of topography along the adjacent coastlines and include cultural information, such as roads, railroads, city plans, outlying settlements, buildings, and prominent landmarks.

This series of numbered charts includes other maps of a more special nature. Among these are large-scale detailed topographic maps and plans of Washington, D.C., including published versions of the King plats and plans of the city by Ellicott, L'Enfant, and Dermott; a map of Wakefield, Va., the birthplace of George Washington; base and outline maps of the United States, Alaska, and the Philippine Islands; outline maps of the North Atlantic and North Pacific Oceans; maps showing great-circle routes; maps of the United States showing drainage features; maps of the United States showing airline distances and of the world showing air routes; isogonic charts of the Caribbean Sea, Alaska, and the United States; and diagrams showing the coordinates for different types of map projections.

There is also a series of unnumbered published charts. Some of these are nautical charts, and others are special chart publications. Among these are some maps and charts of the Confederate States prepared during the Civil War. Included are charts of the navigable waters in those States, maps showing naval activities, city plans, and topographic maps of States or groups of States. There is also a folio of published facsimiles of charts prepared during the Civil War by the C&GS.

There are a few of the manuscript compilations of some of the published charts. The majority of the manuscript maps prepared from surveys and the manuscript compilations for the original charts are in the custody of the Coast and Geodetic Survey.

A set of catalogs containing lists of the numbered series of charts, with index maps locating charts by area covered, is among these records. These catalogs date from 1882.

Arranged in series by kind of map. The numbered series is arranged by chart number assigned in the agency.

Office of Physical Science

379. DIVISION OF PHOTOGRAMMETRY. 1927-61. 3,000 items.

This Division is responsible for the mapping of terrestrial features to obtain the shoreline and other land features that are necessary for control for hydrographic surveys and that are included on nautical charts as aids in coastwise navigation. The records of this Division include record sets of prints of three kinds of maps covering the coastal United States and constructed from aerial photographs. These are: shoreline maps which show accurate delineations of the shoreline of navigable waters with topographic details of navigational importance within a narrow zone along the shore; planimetric maps (also called air compilation maps) which are complete for all shore and inshore details within their limits and show topographic features except contours, shoreline detail, drainage features, towns, buildings, roads, railroads, field boundaries, and prominent landmarks; and topographic maps which include contours in addition to the information described for the planimetric maps.

This Division is also responsible for the construction of the Airport Obstruction Plans. These are plans of individual airports and show runways and flight paths for landing and takeoff, together with the positions and elevations of objects near the airport that are potential hazards to air traffic.

Arranged in series by type of chart and thereunder by file number assigned in the C&GS.

Field Records

380. PHILIPPINE ISLANDS FIELD STATION. 1913-34. 14 items.

Large-scale topographic maps of individual islands in the Philippines. These maps, prepared from surveys made by C&GS personnel stationed at Manila, were published in the Manila office. Nautical charts of the Islands dating to 1951 are among the numbered series described in entry 378. Nautical charts issued since 1951 are among the records of the Hydrographic Office (see entry 188). Arranged numerically by assigned chart number.

RECORDS OF THE ENVIRONMENTAL SCIENCE SERVICES ADMINISTRATION. RG 370

The Environmental Science Services Administration was established in the Department of Commerce in 1965 through the consolidation of the Weather Bureau and the Coast and Geodetic Survey. Its mission is to describe, understand, and predict the state of the oceans, the state of the upper and lower atmosphere, and the size and shape of the earth, and to assist those Federal departments concerned with the national defense, the exploration of outer space, and the management of natural resources.

The records in Record Group 370 include chiefly continuations of map series in Record Group 23 and Record Group 27 already established by the predecessor agencies.

Weather Bureau

381. WEATHER ANALYSIS AND PREDICTION DIVISION. 1965-66. 1,560 items.

Base maps of the United States and Canada annotated to show surface weather conditions at eight different times during each day in 1965-66. Published daily surface weather maps of the United States, 1965, including also maps showing precipitation areas and amounts, and highest and lowest temperatures. These are continuations of map series described in entry 403 under the former Division of Synoptic Reports and Forecasts.

Coast and Geodetic Survey

382. OFFICE OF AERONAUTICAL CHARTING AND CARTOGRAPHY. 1965-66. 376 items.

Continuations of the World, Sectional, and Local Aeronautical Chart series described in entry 377 under the former Aeronautical Division; Aircraft Position Charts; and IFR-VFR Planning Charts.

383. OFFICE OF HYDROGRAPHY AND OCEANOGRAPHY. 1965-66. 535 items.

Continuations of the numbered Nautical and Small Craft Chart series described in entry 378 under the former Nautical Division.

384. OFFICE OF GEODESY AND PHOTOGRAMMETRY. 1965-66. 184 items.

A continuation of the Airport Obstruction Plans series described in entry 379.

RECORDS OF THE BUREAU OF FOREIGN AND DOMESTIC COMMERCE. RG 151

The Bureau of Foreign and Domestic Commerce was formed in 1912 through a consolidation of the Bureau of Statistics and the Bureau of Manufactures. Its functions included the preparation and publication of official statistics on foreign commerce and the promotion of manufacturing by the compilation of information on industries and on foreign and domestic markets. It was abolished in 1953.

Bureau of Statistics

385. GENERAL RECORDS. 1905-8. 3 items.

Published maps of the world showing principal land and sea transportation routes for the years 1905, 1906, and 1908. The editions of 1905 and 1908 include tables showing the mileage and costs of the principal railroads by country; mileages of railroads in the United States for the period 1832-35, quinquennially during the period 1840-1905, and for the years 1906 and 1907; and the distances from New York, New Orleans, Port Townsend (Wash.), and San Francisco to the principal ports of the world and the principal cities in the United States.

Bureau of Foreign and Domestic Commerce

386. GENERAL RECORDS. 1929-31. 2 items.

A published map of the United States overprinted to show territories administered by the district offices of the Bureau, 1931; and a photoprocessed map of the United States showing consumer trading areas determined by the Marketing Division of the International Magazine Co., Inc.; used to accompany the "Market Data Handbook of the United States," Domestic Commerce Series No. 30, issued by the Bureau.

387. DIVISION OF STATISTICAL RESEARCH. 1931. 6 items.

An incomplete set of mimeographed publications entitled "Geographic News" containing information about foreign map publishers compiled by American commercial attachés abroad. The publication of the "Geographic News" was expanded and continued by the Economic Research Division, 1932-33, and the Division of Regional Information, 1933 (see entries 388 and 389).

388. ECONOMIC RESEARCH DIVISION. 1932-33. 15 items.

An incomplete set of mimeographed monthly publications of the Geographic Section entitled "Geographic News." These contain news relating to geographic events of interest. They also include information about map, atlas, and geographic book accessions (see also entries 387 and 389).

389. DIVISION OF REGIONAL INFORMATION. 1933. 3 items.

Mimeographed publications entitled "Geographic News." The format and content of these publications are the same as earlier issues, described above. A published map of Colombia, Ecuador, Panama, and western Venezuela shows chief transportation routes.

390. PETROLEUM DIVISION. n.d. 1 item.

A published map of the Netherlands East Indies and British Borneo showing proven oilfields, prospective fields, and facilities for handling petroleum.

391. OFFICE OF DOMESTIC COMMERCE. 1947. 1 item.

A published map of the United States with insets of parts of Pennsylvania and the area covered by Ohio, Indiana, and Illinois, showing graphically the capacities of steel furnaces in thousands of net tons of steel produced and indicating the ownership of the furnaces.

392. AREA DEVELOPMENT DIVISION. 1950. 1 item.

An atlas showing changes in the economic development of States and regions during the period 1929-48. Included are maps relating to various aspects of population distribution and change, manufacturing, farm economics, income, and consumer costs.

RECORDS OF THE NATIONAL BUREAU OF STANDARDS. RG 167

The National Bureau of Standards, established in 1901 as a successor of the Office of Standard Weights and Measures, acts as one of the principal research and testing laboratories of the Federal Government; its functions include the development and maintenance of working and reference standards in weights and measures and the quality of materials and the application of these standards in science and engineering. Much of its work is conducted in cooperation with other Federal agencies.

393. GENERAL RECORDS. 1935, 1948. 2 items.

Base maps of the United States and adjacent parts of Canada and Mexico, dated 1935 and 1948, overprinted to show standard time zones established by the Interstate Commerce Commission.

RECORDS OF THE BUREAU OF PUBLIC ROADS. RG 30

The Bureau of Public Roads originated in 1893 as the Office of Road Inquiry. Until 1912 its functions were limited to the collection and dissemination of information but they have since been enlarged to include the administration of Federal grants to the States for aid in road construction; cooperation with the Departments of the Interior and Agriculture in the construction of roads in national parks and forests; participation in highway construction projects abroad as a part of U.S. military and economic aid to friendly nations; research in problems of transportation and highway design; and participation with other Government agencies in special projects relating to roads. From 1915 to 1931 the Bureau and its predecessors were responsible for agricultural engineering activities; the records relating to those activities are in Record Group 8, Records of the Bureau of Agricultural Engineering.

The major map-related functions of the Bureau are the financing of State and county highway maps and the supervision of their preparation by the State highway departments following the Bureau's standard specifications. In addition, the Bureau's central office is responsible for compiling and maintaining current highway and traffic maps of the United States.

Office of Public Roads

394. GENERAL RECORDS. 1906. 1 item.

A photoprocessed map of Morehouse Parish, La., annotated to show settled and unsettled areas, high and low alluvial areas, and public roads.

Office of Public Roads and Rural Engineering

395. GENERAL RECORDS. 1918. 1 item.

A photoprocessed map prepared for use in showing the progress of the economic highway survey for Florida.

Bureau of Public Roads

396. GENERAL RECORDS. 1920-65. 3,187 items.

Published maps of the United States showing the Federally aided highway system, the U.S. numbered highways system, interstate highways, and defense highways, 1922-58, including a copy of a map showing the project for the development of national highways, approved by Gen. John J. Pershing, Chief of Staff, 1922. This map represents the basic highway study that led eventually to the adoption of the national system of interstate and defense highways covered in the 1956 Federal-Aid Highway Act. Published and annotated maps of the United States showing the Federal-aid highways initially proposed by the States, 1922; roads, by type of construction, in each State, 1920; the progress of construction of principal interstate highways, 1930; the prevailing subgrades by soil types; existing and proposed toll roads, 1955; modern express highways as proposed by President Roosevelt, 1938; locations of public-works highway projects, 1934; traffic flow; the number of carlot equivalents, by State, of oranges shipped by motor truck from California and from Florida, 1950; and the status of the production of tracings for county base maps, 1939-40.

Published and annotated maps of the Western States showing proposed, approved, and existing Federal-aid highways and highways administered by the Forest Service, 1921-45. Maps of the United States and of the Northeastern States showing roads considered in snow-removal programs, 1920-30. Maps of States, parts of States, and counties annotated to show progress in improvements made with Federal aid for the construction of highways. Published maps of States showing highway systems, the status of highway construction, and highways improved with Federal aid.

Published maps from local planning surveys in Connecticut, Pennsylvania, and the District of Columbia. Maps showing the details of the Baltimore-Washington Parkway, 1951; the Mount Vernon Highway, 1927-32; and the road network leading to the War Department buildings in Arlington, Va., 1943. Maps of Central and South America showing the status of construction of the

Inter-American Highway, 1940-50, and copies of aerial photomosaics of the routes surveyed for an inter-American highway in Mexico and Central America, 1933.

Arranged in series by map coverage or kind of map.

397. RECORDS FROM STATE HIGHWAY DEPARTMENTS IN COOPERA-TION WITH THE BUREAU OF PUBLIC ROADS. 1920-65. 44,236 items.

Published, photoprocessed, and annotated maps of States and of individual counties showing highway systems. These maps show all roads, by type of construction, within a given State or county. They contain a variety of information about railroads, bridges, bus routes, and commercial carrier routes, and they also show political boundaries, Federal and State reservations, Indian reservations, national parks and forests, private land grants, city limits, reservoirs and dams, airfields, and township lines. Many of the more detailed county maps show buildings, residences, farm units, schools, churches, cemeteries, and land-utilization projects. Many of the county maps include insets of metro-politan areas or are accompanied by supplemental sheets on which the metropolitan areas are shown in detail.

A series of diagrammatic traffic maps of States showing a 24-hour average volume of commercial traffic on the primary and secondary roads. Figures give the numbers of vehicles traveling the roads.

Arranged in series by type of map and thereunder alphabetically by State and, where applicable, by county.

RECORDS OF THE WEATHER BUREAU. RG 27

The primary purpose of the Weather Bureau, established originally in the Office of the Chief Signal Officer in 1870, is the systematic forecasting of weather conditions. In conducting its forecasting and related activities it prepares and uses maps as basic tools.

The systematic presentation of weather patterns on daily maps was pioneered by Cleveland Abbe, Sr., and was aided by the development of the telegraph, which made possible the rapid collection of observations from distant points. The Western Union Telegraph Co. issued daily weather maps under the direction of Abbe during the few months in 1870 before the U.S. Army Signal Corps undertook weather observation activities. The Signal Corps used those maps in launching its own weather-mapping program.

The weather forecast service originally was intended for the use of coastal and Great Lakes navigators. Before long, however, the demands of agriculture, commerce, and transportation, and those of navigation, became so heavy that the Weather Service activities were greatly expanded in scope, and the Service eventually was transferred to the Department of Agriculture, where in 1891 it was established as the Weather Bureau. In 1940 it was transferred to the Department of Commerce.

Since its establishment the Bureau's forecasting and mapping functions have increased continually in scope and complexity. In 1958 the National Meteorological Center was established in Suitland, Md., for the purpose of bringing about a greater degree of centralization in Weather Bureau mapping. The Center provides analyses of current weather and forecasts of the future state of the atmosphere at different levels over areas as large as the Northern Hemisphere, and it issues 5-day forecasts and 30-day outlooks. In producing its weather maps and forecasts the Meteorological Center assembles weather data from its network of stations throughout the United States and arctic regions, compiles from that data its synoptic maps, and transmits the maps back to the individual weather stations, both civil and military.

The Bureau also conducts a considerable meteorological research program, in the course of which maps are produced. Studies include research on severe storms, worldwide atmospheric circulation, atmospheric physics, and meteorological instruments and communications systems.

In 1965 the Weather Bureau became a part of the newly organized Environmental Science Services Administration. The records created by the Weather Bureau since that time are in the National Archives with the records of ESSA, in Record Group 370.

Office of the Chief Signal Officer

398. DIVISION OF TELEGRAMS AND REPORTS FOR THE BENEFIT OF COMMERCE. 1870-91. 32,964 items.

A small series of base maps of the United States annotated by the Western Union Telegraph Co. to show surface weather conditions, November 16 to December 5, 1870, with some gaps in dates. Two bound volumes and some loose maps showing surface weather in the United States identified as manuscript (annotated base) maps by Cleveland Abbe, Sr., for November and December 1870 and the first part of January 1871. Base maps of the United States annotated to show surface weather conditions daily from November 1870 to June 1891. Many of the maps in this later series, which are bound into consecutively numbered volumes, were prepared by Cleveland Abbe, Sr., particularly those from November 1870 to December 1871, and a few are identified as having been prepared by Increase Lapham. A sampling of base maps of the United States annotated in certain field offices, particularly Milwaukee, Wis., and New York City, to show surface weather conditions.

A published record set of the surface weather maps of the United States issued daily and sometimes two or three times a day. These published maps include tables giving pressure readings, temperature, humidity, and rainfall at selected localities, summaries of preceding weather, and forecasts for future weather. Included is a series of corrected thrice-daily weather maps, issued separately from the daily weather maps, for the year 1878. Other published maps of the United States illustrate studies of temperature and precipitation, isobars, isotherms, cloudiness, and wind directions and velocities.

Base maps of the Northern Hemisphere annotated to show surface weather conditions daily, 1877-86. Base maps of the Northern Hemisphere annotated daily to show direction and velocities of winds over the North Atlantic Ocean, with occasional references to icebergs sighted by ships at sea, 1888-91. Base maps of the Northern Hemisphere with manuscript overlays showing the daily paths of storms over the North Pacific Ocean and Canada.

Arranged in series by type of map. Within series, usually arranged chronologically.

Weather Bureau

399. GENERAL RECORDS. 1891-1957. 3,266 items.

Published maps of the United States showing administrative districts and facilities of the Weather Bureau. Published manuals on forecasting, the preparation and use of weather maps, meteorology, observing and coding weather, and the making of marine meteorological observations. Published base and outline maps of the United States, Alaska, and the Northern Hemisphere prepared for use in reporting weather.

Published maps of the United States showing weather and climate in general; maps relating to storms, such as studies of storms over New England and studies of hurricanes and cyclones; maps of the Ohio River drainage basin showing hydrologic stations, amount of precipitation during January 1937, and heights of the river during the months of January and February 1937; an atlas of maps of the Northern Hemisphere summarizing international meteorological observations, 1878-87; atlases of maps of the Great Lakes showing currents based on the courses of bottles thrown into the lakes, 1892-94; maps relating to floods, particularly those in the Mississippi and Ohio River Valleys in 1912 and 1922; charts of the Great Lakes showing locations of wrecks, 1886-94; maps illustrating temperature, precipitation, wind frequency, cold waves, and frost in the United States; and a series of published maps of the United States prepared for inclusion in the *National Atlas* showing by months standard deviations of temperature.

Base maps of the Northern Hemisphere annotated to show daily barometric pressures and the directions of prevailing winds over the North Atlantic Ocean, 1891-95, with frequent references to icebergs sighted by ships at sea. Base maps of the United States annotated to show atmospheric weights daily for December 1939 and February 1940.

Arranged in series by kind of map and thereunder chronologically where applicable.

400. OFFICE OF CLIMATOLOGY AND ITS PREDECESSORS. 1891-1914. 1,337 items.

An incomplete published record set of maps relating to climate in the United States, especially prepared for the use of farmers. Among the records are an atlas of climatic maps of the United States showing average rainfall, temperatures, pressures, and typical storms, published in 1904 from observations dating back to 1870; crop weather bulletins with maps of the United States showing temperature and rainfall departures by weeks during the planting, growing, and harvesting seasons, 1891-95; climate and crop bulletins, 1896-1907, and national weather bulletins, 1908-14, based on the weather crop bulletins but including additional information on temperature and precipitation; ice and snow bulletins for the years 1892-1911, with maps showing the limits of ice and snow; and maps showing dates of killing frosts, wind directions and velocities, and numbers of thunderstorm days. There is also a map of the world showing lines of equal sunshine duration.

Base maps of the United States annotated to show dates for planting each of several crops, 1895.

A two-volume "Oceanographic Atlas for Mariners"; Volume 1, published in 1959, covers the North Atlantic Ocean; Volume 2, published in 1961, covers the North Pacific Ocean. Included are various types of climatic maps and charts and oceanographic charts pertaining to waves, currents, water temperatures, and ice.

Arranged in series by type of map and thereunder chronologically.

401. DIVISION OF OPERATIONS AND REPORTS. 1909-14. 855 items.

Published charts of the oceans and the Great Lakes showing wind directions and velocities, currents, fog, temperatures, storm tracks, and shipping lanes. These charts were published by the Marine Section and were issued monthly. They are similar to the Pilot Charts issued by the Hydrographic Office (see entry 191). Arranged by name of ocean or lake and thereunder chronologically.

402. FORECAST DIVISION. 1891-1941. 63,400 items.

Base maps of the United States annotated to show surface weather conditions daily and sometimes two or three times a day, 1891-1928. Base maps of the United States and Canada annotated to show surface weather conditions, 1928-41. Some of the surface weather maps prepared during the period 1936-41 were made at the Washington National Airport and include air-mass data.

Base maps of the United States annotated to show semidaily wet-bulb temperature readings, 1896-97. Base maps of the United States and Canada annotated to show barometer readings, 1937-39.

An incomplete record set of the published daily, semidaily, or tridaily weather maps of the United States, 1891-1941. These maps show surface weather conditions and include tables giving river levels, wind velocities, pressure readings, precipitation amounts, and temperatures at certain localities.

A collection of published papers, with maps, giving information about storms and their relationships with other weather phenomena.

Arranged in series by kind of map and thereunder chronologically.

403. DIVISION OF SYNOPTIC REPORTS AND FORECASTS. 1941-65. 79,393 items.

Records from the WBAN (Weather Bureau, Army and Navy) Analysis Center and its predecessors, including published base and outline maps of the United States, North America, and the Northern Hemisphere used for reporting weather for different purposes; reports on the preparation of prognostic weather maps; and base maps of the United States and Canada annotated to show surface weather conditions for 8 different hours a day. Some of these maps include air-mass data.

The records of the Weather Forecasting and Services Section are a continuation of the daily published surface-weather map of the United States. They also include inset maps showing temperatures, rainfall, pressure, and fronts. Forecasts are given for Washington, D.C., Maryland, Virginia, and Delaware.

Arranged in series by kind of map and thereunder chronologically.

404. DIVISION OF HYDROLOGIC SERVICES AND ITS PREDECESSORS. 1897-1956. 87 items.

Published maps of river basins in the United States showing hydrologic stations, dams, and precipitation gages, 1939-40; a map of the lower Mississippi River Valley showing inundated areas, 1897; and reports with map illustrations on the meteorology of flood-producing storms in the Mississippi River Basin, 1956, winds over Lake Okeechobee, Fla., during a storm in August 1949, and the seasonal variation of the standard storm project.

405. DIVISION OF STATION FACILITIES AND METEOROLOGICAL OBSERVATIONS AND ITS PREDECESSORS. 1944-56. 10 items.

Published maps of the United States showing locations and types of airway, synoptic, and supplemental weather-reporting stations operated by the Weather Bureau and other Federal and State Government agencies, forecast centers, flight advisory weather service units, and Weather Bureau headquarters, airport stations, and city centers. A published map of North America showing the direction and character of principal air currents.

406. METEOROLOGICAL RESEARCH OFFICE AND ITS PREDECESSORS.
    1941-56. 58,000 items.

This Office was responsible for supervising publication of the historical maps showing synoptic weather of the Northern Hemisphere and related information. Most of these records were prepared in cooperation with the Army, the Navy, and the Air Force and were executed by meteorological staffs of certain colleges and universities.

Among the records relating to this project are base maps of the Northern Hemisphere overprinted to show time, time variations, and lines of sunrise and sunset, 1899-1928. Base maps annotated to show a synopsis of daily weather at sea level, 1899-1945; base maps annotated to show a synopsis of weather at sea level with corresponding maps showing a synopsis of weather at 500 millibars, 1946-57; base maps annotated to show tracks of high-pressure areas over 10-day periods and another series annotated to show tracks of low-pressure areas over 10-day periods, 1899-1939; and base maps annotated to show weather conditions at 3,000 dynamic meters.

Many of these maps appear in published volumes, although at a much-reduced scale. The published record set includes the following series: synoptic daily maps, sea level, and sea level with 500 millibar, 1899-1960; a volume of errata maps containing revisions for certain dates covered in the previously described series; daily maps showing weather conditions at 3,000 dynamic meters, October 1932 and October 1940; maps showing normal weather conditions at sea level by months; maps showing normal weather conditions, upper levels, by months; maps showing extreme temperatures, upper levels, by months; and maps showing daily weather conditions at 13 kilometers for February 1941.

Related to these series are two volumes showing daily weather conditions, sea level, in the Southwest Pacific for January 1932 and June 1933. There is also a series of base maps of the Southern Hemisphere annotated to show surface weather conditions for the years 1948-52. This activity is now being conducted in the Union of South Africa.

Arranged in series by kind of map and thereunder chronologically.

407. FIELD OFFICES. 1910-49. 271 items.

Published daily weather maps of the United States showing forecasts for Wisconsin during October 1910.

Atlases prepared under the supervision of the Weather Bureau Office at New Orleans consisting of an atlas of climatic charts of the oceans and an airways meteorological atlas of the United States.

Base maps of the United States annotated at the Cleveland, Ohio, Airport to show surface weather conditions for February 1937. A base map of the United States annotated at the Providence, R.I., Airport to show surface weather conditions on December 2, 1942. These maps are retained as representative samples of the mapping activities of the field offices.

A published map of the Salt River Valley showing mean minimum temperatures for December and January, issued by the Weather Bureau Office at Phoenix, Ariz.

408. STATISTICS DIVISION. ca. 1945. 48 items.

Published maps of eastern Siberia, the North Atlantic Ocean, and the Barents Sea showing average monthly occurrences of various ceiling heights and visibility limits. These maps were prepared by the Work Projects Administration under the direction of the Weather Bureau in cooperation with the Weather Information Branch, U.S. Army Air Forces.

409. AEROLOGICAL DIVISION. 1937. 1 item.

A report issued as Supplement No. 26 to the *Monthly Weather Review* on "Winds in the Upper Troposphere and Lower Stratosphere over the United States." Included are 20 maps showing wind directions and velocities at selected heights.

410. WASHINGTON NATIONAL AIRPORT FLIGHT ADVISORY WEATHER SERVICE. 1946. 46 items.

A volume of plans of airway terminals and weather-reporting stations in the East Central, Middle Atlantic, and Southern States prepared for the use of forecasters in studying modifications of weather due to local factors.

DEPARTMENT OF LABOR

RECORDS OF THE BUREAU OF LABOR STANDARDS. RG 100

The purpose of the Bureau of Labor Standards, established in 1934, is to coordinate the efforts of States and interested organizations to improve the working and living conditions of wage earners. It investigates and reports on labor standards in industry, labor legislation, and labor-law administration.

411. DIVISION OF STATE SERVICES. 1935-58. 18 items.

A published map of the United States showing, by State, the extent and nature of occupational disease insurance coverage. Two sets of published maps of the United States, one issued in 1946 and the other in 1958, showing by State compulsory or elective occupational disease compensation coverage, numerical limitations on coverage, source of insurance provisions, types of provisions, second-injury funds or equivalent arrangements, and types of administration; that is, by court, board, or commission. The 1946 series includes a map showing the States where silicosis was covered and the 1958 series includes a map showing the States where diseases resulting from ionizing radiation were covered.

DEPARTMENT OF HEALTH, EDUCATION, AND WELFARE

RECORDS OF THE OFFICE OF COMMUNITY WAR SERVICES. RG 215

The Office of Community War Services, established in 1943 to succeed the Office of Defense Health and Welfare Services, served as a coordinating center for health, medical care, welfare, recreational, educational, and related services made necessary by the war effort. It was abolished in 1946.

Office of Defense Health and Welfare Services

412. GENERAL RECORDS. 1942. 1 item.

A photoprocessed map of the area around Blackstone, Va., annotated to show the boundary of the U.S. Army Reservation and the boundary of part of Camp Lee near Petersburg.

RECORDS OF THE OFFICE OF EDUCATION. RG 12

The Office of Education, established in 1867 as the Department of Education, was originally organized to collect and disseminate information on education in the United States and abroad and to promote the cause of better education throughout the country. Functions assigned later include the administration of funds appropriated as aids to education. From 1885 to 1931 the Office also was responsible for the educational program in Alaska.

413. GENERAL RECORDS. 1933. 1 item.

A published map of the United States showing the percentage of illiteracy in each county. The map was compiled from the 1930 census by the National Advisory Committee on Illiteracy and the National Illiteracy Crusade.

RECORDS OF THE PUBLIC HEALTH SERVICE. RG 90

The Public Health Service, which originated in 1798 as the Marine Hospital Service, is responsible for protecting and improving public health in the United States. Its activities include controlling the spread of diseases, conducting research into the causes and prevention of diseases, extending and improving State and local health services, supervising the manufacture of biological products, and disseminating health information.

414. GENERAL RECORDS. 1918. 2 items.

Photoprocessed maps from sanitary engineering surveys, including a map showing airfields and military camps in the vicinity of Fort Worth, Tex., and a photoprocessed plan of "Carruthers Field and anti-malarial zone," Tex.

415. DIVISION OF WATER POLLUTION CONTROL. 1942-51. 17 items.

Published maps of the Pacific Northwest drainage basins, the Great Basin in California, Nevada, Utah, and Idaho, the western Gulf drainage basin in Texas and New Mexico, and the California drainage basins, showing sources of pollution, existing treatment works, projects required, and existing water uses. A map of the Ohio River Basin showing major reservoirs and proposed reservoirs with a legend identifying the major purpose and ownership of each.

INDEPENDENT AGENCIES

EXISTING AGENCIES

RECORDS OF THE FARM CREDIT ADMINISTRATION. RG 103

The Farm Credit Administration was established in 1933 as an independent agency to coordinate the activities of several agencies engaged in making loans to farmers and to provide easy credit to various farmers' cooperative corporations and associations. Among its component units was the Office of the Land Bank Commissioner, which supervised the operation of the Federal land banks that had been set up in 1916. Upon its establishment the Administration took over the activities of the Federal Farm Board, and later in 1933 it assumed control of the regional agricultural credit corporations from the Reconstruction Finance Corporation.

416. GENERAL RECORDS. n.d. 12 items.

Published maps of the twelve Farm Credit Administration districts showing counties and crop reporting districts.

417. OFFICE OF THE LAND BANK COMMISSIONER. 1931-42. 12 items.

Records from the Federal Land Bank of St. Louis, Mo., including photoprocessed maps of drainage districts in Clay and Greene Counties, Ark., showing the boundaries of subsidiary drainage districts, drainage ditches and canals, natural drainage features, existing and proposed levees, and earlier meander lines of rivers. Published maps of the Grand Prairie rice region of Arkansas, including a geological map, a ground-water profile, maps showing the spring water tables for 1936 and 1939, and maps showing average ground-water recession, 1929-39.

418. DIVISION OF FINANCE AND RESEARCH. 1933-35. 11 items.

Published base maps of several States showing county boundaries, 1932. A published map of the United States showing the average dollar value of farmland and buildings per acre, by minor civil divisions, 1935.

419. DIVISION OF ECONOMICS AND STATISTICS. n.d. 28 items.

Photoprocessed maps of various States showing by minor civil divisions the value of farmlands and buildings in dollars per acre. The figures are based on the census of 1930.

RECORDS OF THE FEDERAL AVIATION ADMINISTRATION. RG 237

In 1938 the Civil Aeronautics Authority (CAA) was established through a merger of the Bureau of Air Commerce of the Department of Commerce and the Bureau of Air Mail of the Interstate Commerce Commission. The CAA was succeeded in 1940 by two new agencies, the Civil Aeronautics Board and the Civil Aeronautics Administration. These agencies were in turn superseded by the newly formed Federal Aviation Agency in 1958, which later became the Federal Aviation Administration (FAA).

The FAA and its predecessors have been responsible for the regulation of air commerce for safety purposes and for the fulfillment of national defense requirements; the promotion and development of civil aeronautics; the consolidation of research and development relating to air navigation facilities, as well as the installation and operation of such facilities; and the development and operation of a common air traffic-control system for both civil and military aircraft.

420. UNIDENTIFIED RECORDS OF PREDECESSOR AGENCIES. n.d.
     5 items.

Undated, unidentified maps, including a part of a map of the New York City-Atlanta, Ga., air route annotated to show airports and airfields; a map of the Las Vegas area in Nevada and California, annotated to show beacon lights to remain and lights to be removed; a map of Helena, Mont., and vicinity annotated to show beacon lights; a map of the Washington, D.C.-Martinsburg, W. Va., air route annotated to show airfields; and a photoprocessed map showing lighted airways of the U.S. Air Mail Service.

Aeronautics Branch of the Department of Commerce

421. GENERAL RECORDS. 1926-36. 37 items.

Published maps of the United States showing airway routes, proposed routes, lighted routes, airmail routes, and Army air routes. A photoprocessed map of Pennsylvania showing air routes and airports and other air navigation facilities. Annotated and photoprocessed maps of parts of the Southwestern United States showing air routes and beacon sites covered by bills of sale. Maps of air routes around Los Angeles annotated to show airfields and beacon sites. Published airway strip maps covering various regions of the United States. Manuscript plans of airfield and beacon sites along the Salt Lake-Pasco Airway and photoprocessed plans of sites on the El Paso-Fort Worth Airway.

422. AIRWAYS DIVISION. 1931. 2 items.

A manuscript profile of the Amarillo-Oklahoma City section of the Amarillo-St. Louis airway showing airfield and beacon sites; and a map of Illinois overprinted to show Airway Route No. 2 between St. Louis and Chicago and airfields and beacon lights along the route.

Bureau of Air Commerce

423. GENERAL RECORDS. 1934-37. 10 items.

Published airway maps of the United States showing scheduled airlines with a list of operators, Federally lighted airways existing or under construction, State or commercially lighted airways, and Federal airways equipped for day operators. A map of the Los Angeles-Salt Lake City air route annotated to show the radio plan, and a map of the Glendale-Enterprise section of the Los Angeles-Salt Lake City air route annotated to show beacon sites.

424. AIRWAYS OPERATIONS DIVISION. 1938. 1 item.

A published map of the United States showing "Schedule B" aeronautical communication stations.

425. AIRWAYS ENGINEERING DIVISION. 1936-38. 50 items.

Manuscript and photoprocessed plans of airfield sites in Iowa and Utah consisting of general plans, grading plans, plans showing borings, plans of drainage designs, plans showing obstructions, and fencing plans. Manuscript profiles of the Washington-Cleveland airway showing beacon sites and profiles of individual beacon sites located on the route. A manuscript lighting sketch for the airport at Celina, Ohio. Manuscript diagrams of the Nashville-Washington airway runway at Gordonsville, Va.

426. DIVISION OF AIR NAVIGATION. 1937. 4 items.

Photoprocessed sketches submitted for a proposed beacon site at Adairsville, Ga.; and manuscript plans of beacon sites at Stony Point and Hauser Lake, Mont.

Civil Aeronautics Authority

427. GENERAL RECORDS. 1938. 2 items.

Published airways maps of the United States, as described under entry 423 above, annotated with changes.

428. PROJECTS AND SURVEYS DIVISION. 1939-40. 6 items.

Five field notebooks relating to a survey of the Washington, D.C., alternate airport. These notes contain references to bench marks and bearings, topographic levels, and topographic sketches. A volume of field notes from a survey of Alvin Field, Colo., with notes on bench marks and levels and sketches of beacon sites.

429. AIRWAYS ENGINEERING DIVISION. 1939. 30 items.

Manuscript profiles of the runway and plan of possible "ML" radio sites for Alvin Field, Colo. A manuscript plan showing grading details for the airfield site at Zeeland, N. Dak. Manuscript profiles of the runway at Hinde Airport, Sandusky, Ohio. Manuscript plans of airfield sites in Pennsylvania and Utah.

430. BUREAU OF ECONOMIC REGULATION. 1939. 1 item.

A published map of the United States showing selected cities. Compiled by the Accounts and Analyses Division for an airline traffic survey of domestic airline revenue passenger originations and destinations.

431. REGIONAL OFFICES. 1939. 1 item.

A photoprocessed map of the CAA's Third Region, composed of the States in the vicinity of the Great Lakes from Ohio west to North Dakota and including Kentucky, showing radio facilities for air navigators by kind, fan markers, and teletype stations with a list of the stations by call numbers and a list of the frequency of fan markers.

Civil Aeronautics Administration

432. OFFICE OF AVIATION INFORMATION. 1941. 1 item.

A published airway radio facility planning chart of the United States issued by the Flight Information Section showing radio directions and frequencies, power ranges, airways, airports, airport localizers, controlled and noncontrolled airways, minimum safe altitudes, mileages between radio fixes, and danger areas.

433. REGIONAL OFFICES. 1952. 2 items.

Records of the Ninth Regional Office, Honolulu, Hawaii, consisting of a publication entitled *Survey of Requirements for Support of Civil Air Routes, Central and South Pacific Ocean*, with an accompanying volume of maps showing plans for the proposed development of Wake and Canton Islands for use as fueling stations in transpacific air commerce. The textual publication includes maps showing principal air routes and rhumb-line distances in the Pacific, plans of terminals, aerial views of Wake and Canton Islands, graphs showing the volume of transpacific flights, and photographs of the buildings in use on the islands. The accompanying volume contains plans of both islands showing existing conditions and master development plans with overlays showing the several stages of development proposed. A tabulation of fiscal data for the proposed development is included.

RECORDS OF THE FEDERAL COMMUNICATIONS COMMISSION. RG 173

The primary objective of the Federal Communications Commission, established in 1934, is to regulate radio broadcasting and interstate and foreign communication by radio or wire. Similar regulatory functions previously had been performed by the Interstate Commerce Commission, the Federal Radio Commission, and the Post Office Department.

Federal Radio Commission

434. GENERAL RECORDS. n.d. 1 item.

A published map of the United States showing the commercial aviation communications system.

Federal Communications System

435. GENERAL RECORDS. 1937. 1 item.

A published map of the United States, with insets of the territories and possessions, showing the commercial aviation communications system and radio stations.

436. ENGINEERING DEPARTMENT. 1942. 1 item.

A published map of Cuba showing the locations of radio facilities, by ownership or use, and the number of transmitters.

RECORDS OF THE FEDERAL HOME LOAN BANK SYSTEM. RG 195

The Federal Home Loan Bank System was established in 1932 to provide credit reserves for savings and home finance institutions. It now consists of the Federal Home Loan Bank Board, 11 regional Home Loan Banks, and private member institutions.

Record Group 195 also includes records of the terminated Home Owners Loan Corporation, a subsidiary of the Federal Home Loan Bank Board. The records of another subsidiary, the United States Housing Corporation, are in Record Group 3.

Home Owners Loan Corporation

437. GENERAL RECORDS. 1933-39. 13 items.

Published maps of selected cities in the United States annotated to show neighborhood types, including business and industrial areas and high-, medium-, and low-income residential districts.

Federal Home Loan Bank Board

438. DIVISION OF RESEARCH AND STATISTICS. 1941. 1 item.

A map of the United States overprinted to show where defense housing funds were allocated by the Defense Housing Coordinator, areas approved as defense localities where houses could be financed under Title VI of the National Housing Act, and localities in which the two types of areas coincided.

RECORDS OF THE FEDERAL POWER COMMISSION. RG 138

The Federal Power Commission (FPC), organized in 1920, was initially charged with exercising control over the location of all waterpower projects on navigable waters and on public lands and reservations of the United States. Subsequent legislation added to its duties the regulation of electric utilities engaged in interstate commerce, the investigation of power potentials in the flood-control projects constructed by the Department of the Army, and the regulation of interstate commerce in natural gas. It also has emergency control and supervisory functions over the power industry in times of national emergency or war.

439. GENERAL RECORDS. 1941-42. 4 items.

A published map of the United States showing power projects under major license as of June 30, 1941, with a list giving license number, name of plant, and name of stream or river upon which each project was located; and a copy of the same map overprinted to show regional boundaries and headquarters of the Federal Power Commission. A published map of the United States showing principal generating plants by type of ownership (governmental or private) and capacity, and principal electric transmission lines, by voltage, with insets of major cities showing this information in detail. A published map showing natural-gas pipelines in the Middle Atlantic and Ohio Valley States by size and ownership.

440. CHIEF ENGINEER. 1924. 5 items.

Published maps prepared by the Federal Power Commission from information gathered by the Northeastern Super Power Committee and correlated under the supervision of Col. William Kelly, Chief Engineer of the FPC. The purpose of the Super Power Committee was to consider what contribution could be made to further power development by cooperation between State and Federal agencies. The Committee was composed of the heads of various State and Federal agencies under the leadership of the then Secretary of Commerce, Herbert Hoover.

The area chosen for study covered the 11 States of Maine, New Hampshire, Vermont, Massachusetts, Connecticut, Rhode Island, New York, Pennsylvania, New Jersey, Delaware, and Maryland and the District of Columbia. The records of this study consist of maps of the northeastern region showing developed and potential power, transmission systems and primary transmission lines, the amounts of electric and nonelectric power consumed, and a comparison of costs of power from different sources.

441. ENGINEERING DIVISION. 1932. 10 items.

In 1930 applications by private companies desiring to perform construction work on navigable rivers or on public lands were considered by the Engineering Division of the FPC. Later reorganizations of the Commission gave that authority to the Bureau of Power. The records of this Division include a published 10-sheet topographic map of the vicinity of Flathead Lake, Mont., prepared by the Rocky Mountain Power Co. and submitted to the FPC as evidence in accordance with the provisions of article 23 of the license issued May 23, 1930, to that company for Project No. 5.

442. NATIONAL POWER AND ELECTRIC RATES SURVEYS. 1934-35. 5 items.

In 1933 the Commission was directed to undertake a survey of the power resources and requirements of the United States and of the costs of power generation, transmission, and distribution. The Electric Rates Survey compiled and analyzed the rates charged for electric energy and the service furnished by both private and municipal corporations to consumers of all classes throughout the United States.

The records include published maps of the United States compiled by the Research Division of the Survey showing existing and proposed generating plants by type and by ownership, electric transmission lines by capacity for 1934 and 1935, and the areas served by the principal electric utility companies in the United States in 1935. Photoprocessed maps of the United States showing graphically the production of copper, lead, and zinc in 1930 and the locations of electrolytic plants in 1934.

443. BUREAU OF POWER. 1940-54. 55 items.

The Bureau of Power is a part of the Commission's technical staff. Through its three divisions in Washington and its five regional field offices it handles power requirements and supply, licensed projects, and project cost work.

The cartographic records of the Bureau include published and photo-processed maps of the 11 regions and subregions of the FPC in the United States showing electric utility generating stations by ownership and capacity, and transmission lines for 1940-43 and 1953. In addition, there are published State maps showing principal electric facilities by type, capacity, and ownership, 1949-52. This project was never completed; only 24 States were mapped. The regional maps are arranged numerically by region number; and the State maps, alphabetically by State.

444. DRAFTING AND DUPLICATING SECTION, OFFICE OF
      ADMINISTRATION. 1924-52. 800 items.

The Drafting and Duplicating Section, Office of Administration, was responsible for the drafting of the manuscript maps compiled from information gathered by the technical bureaus and divisions of the Commission.

The cartographic records of this Section include manuscript maps, profiles, and graphs pertaining to the development of rivers in the United States. Many of these records illustrate activities undertaken as a result of the Flood Control Acts of 1938 and subsequent years. Maps and related records pertaining to river basins predominate in this series. Included are maps and profiles of major rivers and their tributaries showing power and flood-control projects; general maps of river basins and watersheds showing existing and proposed power and flood-control projects, many of which were proposed by the Corps of Engineers, U.S. Army; topographic maps of individual project areas showing facilities of the projects; plans of dams and other facilities showing details of construction; maps showing the effects of the dams upon navigation; graphs showing river stages at specific sites and dates; graphs showing normal and abnormal flows of water at dams; graphs showing normal output of power at specific developments; maps and graphs showing the extent of damage caused by floods; charts showing the growth and predicted trends in electrical output in different project areas; and other records relating to individual projects. There are a few maps of Alaska showing precipitation characteristics and a few maps and graphs relating to electrical systems in California.

Manuscript maps of foreign areas, prepared during World War II at the request of the State Department. Included are maps showing electrical facilities; charts and graphs showing existing and potential electric-power production in various countries; a map of the world showing potential waterpower, 1941; and maps showing pre-World War II electrical facilities in Canada.

Manuscript maps of States and cities in the United States showing electrical generating plants and transmission lines.

A published map of the United States showing natural-gas pipelines and communities served with natural, manufactured, or mixed gas.

RECORDS OF THE FEDERAL TRADE COMMISSION. RG 122

The Federal Trade Commission (FTC), established in 1914, is authorized to prevent unfair methods of competition and undue restraint of trade in interstate commerce; to compile factual data about the Nation's industries as a basis for remedial legislation and for the guidance and protection of the public; to prohibit the dissemination of false advertisements of food, drugs, curative devices, and cosmetics with a view to safeguarding life and health; and to promote the adoption of trade-practice rules that improve business ethics.

The Federal Trade Commission prepares maps primarily to illustrate its publications. Other cartographic records of the FTC were received with correspondence or were submitted as exhibits in FTC investigations.

445. GENERAL RECORDS, MAIL AND FILES SECTION, ADMINISTRATIVE DIVISION. 1923-34. 57 items.

Published and photoprocessed maps, many with annotations, of the United States and parts thereof containing information relating to public utilities and the companies owning those utilities. Among these records are a map of the United States showing electric transmission lines, natural-gas pipelines, and the fields of operation of the principal power companies; maps showing local areas served by specific electric or gas utility companies and the locations of facilities owned by those companies; maps of the Northwestern States showing the locations of large timber holdings; maps showing grain elevators in Chicago keyed to a list showing the type of ownership of each; a map showing trackage rights and collieries served by railroads in Pennsylvania; a map dated 1933 showing natural gas developments in the central United States; and a map showing the routes of two unidentified trips in Puerto Rico.

The origins of most of these maps are unidentified. Some may have been forwarded to the Federal Trade Commission by the utilities concerned and others may have been gathered by the Commission during its general investigations of the public utility companies. A few are noted as having been submitted in reports, particularly those relating to timber holdings in the Northwest.

Arranged by map number assigned in the National Archives. A card catalog describes each map by subject.

446. CHIEF COUNSEL. 1931-36. 80 items.

In 1928 the Federal Trade Commission was directed to undertake investigations of public utility corporations engaged in interstate or international commerce and of holding, service, and management companies. These investigations were conducted in the FTC through the Chief Counsel and the Economics Division. The records of the Chief Counsel comprise those that were filed as exhibits during the investigations. Each item has either a stamp giving necessary data regarding its use or an exhibit number and a note that it is a copy of the original.

Among the records are charts showing the corporate structure of individual utility companies; maps showing territories served by the utility companies and the facilities owned by each; maps showing electric transmission lines and natural-gas pipelines crossing State boundaries; and maps of the United States showing major electric transmission lines and natural-gas pipelines, and areas controlled by the major utility companies.

Arranged numerically by exhibit number. A card catalog describes the records in alphabetical order by name of corporation or by subject where applicable.

447. ECONOMICS DIVISION. 1928-36. 156 items.

The records of the Economics Division are composed of the files for general inquiries undertaken by the FTC on its own initiative or at the request of Congress, the President, or departmental heads. Among the records are diagrams summarizing the corporate structure of the major utility companies; graphs presenting the distribution of the consumer's average costs for the purchase of farm products and of the average returns to growers for the sale of farm products; maps of the United States showing principal crop-producing areas by type of crop; a map-graph of the world showing the comparative crude petroleum production of the Royal Dutch Shell group and various American producers, 1921; maps of the United States showing principal oilfields and natural gas fields; maps of the United States showing holdings and facilities of the major manufacturers of farm machinery; graphs showing the distribution and source of the national wealth; and maps of the United States and of local areas showing the facilities of the various utility companies and the areas served by those companies.

Many of these are manuscript records prepared to illustrate reports. The reports are summarized in the appendix to the *Annual Report of the Federal Trade Commission for the Fiscal Year Ending June 30, 1938*, p. 173-193. In addition, these summaries list the publications issued by the Commission in which the individual reports are located.

Arranged by file numbers assigned in the National Archives. A card catalog lists the records by subject.

RECORDS OF THE NATIONAL ARCHIVES AND RECORDS SERVICE. RG 64

The primary function of the National Archives, established in 1934, is to assemble, preserve, arrange, and describe those noncurrent records of Federal agencies that have sufficient administrative, legal, research, or other value to warrant their continued preservation and to make them available for use by Government officials, scholars, and the general public. The Archives also is authorized to appraise records proposed for disposal by Federal agencies as lacking sufficient value to warrant their continued preservation. Record Group 64 includes those records created by the National Archives as the custodial agency for noncurrent records of the Federal Government.

From time to time the Cartographic Branch and its predecessors have prepared maps and other records for administrative purposes, for use as finding aids to records in their custody, and in response to special requests. More information about the activities of this Branch is found in the introduction to this guide.

448. CARTOGRAPHIC BRANCH AND ITS PREDECESSOR. 1937-54.
125 items.

Charts and plans relating to the administrative functions of the Branch (formerly the Division of Maps and Charts), including stack-area plans, forms relating to accessioning, and disposition lists for cartographic records of Federal agencies. A series of looseleaf binders containing a daily journal of the activities of the Branch Chief (formerly Division Chief) during the period 1937-54; most of these concern the work of W. L. G. Joerg. Notebooks containing forms relating to the accessioning of cartographic records during the period 1943-51. A manuscript overlay for a map of the United States indexing the cities for which there are cartographic records in Record Group 31, Records of the Federal Housing Administration, and in Record Group 69, Records of the Work Projects Administration. A manuscript map of northern Canada and Greenland showing the activities of Robert E. Peary and indexing maps prepared by Peary that are in Record Group 37, Records of the Hydrographic Office. A photocopy of a map prepared in the Branch showing the routes of transarctic and subarctic flights during the period 1930-40, by nation of origin, and a card file of bibliographic sources documenting the flights. A series of blueprint copies of a map of Spitsbergen Island annotated to show the extent of topographic mapping for various years during the period 1906-26; attached to each map are bibliographic slips identifying sources used in its compilation. Manuscript index maps to topographic maps and roadmaps of the Dominican Republic compiled by the U.S. Marine Corps.

Other records of the Branch include a manuscript map showing several versions of the Louisiana Purchase boundary and the U.S.-Texas boundary; a series of manuscript maps summarizing selected information shown on David Dale Owen's map of southeastern Wisconsin (Record Group 46, Records of the United States Senate); statistical maps relating to National Archives microfilm projects and to volumes of Federal records in the various States; and several copies of a published Army Air Forces map of the Northern Hemisphere annotated by Herman R. Friis to show selected transportation routes and other economic features in the arctic and subarctic areas, and scientific explorations by aircraft during the period 1945-54.

RECORDS OF THE FEDERAL HOUSING ADMINISTRATION. RG 31

The Federal Housing Administration (FHA) was established in 1934 to improve housing standards and to stabilize the housing market.

The Federal Housing Administration prepares maps as a method of illustrating housing data collected by the agency. The maps accessioned as records relate primarily to two programs conducted by the FHA: the Real Property Surveys conducted from 1934 to 1941 by the FHA and other Federal agencies; and the Housing Market Analyses conducted from 1937 to 1942.

The Real Property Surveys of cities in the United States were first conducted by local governments under the direction of the Bureau of Foreign and Domestic Commerce. The information gathered by this Bureau was turned over to the FHA where it was plotted on maps. In 1935 the Administration's Division of Economics and Statistics (later the Division of Research and Statistics), with the help of other Federal agencies, evolved a standard procedure for conducting these surveys and presenting the data. From 1935 to 1941 the surveys were administered by the Work Projects Administration; personnel employed by that agency prepared the maps, following the standardized procedures established in the FHA. Most of the maps thus prepared were turned over to the FHA; a few covering certain cities in Georgia were retained by the WPA (see entry 528).

The Housing Market Analysis maps were prepared in the Division of Research and Statistics in the FHA from data gathered by the agency. The FHA retains custody of those completed since 1942.

The National Archives, *Cartographic Records of the Federal Housing Administration*, Preliminary Inventory No. 45 (Washington, 1952) is out of print, but reference copies are available in many public and university libraries.

449. GENERAL RECORDS. 1934-36. 117 items.

Manuscript and published maps of the United States showing the jurisdictional districts of the FHA, World War II defense areas, trading centers, mortgages insured, urban and rural population, summaries of housing research, and economic characteristics of industry and agriculture; and graphs summarizing characteristics of selected urban areas and FHA data on foreclosures and mortgages. Arranged in series by subject.

450. DIVISION OF RESEARCH AND STATISTICS. 1934-42. 3,855 items.

Manuscript, annotated, and published maps prepared to show the results of the Real Property Surveys conducted in about 260 cities throughout the United States. Most of the maps are large-scale cadastral maps showing by blocks certain aspects of housing, such as physical condition of structures, average rental, occupancy by owner or tenant, occupancy by race, income of occupant, age of structure, duration of occupancy, number of persons per room, extent of mortgages, and sanitary facilities. Other maps show special characteristics of cities, such as spatial patterns of city growth, settled areas, growth of population, transportation facilities, neighborhood conditions, land use, industrial areas, and business areas.

Manuscript and published maps prepared from the Housing Market Analyses showing areas around selected cities considered financially safe for underwriting mortgages. The maps prepared after 1939 also show major defense industrial areas and the practicable commuting distances for workers residing in nearby areas.

These two series have been merged to form a single series, filed alphabetically by State and thereunder by city. A card catalog listing each map is arranged in the same way.

There are also a few manuals describing the methods for conducting real-property surveys and the preparation of real-property maps.

RECORDS OF THE INTERSTATE COMMERCE COMMISSION. RG 134

The Interstate Commerce Commission, organized in 1887, is authorized to regulate the services, safety precautions, rates, facilities, equipment, financial structure, accounting practices, and records of all common carriers engaged in interstate commerce except airplanes.

The records described below were furnished to or acquired by the Commission for use in its activities relating to investigations of interstate commerce.

451. BUREAU OF FORMAL CASES. 1900-34. 414 items.

The "formal cases" are those cases involving controversies between carriers and shippers and cases instituted by the Commission itself regarding rates or other matters over which it has cognizance. The cartographic records of this Bureau consist of manuscript, annotated, published, and photoprocessed maps of the United States and parts of the United States which were submitted as exhibits in the cases. Most of the maps pertain to the railroad industry. Among the records are maps of the United States and parts thereof showing railroad lines and systems, maps of areas covered by individual railroad systems showing the lines of the railroads, maps showing industrial sites and the railroads serving the industries, maps showing freight association districts, maps showing terminal points and railroad properties, maps showing corporate ownership of railroad lines, maps showing information about rates charged for the shipment of specific commodities and rates charged between given points, and maps showing maintenance costs and operating expenses for railroad lines.

Maps pertaining to subjects other than railroads include maps of the United States and of local areas showing coastal steamship lines and in many instances their relationship to railroad lines, maps pertaining to the coal industry showing the locations of coalfields and collieries within coalfields and including plans of coal mines, maps relating to the timber industry showing the extent and amount of timber in the United States and in local areas, maps of Kansas City showing the extent of the stockyards and the railroads serving them, a map of the United States showing the flow of copper in 1928, a map showing oil pipelines in the northeastern United States, a map showing sheep grazing grounds in Arizona, and a map showing creameries and cheese factories in Wisconsin.

Arranged numerically by "I and S" docket number. A card catalog lists the records by name of company.

452. BUREAU OF FINANCE. 1910-41. 131 items.

The finance cases related to actions taken by the Commission on requests by carriers for permission to issue bonds, make loans, effect consolidations, or undertake basic financial obligations. The maps filed with these cases consist of manuscript, annotated, published, and photoprocessed maps and profiles of railroad lines; maps showing railroad rights-of-way; and maps showing proposed railroad routes.

One large group of maps accompanied the application of the Pennsylvania Railroad and the Pennsylvania Co. to acquire control of the Wabash Railway through purchase of common stock. They include maps showing the corporate structures of the railroad systems involved and plans of cities showing railroad facilities.

Arranged numerically by docket number. A card catalog lists the maps by name of company.

453. VALUATION DIVISION. 1913-38. 138 items.

Representative samples of manuscript, photoprocessed, and annotated right-of-way maps and centerline profiles of railroad lines prepared by the railroad companies and forwarded to the Interstate Commerce Commission for use in connection with valuation surveys. These maps, selected at random from a large mass of maps authorized for disposal, were retained to illustrate an important activity of the Commission. Complete files of these records, with subsequent annotations, are retained permanently in the Lands Section of the Commission.

RECORDS OF THE PANAMA CANAL. RG 185

The first two organizations to engage in the construction of an isthmian canal were the Compagnie Universelle du Canal Interoceanique (1881-89) under the control of Ferdinand de Lesseps, and the Compagnie Nouvelle du Canal de Panama (1894-1904), both French companies. Partly to forestall a French monopoly of transisthmian transportation, the Nicaragua Canal Commission was appointed by the President of the United States in 1897 to survey a route for a Nicaragua canal. This body was superseded in 1899 by the first Isthmian Canal Commission, which investigated several proposed routes and recommended early in 1902 that the French Compagnie Nouvelle be purchased and work continued on the Panama canal. This was accomplished in 1904. Three more Isthmian Canal Commissions followed, the last of which saw the completion of construction work in 1914 under the chairmanship of Lt. Col. George W. Goethals. An organization known as The Panama Canal was set up in that year to serve as the permanent governing agency for the canal, the Panama Railroad Co., and the territory of the Panama Canal Zone.

In 1950 The Panama Canal became known as the Canal Zone Government, its functions limited to maintaining civil government. The operation and maintenance of the canal itself was charged to a new organization, the Panama Canal Company. The Governor of the Canal Zone also is president of the Panama Canal Company.

Most of the maps and related records in Record Group 185 are in manuscript form and were prepared in the field by engineers in the employ of the French companies and the U.S. Commissions, or by draftsmen in the Panama offices of the companies and commissions. Within each series of records the individual items are arranged by the letter or number designation assigned to them by the agency of origin.

For a detailed listing of these cartographic records, see The National Archives, *Cartographic Records of the Panama Canal*, Preliminary Inventory No. 91 (Washington, 1956). This inventory includes two appendixes, one of which lists each record by file number in each series; the other lists place names alphabetically and correlates them with the record items listed in the first appendix.

454. COMPAGNIE UNIVERSELLE DU CANAL INTEROCEANIQUE.
    1881-1900. 6,774 items.

The cartographic records of this organization consist of two major series. The first includes general maps, progress and status maps, harbor plans, city plans, and cross sections and profiles of terrain that were prepared during preliminary surveys of the route for the proposed sea level canal across the Isthmus of Panama. Other maps in this series are detailed maps prepared from surveys of rivers that were to be used in building a canal.

The second series of records contains the detailed working maps and plans for the Panama Canal route. Among these records are topographic maps of selected areas, harbor plans, cross sections and profiles of excavations, and plans of dams, locks, hospitals, shops and other buildings, equipment, and machinery.

455. COMPAGNIE NOUVELLE DU CANAL DE PANAMA. 1889-99. 730 items.

The cartographic records of this company consist of seven series. Among these series are area maps of the Panama Canal route with some maps of the Panama Railroad line; plans, cross sections, and profiles of terrain, rivers, locks, dams, and excavations; profiles of canal excavations at close intervals from the Atlantic to the Pacific coast; sectional maps of the route of the canal showing topographic and cultural features adjacent to the route; large-scale maps of Lago de Alhajuela and Lago de Bohio; and published portfolios and reports of the Technical Committee including general maps, plans, profiles, and cross sections showing the progress of the work on the canal. Most of these records are manuscript and were prepared by the chiefs of the geographical sections and were approved by the chief engineer, who was Director of the Administrative Service.

456. NICARAGUA CANAL COMMISSION. 1895-99. 417 items.

There are two series of cartographic and related records for this Commission. The first is composed of general maps, profiles, and cross sections of the routes proposed by members of the Commission. Among these are large-scale sectional maps of the Nicaragua Canal area showing some of these proposed routes. The second series is composed of detailed cross sections, profiles, and maps of the projected routes across Nicaragua. Other records in this second series are harbor plans for Greytown (San Juan del Norte) and Brito, sounding records for Greytown Harbor made by the U.S.S. *Newport*, excavation notes, technical estimates and computations, statistics about rainfall, and what appear to be fragmentary records of the Maritime Canal Co. of Nicaragua, a privately financed company incorporated by the U.S. Congress in 1889 and terminated in 1893 because of lack of funds.

457. ISTHMIAN CANAL COMMISSIONS. 1899-1913. 1,284 items.

Most of the records among these 11 series are from the first of the Isthmian Canal Commissions. Included are maps, profiles, and cross sections of the whole of the proposed Nicaragua Canal route and of the Eastern, Middle, and Western Divisions of the route; maps, profiles, and cross sections of the proposed Panama Canal route and of the routes through the Isthmuses of Darien and San Blas;

boring records for the Nicaragua and Panama Canal routes; and plans of canal lock construction. There are separate series of manuscript maps, profiles, and cross sections used to accompany the report of the First Isthmian Canal Commission and to appear in the appendixes of the report. There is also a series of maps published by the last of the Commissions in 1913 showing the route of the Panama Canal and the topography of the adjacent areas.

458. CARTOGRAPHIC RECORDS OF THE PANAMA CANAL. 1921-57. 10 items.

Published and photoprocessed topographic maps of the Canal Zone showing boundaries of the Canal Zone, the route of the canal, roads, and railroads, editions of 1924, 1938, and 1957. A photoprocessed plan of Fort Sherman showing the officers' quarters at Toro Point, compiled by the Department of Operations and Maintenance of the canal, about 1921. A series of six photoprocessed plans and cross sections showing the existing locks and the projected new locks compiled for a study of the steps necessary to convert the existing canal to a sea-level canal, 1931.

RECORDS OF THE SMITHSONIAN INSTITUTION. RG 106

The Smithsonian Institution, established in 1846, conducts explorations and scientific research, maintains museum and gallery exhibits, and issues publications based on its research and collections. The Institution is the overall administrator for the United States National Museum; the Astrophysical Observatory; the Radiation Biology Laboratory; the Tropical Research Institute; the National Zoological Park; the National Air and Space Museum; the International Exchange Service; the National Collection of Fine Arts; the Freer Gallery of Art; the National Portrait Gallery; the Joseph H. Hirschhorn Museum and Sculpture Garden; and, under separate Boards of Trustees, the National Gallery of Art and the John F. Kennedy Center for the Performing Arts.

459. GENERAL RECORDS. 1874. 3 items.

Published isothermal maps showing mean temperatures in the United States annually and for the winter and the summer; constructed from observations made and materials collected by Charles A. Schott, Assistant, U.S. Coast Survey.

460. BUREAU OF AMERICAN ETHNOLOGY. 1884-1950. 4 items.

Published maps showing the territorial limits and cessions of the original land occupied by the Cherokee Nation and a map showing the territory assigned to the Cherokees west of the Mississippi River and the lands owned or occupied by them in 1884. Both of these maps were prepared by C. C. Royce in 1884 and appeared in the Bureau's Fifth Annual Report. A published map prepared by

J. W. Powell for the Seventh Annual Report of the Bureau, showing the distribution of the American Indian linguistic stocks in North America, excluding Mexico, and in Greenland. A published map of South America showing the distribution of Indian tribal and linguistic groups. This appeared as map 18 in volume 6 of Bulletin No. 143, published in 1950.

RECORDS OF THE TENNESSEE VALLEY AUTHORITY. RG 142

The Tennessee Valley Authority (TVA), a corporation created by Congress in 1933, was directed to take over and operate the already existing Wilson Dam and associated powerplants at Muscle Shoals, Ala., in the interest of national defense and for the development of new types of fertilizers for agricultural use; to develop the Tennessee River and its tributaries in order to improve navigation, control floods, and generate and dispense hydroelectric power; and to conduct investigations upon which additional legislation could be based in order to aid further the proper conservation, development, and use of the resources of the region. The corporation is authorized to cooperate with other Federal, State, and local agencies and institutions in fulfilling these responsibilities.

Base topographic map information required by the TVA falls into two categories: regional coverage for overall planning, and large-scale, detailed mapping used in planning, design, and construction of engineering works. In addition to providing these requirements the Maps and Surveys Branch of the TVA cooperates with the U.S. Geological Survey, the Army Map Service, and other Government agencies in the development of new mapping techniques; it also maintains records of survey control data which are widely used by private and public engineering agencies.

461. GENERAL RECORDS. ca. 1935-43. 34 items.

Published maps of the Southeastern United States and of Johnson County, Tenn., showing cities, towns, roads, highways, railroads, and drainage features. A published map of the Tennessee Valley region showing dams and reservoirs, and a map of the lower Tennessee and Ohio River regions showing locations for possible projects. A series of published maps and diagrams of the Tennessee Valley region, including maps showing the effects of the Norris Dam and other projects under construction on the channel depths of the Tennessee River, previous projects located on the river, the navigation program for the river, existing and proposed river depths after passage of the TVA act, the Tennessee Valley as a potential national defense center, and the watershed protection program through electric power production; and diagrams showing the operation of high dams for flood control and control of storage by high dams on the main river. A series of map-plans of dam sites along the river showing locations of construction camps. A series of panels of maps with profiles of the Tennessee River and its tributaries showing existing, proposed, and possible developments.

A series of mimeographed memoranda on the subject classification system for the central map and drawing services and on grouping and numbering drawings.

462. COMMUNITY PLANNING DIVISION. 1938. 1 item.

A publication entitled *A Brief Graphic Appraisal of the Tennessee Valley ... 1938* containing maps showing, by county, information about income, employment, land use, land values, education and illiteracy, expenditures for education, and use of electricity, telephones, and automobiles on farms.

463. OFFICE OF POWER. 1955. 1 item.

A published map of the Tennessee Valley region showing transmission lines in service, under construction, or to be retired, electrical stations, hydroelectric plants, facilities belonging to the TVA, facilities belonging to private owners, Rural Electrification Administration projects, and service areas of municipalities and of cooperatives.

464. DEPARTMENT OF REGIONAL PLANNING STUDIES. 1939. 1 item.

A published map of the Tennessee Valley area showing retail trade boundaries, tentative retail trade boundaries, public land areas, distribution of population, and the Tennessee River Basin drainage divide.

465. ENGINEERING SERVICE DIVISION. 1934-35. 7 items.

A published map of the Tennessee Valley region showing roads by type, railroads, dams, mountain peaks, the Tennessee River Basin, national parks, Indian reservations, and TVA reservations, 1934. A copy of the same map annotated to show completed dams. A series of photoprocessed maps of the Chickamauga Reservoir showing ownership of lands to be purchased. Maps of the Norris and Pickwick Reservoirs and their surrounding areas showing the boundaries of TVA lands.

466. DEPARTMENT OF FORESTRY RELATIONS. 1941. 2 items.

A published map of the Tennessee Valley region showing areas characterized by principal forest types. A photoprocessed map covering the territory of the Appalachian Forest Experiment Station, Asheville, N.C., colored to show forest tree types.

467. FOREST RESOURCES PLANNING DIVISION. 1939-41. 30 items.

A published map of the Tennessee Valley region showing primary wood-using industries; and a series of published maps of the Tennessee Valley area showing major forest patterns and forest types and maps of individual counties showing forest types and conditions of forests.

468. DIVISION OF LAND PLANNING AND HOUSING. 1934-37. 25 items.

A record copy of "Part 1, Natural Series," published in 1936, of the *Atlas of the Tennessee Valley Region* with 12 maps, each accompanied by a related textual description. Included are a physiographic diagram of the region and maps showing soils, soil erosion, forest cover, amounts of precipitation, average temperatures, average and minimum lengths of the growing season, average dates for the latest killing frost in the spring and the earliest killing frost in the fall, average number of rainy days, and distribution of population.

A published map of the Tennessee Valley region showing information about rural lands relating to types of agricultural areas, the quality and productivity of the lands, and the quality and types of land use. Published maps of the Southeastern United States, including a map showing airways, airports, and landing fields; and a map showing the main highway systems and the tentative through highway system of the Tennessee Valley region. A published city plan of Norris, Tenn. A series of published maps showing scenic recreational areas in parts of the Tennessee Valley.

469. SOCIAL AND ECONOMIC DIVISION. 1937. 36 items.

A series of published maps of the Tennessee Valley area compiled by the Research Section of the Division. These maps give information by county about the amount of taxes levied; population density, distribution, changes, and characteristics; gainful employment by kind of industry; counties with public health services; expenditures by local governments; farm types; farm and crop values; the gross debt; and per capita spendable money income.

470. TRANSPORTATION-ECONOMICS DIVISION. n.d. 17 items.

A series of published maps of the Tennessee Valley area showing the chief transportation facilities in relation to producing centers for bituminous coal, cement, coke, cotton, cotton liners, feldspar, forest resources, fuller's earth, iron, lime, limestone, mica, ochre, phosphate rock, sulphuric acid, talc, soapstone, and titanium. Based on 1932 data.

471. MAPS AND SURVEYS DIVISION. 1934-55. 1,600 items.

Published index maps of the Tennessee Valley region showing the monthly status of topographic mapping from August 1943 to May 1957, and maps showing the availability (to the public) of topographic maps at irregular intervals between July 1943 and April 1957. Published index maps to topographic quadrangles, navigation charts and maps of reservoirs, aerial photographs, and planimetric maps covering the Tennessee Valley. Index maps to general and land maps of the Kentucky Reservoir project.

Published general maps of the Tennessee Valley including one showing national forests in the valley and its vicinity. Photoprocessed maps showing land conveyance and land sales in project areas. Published maps of project areas showing proposed land exchanges between the TVA and the Forest Service. Plans showing lot and block layout for Norris Properties, Inc., Subdivision No. 1, Norris, Tenn. Maps of the Kentucky Reservoir area showing landownership.

Published navigational charts of the Tennessee River and maps of reservoir areas. Published topographic and planimetric quadrangles most of which were compiled in cooperation with the Geological Survey, following the standards established for USGS quadrangles (see entry 242).

RECORDS OF THE UNITED STATES TARIFF COMMISSION. RG 81

The United States Tariff Commission, established in 1916, is responsible for the investigation of technical problems of customs administration, domestic and foreign manufacturing costs, questions relating to commercial treaties, unfair competition in the import trade, and foreign discrimination against American trade. It also cooperates with other agencies in activities pertaining to reciprocal trade and agricultural problems.

472. GENERAL RECORDS. 1943. 1 item.

A published outline map of Mexico and Central America.

473. TARIFF COMMISSION INVESTIGATIONS. 1930. 27 items.

Published Coast and Geodetic Survey nautical charts of the coasts of the continental United States, Alaska, Puerto Rico, and the Hawaiian Islands overprinted with information showing the 3-mile legal limit of territorial waters. Arranged by Coast and Geodetic Survey chart numbers.

WORLD WAR I AGENCIES

RECORDS OF THE AMERICAN COMMISSION TO NEGOTIATE PEACE. RG 256

The American Commission To Negotiate Peace, the official U.S. mission to the Paris Peace Conference of 1919, comprised a group of geographers, historians, political scientists, and economists, known aggregately as "The Inquiry," which in 1917 and 1918 had studied the geographic, historical, ethnographic, economic, and political questions that were likely to be considered at any postwar peace settlement. The Commission, led by President Wilson, Secretary of State Lansing, General Tasker H. Bliss, Edward M. House, and Henry White, contained an Executive Office, a Secretariat, a Division of Territorial, Economic, and Political Intelligence, commonly known as Intelligence, and liaison and technical personnel. When the Treaty of Versailles was signed on June 28, 1919, the Commission's work was completed.

All the separately maintained cartographic records of the Commission in the National Archives were prepared by Intelligence. The Division of Geography and Cartography, a component of Intelligence, assembled and produced a large number of base maps which were made available to other divisions within Intelligence for use in depicting geographic, ethnographic, and political problems as well as in drafting proposed national boundaries. Other agencies of the U.S. Government prepared maps for The Inquiry on request.

Other cartographic records of the Commission are in the custody of the American Geographical Society of New York, and still others may be among the Sidney E. Mezes papers at the College of the City of New York, the Edward M. House papers at Yale University, and the Woodrow Wilson papers in the Division of Manuscripts at the Library of Congress.

The National Archives, *Cartographic Records of the American Commission To Negotiate Peace*, Preliminary Inventory No. 68 (Washington, 1954) describes the records in more detail.

474. ECONOMICS DIVISION. 1917-19. 305 items.

Manuscript, published, and annotated base maps, some of which are in bound atlases, of the world and of specific areas, showing power resources and mineral deposits, prepared by the Geological Survey in cooperation with the Forest Service; graphs showing tonnages of Allied and neutral countries sunk by enemy action, the merchant marine tonnage of the world, the value of forest resources by country, and agricultural and livestock production; maps of Africa showing agricultural production and land resources; maps of Alsace-Lorraine showing information about mining and mineral resources; maps of Asia, Oceania, Europe, and North America showing forest resources; and maps and other records relating to the trade volume and markets of Austria-Hungary and Germany.

Arranged by area or country.

475. HISTORY DIVISION. 1918. 1 item.

A manuscript chart showing colonization in the West Indies from 1600 to 1918.

476. GEOGRAPHY AND CARTOGRAPHY DIVISION. 1917-19. 337 items.

This Division was responsible for assembling, preparing, and maintaining a central file of base and outline maps for the use of other divisions. Its records include an incomplete set of copies of these base and outline maps, with additional copies annotated by other divisions of Intelligence. These maps cover areas throughout the world, particularly Eastern Europe and the Near East. They show ethnic and linguistic distributions, population densities, political subdivisions and boundaries, and information pertaining to various aspects of industry, labor, agriculture, commerce, and transportation.

Arranged by file number assigned by the Division. Some of the smaller maps are in bound volumes. Each map is accompanied by notes on its origin and use.

Another group of maps is identified merely as "Photostats from New York." They are similar in content to the numbered maps and are arranged by area or country.

477. AFRICA DIVISION. 1917-19. 29 items.

This Division, headed by Prof. George Louis Beer, studied colonial problems and made recommendations concerning proposed African mandates. The records include manuscript, annotated, and photoprocessed maps showing population densities, ethnic and religious distributions, areas suitable for colonization, climate, natural resources, and projected Cape-to-Cairo railroad routes. Arranged by file number assigned in the Division.

478. ASIA DIVISION. 1917-19. 9 items.

This Division, headed by Dr. R. B. Dixon, studied the problems of the lands of Central Asia between China proper and Russian Asia. The records consist of photoprocessed maps annotated to show ethnic distributions, population densities, and Russian colonization in Central Asia; a map of Eurasia annotated to show the domains of the German-Russian-Japanese Alliance proposed by Werner Daya in *Der Aufmarsch im Osten* and the general plan advocated by him for the next war against Great Britain; and maps of Sinkiang annotated to show relief, soils, lines of communications, population density, and linguistic distributions. Arranged by file number assigned in the Division.

479. AUSTRIA-HUNGARY DIVISION. 1917-19. 128 items.

This Division, headed by Dr. Charles Seymour of Yale University, studied possible divisions of the Austro-Hungarian Empire, giving particular attention to Czechoslovak and Yugoslav aspirations for independence. The records consist of manuscript and annotated base maps showing population density, areas of highest literacy rates, employment data, industrial development, agricultural production and the size of landholdings, quantity and value of foreign and transit trade in 1912, emigration and immigration, transportation routes, political subdivisions, historical territorial divisions in the Empire, territorial acquisitions of the Hapsburgs, proposed boundaries of new and old states, historic claims of ethnic groups, and the distribution of linguistic and ethnic groups; and physiographic block diagrams of the Trieste-Isonzo region and the Carpathian Mountains. Arranged by file number assigned in the Division.

480. BALKANS DIVISION. 1917-19. 78 items

The Balkans Division, headed by Dr. Clive Day of Yale University, was assigned to work toward a satisfactory solution to the complex boundary problem in the Balkan States. A geographical study of the eastern Adriatic region was made by Maj. Douglas W. Johnson. The records consist of manuscript and annotated maps showing historic and proposed boundaries of the Balkan States, conflicting territorial claims, administration of commerce on the Danube River and work on its Sulina branch, railroad and highway networks and surviving Roman roads, linguistic and ethnic problems, and the distribution of Orthodox Catholic churches; and a physiographic block diagram of Albania. Arranged by file number assigned in the Division.

481. FAR EAST AND PACIFIC DIVISION. 1917-19. 21 items.

The Far East and Pacific Division, headed by Dr. Stanley K. Hornbeck of the University of Wisconsin, specialized in the study of Sino-Japanese relations and of colonial problems in the Pacific islands. The records include maps of China showing the development and ownership of railways, spheres of foreign influence, the relation of outlying provinces to the Republic, and the boundaries and subdivisions of Inner and Outer Mongolia; and maps of the Pacific showing American interests, communications lines, and areas dominated by various naval forces. Arranged by file number assigned in the Division.

482. ITALY DIVISION. 1917-19. 60 items.

The Italy Division, headed by Dr. W. E. Lunt of Haverford College, studied claims involving the boundaries of Italy, with particular emphasis on conflicting claims in the Tirol. The records consist of maps of Italy showing the linguistic problem in the Austro-Italian border region, conflicting claims of Austria and Italy, and the historic boundaries between the nations; a physiographic block diagram of the Trieste-Isonzo and Trentino regions annotated to show proposed boundaries; and maps of the Tirol region showing ethnography, linguistic distributions, population density, historic boundaries, and conflicting Italian and Austrian claims. Arranged by file number assigned in the Division.

483. RUSSIA AND POLAND DIVISION. 1917-19. 152 items.

This Division, headed by Dr. R. H. Lord of Harvard University, studied the problems connected with the establishment of an independent Poland and the problems of western Russia. The records include a base map annotated to show the corridor to the Arctic Ocean ceded to Finland by Bolshevist Russia; maps showing the areas proposed to be included in the new Polish nation; maps of Poland showing political subdivisions, ethnic, religious, and linguistic distributions, economic data relating to agriculture and industry, population density, mineral deposits, climate, topography, forests, historic frontiers, proposed boundaries, and territorial demands; and maps of Russia showing religious and ethnic distributions, population density, political subdivisions, railroads, topography, and soil types; maps showing the historic frontiers of Lithuania, Russian colonization in Asia, new boundaries created by the Treaty of Brest-Litovsk, the sphere of German influence and occupation in Russia, conflicting claims of newly independent states created from former Russian territory, the proposed political division of the Caucasus region, and facilities of the American Relief Administration in the famine areas of Russia. Arranged by file number assigned in the Division.

484. WESTERN ASIA DIVISION. 1917-19. 44 items.

The Western Asia Division was organized primarily to study the political problems connected with the plans for breaking up the Turkish Empire. The Division's first maps were produced under the direction of Dr. Dana C. Munro of Princeton University. Most of its maps were produced later in 1918 and 1919 when Dr. W. L. Westermann of Cornell University was Director of the Division. The records consist of maps of Turkey showing population density, the transportation system, mineral resources, existing and proposed boundaries, ethnic, religious, and linguistic distributions; a map showing the proposed boundaries of part of Anatolia and the area included in the Venizelos claim; maps of Arabia showing proposed boundaries for a Jewish state, areas of British control, linguistic distributions, topography, political boundaries, and railroads; maps of Armenia showing proposed and historic boundaries, population density, and the distribution of members of various religions; maps showing Mesopotamia's strategic world position and its proposed boundaries; and a map of Syria showing the proposed Jewish and Syrian states, the autonomous district of Lebanon, and Jewish agricultural colonies. Arranged by file number assigned in the Division.

485. WESTERN EUROPE DIVISION. 1917-19. 14 items.

The Western Europe Division, headed by Dr. Charles H. Haskins, dean of the Harvard Graduate School, was formed to study particularly the Franco-German border problems. The records consist of maps of Europe showing battlelines on the Western Front, the location for a concrete obstruction proposed by the Allies to be built across the North Sea as a barrier to German submarines, and ethnic and linguistic distributions; a map of the French battlefront showing areas of greatest destruction, two physiographic diagrams of the western war zone, one annotated to show the battlefront at various dates; a map of the northern provinces of the Netherlands; maps showing linguistic and ethnic distributions in North Schleswig and the proposed boundary between Denmark and Germany; and maps of Spitsbergen showing geological information and the geographical and strategic relation of the islands to northern Europe. Arranged by file number assigned in the Division.

RECORDS OF THE UNITED STATES FOOD ADMINISTRATION. RG 4

The functions of the United States Food Administration, established in 1917 and abolished in 1920, were to provide for the supply, distribution, and conservation of foods; to prevent monopolies and hoarding; and to maintain governmental control over foods through voluntary agreements and a licensing system. The Administration also assumed jurisdiction over commodities when they reached commercial channels.

486. GENERAL RECORDS. 1917-20. 8 items.

Published and photoprocessed maps annotated in the Administration to show capacities and conditions of transportation systems in Europe, the political and military situation in Europe on June 30, 1919, and the origin of British wheat imports. A photoprocessed map of the Aroostook Farm Experiment Station in Maine, showing relief, character of the soil, farm buildings, and roads, 1917. A map-graph of Massachusetts showing the relationship between production and consumption of food products and the population in 1912.

487. MILLING DIVISION. 1917-18. 3 items.

Manuscript, photoprocessed, and published maps of the United States prepared by or for the Milling Division showing the amounts of wheat, corn, rye, and barley produced in each State in 1917 and the amount ground in 1914; new and old rates of shipment of grain and flour; and administrative boundaries and offices of regional milling divisions and grain corporation zones.

RECORDS OF THE UNITED STATES GRAIN CORPORATION. RG 5

The chief functions of the United States Grain Corporation, established in 1917 and abolished in 1927, were the regulation of the grain trade through purchasing, storing, and selling grains and grain products and, in cooperation with the War Trade Board, the controlling of grain imports and exports. During and after World War I it cooperated in the relief of famine areas in Europe. In 1919 it was the fiscal and purchasing agent for the American Relief Administration, some of whose records were placed in its custody.

Central Office

488. STATISTICAL DIVISION. 1918. 5 items.

Maps of the world, dated 1918, annotated to show the active and inactive Allied Nations, the Central Powers, neutral areas controlled by the Allies and by the Central Powers, neutral nations, and captive territory of the Allies and of the Central Powers; and undated maps of Europe showing World War I famine areas.

American Relief Administration

489. MAP AND DRAFTING DEPARTMENT. 1918-19. 13 items.

Published base maps of the world and manuscript, photoprocessed, and annotated maps of Europe showing changes in political boundaries, and administrative regions of the American Relief Administration.

RECORDS OF THE UNITED STATES HOUSING CORPORATION. RG 3

The United States Housing Corporation, established in 1918 and terminated in 1952, was authorized to provide housing for war needs. The preparation of maps and plans was an important phase of the Corporation's work.

490. GENERAL RECORDS. 1918-19. 486 items.

Published, photoprocessed, and manuscript maps and plans of numbered project areas. Included are preliminary and final plans of housing developments showing boundaries, street layouts, layouts of houses by blocks, landscape plantings and gradings, topography, and stores, schools, and other facilities. Other records include maps showing ownership of adjacent properties and lands proposed for addition to the developments, plans of buildings, and profiles of streets.

Processed maps of numbered project areas annotated to show the progress of construction of the developments, properties required and properties not required, types of house construction, changes in plans, and proposed electric systems. Many of these records are signed by members of the Corporation and noted as being records of conferences.

Manuscript, published, and photoprocessed maps and plans compiled by or for the Corporation. These records do not have assigned project numbers. Included are preliminary plans of developments and plans of individual buildings.

Processed maps and plans without project numbers but with annotations, including maps of cities or local areas annotated to show industrial sites and potential housing sites, maps annotated to show lands required by and lands no longer needed by the Corporation, and maps annotated to show existing and proposed systems of transportation between housing sites and industrial locations.

Arranged in series by type of map. Within series the maps are arranged numerically by project number or, in the absence of such numbers, alphabetically by name of city in which the developments were located.

491. TRANSPORTATION DIVISION. 1918-20. 4 items.

A manuscript plan of the Newport News, Va., project area showing the main transportation route to the Morrison Aviation Camp; a photoprocessed graph showing the daily flow of traffic and the operating schedules for the Norfolk-Portsmouth, Va., ferries for October 1920; and photoprocessed maps of parts of Washington, D.C., annotated to show steps taken in proposed track construction for the Washington Belt Line.

492. TOWN PLANNING DIVISION. 1918-19. 75 items.

Manuscript and annotated photoprocessed map-plans of parts of specific cities and Corporation project areas showing properties required by and properties no longer needed by the Corporation, proposed and accepted changes in developments, and facilities to be built, including electric lines, sewers, and streets. Many of these plans are signed by members of the Corporation and noted as being records of conferences. Arranged alphabetically by name of city.

493. REAL ESTATE DIVISION. 1918. 2 items.

A manuscript map of the Puget Sound area of Washington, showing lands to be acquired for a housing development and changes in plans for the development; and an annotated plan of properties in the 39th Ward, Philadelphia, Pa.

RECORDS OF THE UNITED STATES SHIPPING BOARD. RG 32

Record Group 32 includes the records of the United States Shipping Board, established in 1917, its successor, the United States Shipping Board Bureau, established in 1933, and the Emergency Fleet Corporation, established in 1917 and controlled by the Shipping Board. The functions of the Shipping Board were to regulate water carriers and to develop a naval auxiliary and a merchant marine. The Emergency Fleet Corporation conducted a vast ship construction program during World War I and also operated ships for the U.S. Government.

United States Shipping Board

494. PORT AND HARBOR FACILITIES COMMISSION. ca. 1917-18.
21 items.

Published plans of harbors in England and Scotland showing harbor facilities. These were prepared to accompany a report of Capt. F. T. Chambers, U.S.N., Chief Engineer.

495. BUREAU OF RESEARCH. 1914-31. 4 items.

Published and photoprocessed maps of the world showing information about American shipping lines, including general trade routes, home ports, foreign ports, trade divisions, and, on a map dated 1931, lines controlled by the United States Shipping Board, lines disposed of by the Board, lines operating vessels acquired from the Board, and lines not operating vessels acquired from the Board.

Emergency Fleet Corporation

496. GENERAL RECORDS. 1918-26. 3 items.

Published maps, including a map of the world showing distances between ports and United States Shipping Board fuel oil stations, 1920; a map of the world showing merchant marine services by routes and names of lines, 1926; and a map of the United States showing districts of the Emergency Fleet Corporation and the locations and names of shipyards constructing vessels for the Corporation, with symbols designating types of vessels constructed within each yard, 1918.

497. DIVISION OF SHIPYARD PLANTS. 1917-19. 220 items.

Published charts of harbors, ports, and coastal areas of the United States annotated to show improved or changed harbor facilities and the locations of shipyards and other marine harbor activities. Arranged alphabetically by name of State and thereunder by name of harbor. A card catalog lists the maps by name of city or area and by name of company.

United States Shipping Board Bureau

498. DIVISION OF SHIPPING RESEARCH. 1934. 1 item.

A published map of the world showing American shipping lines in foreign trade and in trade with U.S. possessions. General trade routes and their relative importance are shown. A listing of the lines indicates their home ports and their trade destinations.

AGENCIES ESTABLISHED 1920-39 AND LATER TERMINATED

RECORDS OF THE FEDERAL COORDINATOR OF TRANSPORTATION. RG 133

The Federal Coordinator of Transportation, a position established in 1933 and abolished in 1936, was authorized to devise plans to assist carriers in reducing duplication of facilities and services, in eliminating practices causing undue impairment of net earnings, and in accomplishing financial reorganization whereby fixed charges could be reduced.

499. GENERAL RECORDS. 1932-36. 22 items.

Manuscript, photoprocessed, and annotated maps and plans consisting of a map of the United States showing time zones; a series of maps of the Western States showing freight and passenger service of the Southern Pacific Railway Co. in relation to lines operated by independent motor truck and motor bus companies and motor truck and bus lines operated by the Southern Pacific and its subsidiaries; diagrams showing present through passenger service between principal points on the Baltimore and Ohio and the Pennsylvania Railroad systems and proposed service on those two systems after consolidation; a map annotated to show the extent of the New River-Pocohantas Coal Field in West Virginia and railroad lines in the vicinity of the field; and plans of railroad terminals at Chicago, Ill., Ogden, Utah, Memphis, Tenn., Columbus, Ohio, Raleigh, N.C., and Pensacola, Fla.

500. THE FEDERAL COORDINATOR. 1933-36. 55 items.

Annotated and photoprocessed maps, including a map of the United States showing through routes under the proposed "Prince Plan" and maps of the individual systems, based on area, showing railroad lines and lines of jointly owned railroads as advocated in the "Prince Plan." Another series includes maps of parts of the United States showing lines of individual railroads as allocated by the Interstate Commerce Commission in 1929.

501. SECTION OF RESEARCH. 1935. 4 items.

Maps of the United States showing federal land-grant, bond-aided, and equalization railroads. Included are a map dated 1930 published by the Engineer

Reproduction Plant, U.S. Army, and annotated with corrections; an undated manuscript map showing railroad routes aided by Federal land grants, classified on the basis of charges collectable for the transportation of Government troops and property; and two photoprocessed maps issued by the Section of Research, one dated January 1935 and the other June 1935.

502. SECTION OF TRANSPORTATION SERVICE. 1934-35. 6 items.

Manuscript and photoprocessed maps of the United States showing trade areas, equigraphic rate blocks, railroad freight traffic department agencies, and selected mileage basing points. A table listing centers of American trade; and a map of Delaware and the eastern parts of Maryland, Virginia, and North Carolina colored to show trade areas proposed for a survey of traffic and commodity movements.

RECORDS OF THE NATIONAL RECOVERY ADMINISTRATION. RG 9

The National Recovery Administration (NRA) was established in 1933 to stimulate industrial recovery through the establishment of operating codes and standard employment practices. The cartographic program of the NRA was a supporting activity to its main functions. Maps were prepared to illustrate data collected and compiled on specific aspects of the Administration's activities. Most of these maps, which include annotated base maps and manuscript maps, were prepared in the Compliance, Review, and Research and Planning Divisions. The latter two had graphic arts sections which were responsible for preparing many of the maps.

A list of the maps, described by subjects, is available in the Cartographic Branch and in the Central Reference Room of the National Archives.

503. GENERAL RECORDS. 1933-35. 49 items.

Manuscript and annotated maps relating to code authority areas. Among the records are maps showing boundaries of the various code authorities in the United States as a whole or by region; code authority divisions within industries such as the coal industry, the wholesale automotive trade industry, the laundry industry, the retail solid-fuel industry, the lumber and paper industries, and the textile industries; and the number of code authorities in individual States and cities. Other maps relate to administrative activities of the NRA and show regional boundaries, review board trade areas, "A-1" to "A-5" establishments, and areas enumerated by the Michigan Unemployment Census. Arranged by file number assigned in the agency. A card index locates individual maps by subject.

504. DIVISION OF COMPLIANCE. 1935. 1 item.

This Division was responsible for enforcing the NRA laws and codes. The records include a map of the United States annotated to show Division regions and offices; the number, by State, of establishments reporting to the President's reemployment agreement of October 14, 1934, and the number per square mile; and the number of employees under NRA codes.

505. DIVISION OF RESEARCH AND PLANNING. 1933-35. 169 items.

This Division was responsible for undertaking studies of industries and trades in the United States. One of the results of its activities was the published atlas entitled *A Study of Natural Areas of Trade in the United States* (Washington, 1935). In addition to the atlas there are other maps pertaining to studies of trade areas and related transportation facilities.

The records also include maps relating to studies of individual industries, such as maps of the United States showing the proportion of business per State for certain industries; and maps of the United States and of specific regions in the United States showing information about the coal industry, such as the volume of production and consumption, transportation facilities, and hourly rates paid to employees.

Arranged by file number assigned in the agency. A card catalog locates each map by subject.

506. DIVISION OF REVIEW. 1935-36. 19 items.

This Division was established in December 1935 to analyze the work performed by the NRA after the Supreme Court invalidated the codes. Among the records are maps of the United States prepared by the Statistics Section showing the productive capacity of active and inactive paperboard and pulp mills, a map of the United States prepared by the Bituminous Coal Section showing minimum price areas and schedules of districts following the Bituminous Coal Conservation Act of 1935, and maps of the United States prepared by the Special Studies Section showing areas of wheat production and centers of the lime industry in the United States.

Arranged numerically by assigned map number. A card catalog locates each map by subject.

RECORDS OF THE OFFICE OF PUBLIC BUILDINGS AND GROUNDS. RG 42

While some of the cartographic records in this record group were prepared by or for the Office of Public Buildings and Grounds, many were inherited from its predecessors and a few were acquired from private sources. There are some records that probably were prepared in the Office of the Superintendent of the State, War, and Navy Building, which was combined with the Office of Public

Buildings and Grounds in 1925 to form the Office of Public Buildings and Public Parks of the National Capital. That Office was abolished in 1933 and its functions were transferred to the Office of National Parks, Buildings, and Reservations (the National Park Service) in the Department of the Interior. Many of the cartographic records inherited from the Office of Public Buildings and Public Parks of the National Capital became a part of the files of the National Capital Parks, the office within the National Park Service concerned with the park system in the District of Columbia (see entries 284-286).

507. NUMBERED FILE. 1771-1894. 61 items.

Manuscript, annotated, published, and photoprocessed maps and plans of Washington, D.C., including early maps of towns now a part of the city; an annotated copy of the Dermott map of 1797-98; a manuscript copy made by Dermott in 1799 of a plan of part of the city used by the Commissioners in conducting sales in 1791; annotated copies of an undated map of the city of Washington engraved by W. J. Stone, about 1852, one of which is colored to show wards; a map published by A. Petersen and J. Enthoffer in 1872 annotated to show areas of unimproved angles, paved areas, and Government reservations; and a map showing public reservations under control of the Office of Public Buildings and Grounds in 1894.

Among these records are maps and plats showing street layout in different parts of the city and proposed plans of improvement; plans of the White House grounds, of the grounds adjacent to the Capitol showing the proposed alteration of the canal, and of proposed improvements in the vicinity of the Washington Monument; a copy of a plan of part of the city of Washington showing Water Street, dated March 8, 1797; a plan of the wharves from Long Bridge to the arsenal as originally established with names shown for leased wharves; diagrams showing the floor plans of the new Treasury Building and the old State Department Building; a plan of proposed alterations to the old jail; a drawing of the proposed facade of the courthouse in Alexandria and floor plans of the courtroom and office floor; a volume of lithographed maps of real estate in the county of Washington outside the cities of Washington and Georgetown as surveyed in 1881; and a volume including tracings of real-estate plats and maps showing the subdivision of large tracts on the outskirts of the two cities dated from about 1840 to 1878. Arranged by assigned numbers corresponding to an accompanying list.

508. PLATS SHOWING WATER STREET, WATER LOTS, AND
     WHARFING PLANS FOR THE CITY OF WASHINGTON.
     1793-1835. 22 items.

A manuscript map of part of the city in the vicinity of Washington Circle prepared in 1793 by order of the Commissioners with the area bordering the Potomac River sketched in pencil and a few wharves added, two sets of plats showing lots in squares 955 and 979 on the eastern branch bounded by O Street and 9th, 10th, and 11th Streets S.E., as surveyed in 1793 and 1796, and one set of plats showing lots in the "Square South of Square 12" bounded by D Street, Water Street, and 26th and 27th Streets N.W., as surveyed in 1797, with copies of agreements between the Commissioners and the original proprietors concerning their sale or retention; plans 1-12 of part of the city showing Water Street, water lots, wharves, and public landings along the Potomac River and a copy of a letter of transmittal by Nicholas King, dated March 8, 1797, explaining the plans to the Board of Commissioners; plans of two wharves belonging to John Nicholson, drawn by King, and a copy of the letter of transmittal dated April 15, 1797; and a plan showing Water Street and water lots with wharves and docks along the river from E to T Street S.W., drawn by William Elliot in 1835 and approved byPresident Van Buren on February 22, 1839.

509. KING PLATS OF THE CITY OF WASHINGTON. 1803. 4 items.

A volume of manuscript plats of the city of Washington prepared by Nicholas King in 1803 showing numbered squares or blocks; names of streets; numbered, appropriated, or reserved areas; and lines of the holdings of original proprietors. A manuscript copy of the King plats made by William P. Elliott in 1834 in agreement with William Noland, Commissioner of Public Buildings of the City of Washington, colored to show lots sold and lots apportioned to the original proprietors; and two sets of photolithographed King plats, one with annotations, and both with published appended copies of the L'Enfant, Ellicott, and Dermott maps of the city of Washington, a preface with a brief history, and a copy of the correspondence relating to their publication as approved by the U.S. Coast and Geodetic Survey Office in 1884.

510. OTHER MAPS AND PLANS OF THE CITY OF WASHINGTON
     AND ITS RESERVATIONS AND GOVERNMENT BUILDINGS.
     1871-1919. 6 items.

A manuscript plan of the city of Washington showing the public reservations as prepared by Maj. O. E. Babcock in 1871; a copy of a map of the city of Washington published by A. Petersen and J. Enthoffer in 1872 with one sheet labeled on reverse "U.S. Exhibit #79"; a published set of statistical maps compiled by Lt. F. V. Greene to accompany the annual report of the Commissioners for the year ending July 30, 1880, showing the valuation of real property, street grades and pavements, types of shade trees along the streets, the locations of gas lamps, water mains, and sewers, public school, police and fire department stations, street railways, telegraph lines, and the schedule of street sweeping; plats of reservations and public spaces under the control of the Commissioner of Public Buildings as compiled by William Forsyth, surveyor of the District of Columbia, in 1883; a published map of the public lands under Federal jurisdiction in the District of Columbia compiled in the Office of Public Buildings and Grounds in 1915 from information obtained from the commission to investigate title of U.S. lands in the District of Columbia; and a map of the

Mall and vicinity prepared by the Public Buildings Commission in 1917 to show buildings occupied by Government agencies and annotated to show buildings occupied by the War Department and space released from November 18, 1918. to June 30, 1919.

511. ARCHITECTURAL PLANS AND DESIGNS. 1879-1903. 59 items.

Manuscript plans of the extension of the Executive Mansion and a chart showing data for heating and ventilating prepared by the Office of Public Buildings and Grounds, 1900-1901. Drawings and specifications, some prepared by private concerns, for a rose house, proposed alteration of the camellia house, designs and preliminary specifications and estimate of the cost of construction of a greenhouse, and plans of the old and new conservatory for the White House, 1879-1903. Arranged by subject.

RECORDS OF THE PUBLIC WORKS ADMINISTRATION. RG 135

The Public Works Administration, established as the Federal Emergency Administration for Public Works in 1933 and abolished in 1943, was authorized to prepare a comprehensive program of public works and was empowered to participate in the financing and construction of public works projects included in the program.

Federal Emergency Administration for Public Works

512. HOUSING DIVISION. ca. 1935. 1 item.

A photoprocessed map of the District of Columbia showing population, by race, for each census tract in the residential areas.

513. MISSISSIPPI VALLEY COMMITTEE. 1934. 1 item.

A published map of the Mississippi Valley drainage basin. The functions of this Committee were later transferred to the National Resources Board.

Public Works Administration

514. GENERAL RECORDS. ca. 1939. 2 items.

Published maps of the United States showing graphically the locations of some of the activities undertaken by the Public Works Administration in rebuilding local areas, conserving natural resources, improving transportation facilities, building ships for national defense, controlling floods, improving internal waterways, improving health facilities, harnessing rivers for power, and building hospitals, schools, and other public buildings.

RECORDS OF THE RECONSTRUCTION FINANCE CORPORATION. RG 234

The Reconstruction Finance Corporation (RFC) was established in 1932 to make loans and to provide other types of financial assistance to banks and other credit institutions and to railroads. It was later empowered to offer financial aid to other types of businesses, public works projects, and local governmental agencies and to public or private agencies, in the event of floods or other catastrophes. In 1940 it was authorized to provide financial aid for the acquisition of strategic and critical materials and for the manufacture of equipment and supplies necessary to the national defense. The Corporation functioned through a central office in Washington, D.C., branch offices, and loan agencies. Many of its programs, chiefly those connected with mortgages and defense activities, were carried out by subsidiary corporations which were legally and financially separate from the RFC. The agency was liquidated in 1957.

The records described below include those of two RFC subsidiaries: the Rubber Development Corporation and the Defense Supplies Corporation.

Reconstruction Finance Corporation

515. GENERAL RECORDS. ca. 1937. 1 item.

A published map of the United States showing loan agency districts and district headquarters.

516. RAILROAD DIVISION. 1934-50. 2,309 items.

This Division was responsible for handling loans to railroads. In the fulfillment of this activity studies were made of individual railroads that applied for loans. Information received during these investigations was shown graphically on maps and charts prepared in a small drafting unit in the central office at Washington, D.C. The information plotted was acquired directly from the railroads; maps and charts prepared by the railroads often were used as sources.

There are records for about 125 railroads. For almost all of these a chart illustrating its corporate structure and a map showing the corporate property ownership are included. Sometimes the chart and the map are on the same sheet. The records include manuscript tracings showing the corporate structure and ownership of the railroads, in most cases corrected to December 31, 1939, and blueline prints of the charts and maps showing information to December 31, 1938. There are a few charts and maps from earlier and later dates.

Maps showing the varying weights of rail used are included for most of the railroads. These maps were revised yearly; the records for a given railroad usually include a manuscript tracing correct to January 1, 1946, and blueline prints, some of them annotated, for each year from 1940 to 1945. The blueline prints were made from the manuscript tracings, corrected each year. The annotated copies are blueline prints which were sent to the railroad companies for revision. These bear notes stating that the tracings were revised in accordance with the changes shown by the annotations.

Exhaustive studies were made of some of the railroad systems. The records for those systems include maps showing kinds of ballast shipped by each line; dispatchers' districts; communications networks paralleling the railroad lines; the distribution of materials carried by the lines; sources of materials carried; passenger, train crew, and locomotive runs; types of ties and tie protection; maximum grades; mortgages existing for each line within the corporate structure of a railroad system; operating divisions; bridges and tunnels, stations, water tanks, signals, and icing installations; railroad crossings; dates of construction of individual lines; and maximum and minimum freight and passenger train speeds.

Among these records are a number from studies for proposed railroad consolidations, including a group of maps from studies of the proposed coordination of the Chicago, Milwaukee, St. Paul and Pacific Railroad and the Chicago and Northwestern. These records include plans of terminals showing properties owned by the companies; maps of the systems and parts of the systems; and maps showing facilities, maximum grades, weights of rail, mileages, and locomotive assignments of the systems. Other maps from consolidation studies show railroad systems in different parts of the United States, the geographical relationships between certain railroad lines, and terminal facilities at selected cities. A group of maps of the Northeastern United States, identified as "System 1," shows suggestions and modifications proposed by the New York Central Railroad.

The maps pertaining to studies of the individual railroad systems are arranged alpha-numerically; the records of a given railroad are usually filed together. Index cards and a list locate the records by name of railroad.

Other records of this Division consist of a series of condensed profiles of the main lines of certain railroad systems; a map of the Wilkes Barre, Pa., area, showing different railroad lines serving the area, noted as submitted with an annual report to the Interstate Commerce Commission, 1938; a map of the Akron System and a map showing its geographical relationship to other systems; a map of the area around Omaha, Nebr., and Council Bluffs, Iowa, showing railroad lines, noted as Exhibit 1; and a map of the area covering Tps. 1 N. and 1 to 3 S., Rs. 6 to 8 W., Willamette meridian, Oreg., showing areas under Reconstruction Finance Corporation mortgages, the fire lines of 1933 and 1939, and outlines of Hammond-Wenton units 11 and 12 and Chehalem units 6 and 13 containing about 100 million foot logs.

A list of these records is available in the Cartographic Branch of the National Archives.

Arranged in series by subject.

Rubber Development Corporation

This subsidiary corporation was owned wholly by the RFC. It was created in 1943 to supervise the Government's program for the development and procurement of natural rubber. On July 15, 1943, it was transferred to the Office of Economic Warfare, which was renamed the Foreign Economic Administration. The Rubber Development Corporation was returned to the Reconstruction Finance Corporation on September 27, 1945. Its certificate of corporation expired on June 30, 1947.

The Rubber Development Corporation produced or procured special maps to assist in its assigned work program. These maps were not made for publication; they may be examined by employees of the Federal Government on official business, but others desiring to use them must obtain permission to do so from the Administrator of General Services or his authorized representative.

517. GENERAL RECORDS. 1943-44. 224 items.

Manuscript and published maps of parts of Brazil consisting of a map of the northern part of the State of Mato Grosso showing vegetation; a plan of the city of Manaus; a general map showing the works erected by the Rubber Development Corporation at Ponta Pelada, Manaus; and a planimetric sketch of the lines of flight of an aerial survey made by the U.S. Army for the Rubber Development Corporation. The area covered by this latter map is from 9°5' to 11°5' S. and 64°10' to 63°52' W. Aerial photographs along the lines of flight are indexed by the identity of the flight and by the number of the photograph.

Manuscript and annotated maps of the Vaupés area in Colombia showing rubber camps and names of camp overseers, zones for intensive exploitation, rapids and other hazards on the Rio Vaupés, and existing and potential landing fields. Other records pertaining to Colombia consist of a plan of the road from San José to Acacias showing public works and the building materials used in these works; and a plan of the landing strip at Miraflores.

Maps pertaining to Peru consist of maps showing flight lines, distances, minimum altitudes for flights, and landing fields between the inland and coastal cities; plans of the City of Iquitos, the airports at Iquitos and Quince Mil, and port facilities at Agua Caliente; a map of western Peru showing principal product and transportation facilities, manuscript maps apparently showing the number of workers in the rubber areas south of Pucallpa; a plan of the Ucayali and Pachitea rivers between Pucallpa and Agua Caliente; maps of the Department of Madre de Dios showing the caucho (a type of rubber) area, concessions, roads and trails, villages and the principal center of the Mashcos Indians, rubber producers with and without loans, Rubber Development Corporation and Peruvian Amazon Corporation centers, and areas for future rubber development; a series of about 200 numbered maps of individual rubber plantations in northern Peru showing the boundaries of the plantations, the acreages, and the names of the overseers; and a map of northern Peru indexing the sketch maps described in the previous statement with a list, by number, of the plantations giving the names of the overseers, the number of workers employed, and the name of the river on which each plantation shipped its rubber.

A manuscript map of the area where Brazil, Peru, and Bolivia join showing the international boundaries, roads and trails, airfields, rubber producers, army posts, Rubber Development Corporation and Peruvian Amazon Corporation distributing centers, and river routes.

Arranged in series by area.

518. EXPLORATION DEPARTMENT. 1943. 3 items.

Manuscript maps of the State of Mato Grosso, Brazil, showing the development of roads and classes of rubber trees.

519. COMMUNICATION AND ENGINEERING DEPARTMENT OF THE AVIATION DIVISION. 1943. 4 items.

Blueline prints of a map of northern South America compiled by the Division with annotations as follows: one copy shows lines of operations of the different airline companies, existing and proposed airports and aircraft fuel depots, existing and proposed radio stations, range stations, stations of the Brazilian Indian Service and other Brazilian Government stations; a second copy shows the same information and also the major and minor rubber-producing areas; a third copy shows radio aids to navigation by type; and a fourth copy shows point-to-point stations.

520. EXPLOITATION DEPARTMENT. 1943. 1 item.

A manuscript map of the departments of Huila, Cauca, Valle del Cauca, Tolima, Caldas, and Nariño, Colombia, showing roads and trails.

521. CONSTRUCTION DEPARTMENT OF THE ENGINEERING DIVISION. 1943. 18 items.

Manuscript and annotated published maps and plans relating to the construction of Rubber Development Corporation properties and an airport at Manaus, Brazil. The maps show boundaries of the property granted to the Corporation by the Brazilian Government and a tract within this property reserved for an existing sawmill; plans of the industrial site and the fuel distribution dock; and detailed topographic plans, profiles, and cross sections of the airport runway. Other maps show proposed changes in the João Zany Road, Brazil, and there are cross sections of the relocation of the Paredao Road.

522. ARCHITECTURE AND ENGINEERING DIVISION. 1943. 8 items.

Manuscript and photoprocessed maps and plans relating to the construction of Rubber Development Corporation properties at Manaus consisting of plans showing the layout of the buildings and other facilities for the American colony, plans showing the status of construction of these properties, plans for port facilities, and maps showing the boundaries of the American property.

Defense Supplies Corporation

This Corporation was formed in 1940 to purchase strategic and critical materials other than metals and rubber to be stockpiled and sold under allocation. In 1942 it was transferred to the Department of Commerce, but it was returned to the RFC in 1945. The Corporation was dissolved on June 30 1945, and its functions, duties, and authority were transferred to the Reconstruction Finance Corporation.

The records of this Corporation may be examined by employees of the Federal Government on official business. Other individuals wishing to use them must obtain permission to do so from the Administrator of General Services or his authorized representative.

523. DIVISION OF AMERICAN REPUBLICS AVIATION. 1943-44. 36 items.

Manuscript, annotated, and photoprocessed topographic maps, profiles, plans, and related field notebooks from surveys of airport sites at Boca do Acre, Canafe, Fonte Bôa, João Pessoa, Manaus, and Teffé, Brazil. One notebook contains sketches relating to construction of buildings.

RECORDS OF THE UNITED STATES MARITIME COMMISSION. RG 178

The general purpose of the Maritime Commission, established in 1936 and abolished in 1950, was to carry out the declared policy of the United States "to foster the development and encourage the maintenance of . . . a merchant marine."

524. GENERAL RECORDS. 1940. 1 item.

A published cartogram of the world showing the relative importance of the routes of American shipping lines in trade with foreign countries and with U.S. possessions. Listed on the map are the companies and their ports of call in the United States and in foreign areas.

RECORDS OF THE WORK PROJECTS ADMINISTRATION. RG 69

A primary function of the Work Projects Administration (WPA), established in 1935 as the successor of the Federal Emergency Relief Administration and the Civil Works Administration, was the creation of jobs for unemployed persons. It supplied map work for many persons and supplied personnel to assist in the mapmaking activities of other Government agencies. Maps prepared by WPA personnel are to be found in the records of other agencies, including the Weather Bureau, the Federal Housing Administration, and Soil Conservation Service. The WPA was terminated in 1943.

Federal Emergency Relief Administration

525. SECTIONAL ECONOMIC RESEARCH UNIT. ca. 1933-35. 4 items.

Photoprocessed maps of the United States showing for each county the major type of economic activity; i.e., industrial or agricultural, the chief industrial product, the principal natural resource, and the principal agricultural crop, based on the 1930 census.

526. COORDINATOR OF STATISTICAL PROJECTS. ca. 1933-35. 1 item.

A published cartogram of the United States showing the numbers and names of cities within each State having real property inventories, together with symbols giving the form or origin of the surveys.

527. IOWA STATE PLANNING BOARD. 1934. 6 items.

A photoprocessed topographic map and profiles of a proposed dam and power plant at Bonaparte, Iowa, prepared by FERA in cooperation with the Iowa State Planning Board.

Work Projects Administration

528. GENERAL RECORDS. ca. 1933-36. 5 items.

Photoprocessed maps of the United States showing Federal aid per capita (excluding AAA payments) by county for the period 1933-36; percentage of population receiving relief, by counties, for the period July 1934-June 1935; and WPA airport and landing-field projects, 1936. A photoprocessed diagrammatic map of the United States showing WPA work districts, proportionate in size to their respective populations; and an unidentified published diagrammatic map of the United States dated 1936.

529. SERVICE DIVISION. ca. 1935-41. 100 items.

The Service Division supervised the Federally sponsored white-collar-work relief projects designed to give work to individuals who had professional training. The Division's cartographic records are from the cartographic study of the United States conducted under the auspices of the WPA's New York City regional office and from the real-property surveys conducted in Georgia.

Among the records of the Georgia real-property surveys are maps of cities showing, by block, housing conditions, average rents, house occupants per room, and sanitary conditions. Other maps show certain aspects of urban geography, such as urban growth patterns, land use and occupancy, property ownership, and industrial and transportation facilities. Most of the records of the real-property surveys conducted by the WPA were transferred to the Federal Housing Administration, which administered the program (see Record Group 31). A card catalog to the records of the FHA also includes cards for the WPA real-property surveys for Georgia. In addition, these records are listed in The National Archives, *Cartographic Records of the Federal Housing Administration*, Preliminary Inventory No. 45 (Washington, 1952).

The records from the cartographic study include a bound report entitled "The Cartographic Study; A Review of Accomplishments and Prospects," dated 1939, and a microfilm copy of the report; a processed "Descriptive Guide to the Engineering Projects," of the Manhattan District Office of the WPA, 1940; a processed report on the engineering surveys of that Office during the period October 1939-June 1940; and negatives from photographs of project models.

WORLD WAR II AGENCIES

RECORDS OF THE AMERICAN COMMISSION FOR THE PROTECTION AND SALVAGE OF ARTISTIC AND HISTORIC MONUMENTS IN WAR AREAS. RG 239

This Commission, established in 1943, operated in conjunction with other Government agencies and museums, universities, and individual scholars to prevent the destruction by American forces in war zones of buildings or areas of cultural, historic, or artistic importance. In addition, the Commission compiled data on cultural property appropriated by the Axis Powers, and cooperated with the U.S. Army in encouraging the restitution of such property. Among the private organizations active in assisting the Commission were the American Defense-Harvard Group and the American Council of Learned Societies' Committee on the Protection of Cultural Treasures in War Areas; the latter body made its research files available to the Commission. The maps were prepared by the Commission largely on the basis of this information. The activities of the Commission were assumed by the Department of State in 1946.

530. GENERAL RECORDS. 1943-46. 1,489 items.

A major activity of the Commission was the compilation of maps showing locations of areas or sites in enemy or enemy-occupied areas which were to be spared destruction if possible during World War II. Base maps of provinces, regions, and cities were acquired and tissue overlays were made on which numbers were placed indicating these areas or sites. Photocopies were then made of the base maps and accompanying overlays. Lists identifying each site or area shown were typed. The records consist of a set of instructions for the preparation of maps, lists of maps prepared, and a set of the photoprocessed maps and accompanying identification lists. In a few instances a base map with a manuscript overlay substitutes for a photocopy. The countries and regions for which there are records are Albania, Austria, Belgium, Bulgaria, Corsica, Czechoslovakia, Dalmatia, Denmark, France, Germany, Greece, Hungary, Indochina, Italy, Japan, Java, Korea, the Netherlands, Norway, the Philippine Islands, Rumania, Sardinia, Sicily, and Yugoslavia. Arranged by continent, thereunder alphabetically by name of country, and thereunder alphabetically by name of city or province.

RECORDS OF THE OFFICE OF CIVILIAN DEFENSE. RG 171

The Office of Civilian Defense was established in 1941 to coordinate Federal, State, and local activities pertaining to civilian defense during World War II. The Office functioned through regional offices set up in nine cities, each located within an area corresponding to the Army Corps Areas (later Service Commands). The Office was abolished in 1945.

Headquarters Records

531. GENERAL RECORDS. 1941-45. 111 items.

Published and photoprocessed maps of the United States annotated to show regional boundaries and administrative offices of the Office of Civilian Defense, the Air Warning Service, and the War Department. A map of the United States annotated with pins to show target communities for the purpose of allocating civil defense equipment. Aviation strip maps of the United States annotated to show boundaries of areas apparently assigned to local civil defense or air warning groups. Symbols indicate what appear to be the home stations of these groups.

Published and photoprocessed maps of urban areas annotated with information about the locations of industries, often in relation to schools, roads, housing, and sanitary facilities, or with the location, installation, or improvement of these facilities in relation to industrial locations.

A published map of Puerto Rico annotated with pins to show medical facilities operated by civilian defense units.

Regional Office Records

532. NINTH REGION. 1941-45. 422 items.

The Ninth Civilian Defense Region was composed of the three west coast States: Washington, Oregon, and California. Some of the records are identified as having been compiled by or for the Region's Planning Division. These include maps of the Region annotated to show distribution of supplies of blood plasma, the distribution of population, target areas, and industrial and military installations for the purpose of distributing civil defense equipment.

The records of the Division of Property Protection of this Region include maps of areas in California, in Los Angeles County and in the San Francisco and Sacramento areas, annotated to show plans for the protective concealment of certain properties.

Published and photoprocessed maps of urban areas in California, Oregon, and Washington showing plans for the improvement of roads, sewage facilities, recreation facilities, and school facilities in relation to industrial locations; plans for camouflaging selected areas; plans for emergency evacuation of urban areas;

locations of civilian defense facilities; and plans for storm drainage facilities for the protection of property. Some of these maps were prepared and submitted by local governments in support of requests for Federal assistance in financing defense-connected expansion programs.

Arranged in series by division of origin, where known, or by State.

RECORDS OF THE OFFICE OF DEFENSE TRANSPORTATION. RG 219

The Office of Defense Transportation was established in 1941 to succeed the Transportation Division of the Advisory Commission to the National Defense Council. It was given authority over all railroads, motor vehicles, inland waterways, pipelines, air transport, and coastwise and intercoastal shipping within the continental United States to insure that those facilities were being used with maximum efficiency during World War II. The Office was terminated in 1949.

533. GENERAL RECORDS. 1942-43. 3 items.

A manuscript map of the railroad terminal at Toledo, Ohio, showing railroad lines, properties, and terminal facilities, 1934. A photoprocessed map of the United States showing the traffic density on certain major rail systems, and an enlarged copy of that part of the map showing the northeastern and north-central parts of the United States. Notes on these maps indicate that the information was furnished through the courtesy of H. H. Copeland and Son, New York City.

534. ADVISOR ON RAILROAD ABANDONMENTS. 1944. 1 item.

A published map of parts of Missouri and Arkansas showing roads and highways and the routes and connections of the Missouri and Arkansas Railway Company.

535. DIVISION OF PETROLEUM AND OTHER LIQUID TRANSPORT. ca. 1941-45. 1 item.

A photoprocessed schematic diagram and flow chart showing crude-oil pipelines and the flow of oil measured in barrels for each of the lines in Districts 1 and 2, covering approximately the northeastern quarter of the United States.

536. DIVISION OF RAILWAY TRANSPORT. 1941. 2 items.

Diagrammatic maps showing the volume and direction of shipments of bituminous coal on the Great Lakes and the St. Lawrence River.

RECORDS OF THE FOREIGN ECONOMIC ADMINISTRATION. RG 169

The Foreign Economic Administration was established in 1943 to consolidate Government activities relating to foreign economic affairs. Among the agencies that it succeeded was the Office of Economic Warfare, which in turn had succeeded the Board of Economic Warfare.

Board of Economic Warfare

537. ENEMY BRANCH. 1942. 1 item.

A published map showing land utilization in Japan, Korea, and Formosa. This map, identified as GDSS Map No. 819, apparently was drawn by the Geography Division of the Office of Strategic Services from information supplied by the Enemy Branch of the Board of Economic Warfare before the Board had a cartographic section. Other maps compiled from information supplied by the Enemy Branch are among the numbered maps prepared in the Cartographic Section of the Board (see entry 540).

538. FAR EASTERN DIVISION. n.d. 1 item.

A photoprocessed map of Quelpart (Cheju) Island showing roads, trails, streams, and geographic regions.

539. OFFICE OF IMPORTS. 1942. 1 item.

A published map of Peru showing the locations of producing and prospective mines. Included is a list of the leading producers of copper, zinc, lead, and other minerals and their respective volumes of production.

540. CARTOGRAPHIC SECTION. 1943. 4 items.

An incomplete set of the numbered series of maps published by the Cartographic Section. Among these are maps of Africa, the Caribbean Sea, and South America showing commodities under directives of the Board of Economic Warfare and a map compiled from information furnished by the Enemy Branch showing the economic situation in the Southwest Pacific.

Office of Economic Warfare

541. CARTOGRAPHIC SECTION. 1943. 8 items.

A photoprocessed copy of a map of Singapore which had been annotated to show hotels, consulates, and headquarters of American companies. The map is identified as belonging to the files of the Map Information Unit of the Cartographic Section.

The remaining records form an incomplete series of numbered maps published by the Cartographic Section. Among these are maps compiled from information furnished by the Supplies and Resources Division, consisting of maps of Central and South America showing the distribution of mahogany, a map of Mexico showing forest regions, a map of Brazil showing climatic zones, and a map of India showing percentages of cultivated areas growing rice. Maps compiled from information furnished by the Metals and Minerals Branch show principal metallic ore deposits of the Gold Coast and Nigeria. Other maps, of unidentified origin, include one of Cuba showing transportation routes, one of the Southwest Pacific showing mines and mineral deposits, and one of southwestern China showing mining and metallurgical enterprises.

Foreign Economic Administration

542. MAPS AND GRAPHICS DIVISION. 1943-45. 26 items.

An incomplete set of the numbered series of maps and other graphic items published by the Maps and Graphics Division and its predecessor, the Cartographic Section. Among these records are general maps of the Middle East, Ethiopia, China, Manchuria, Nigeria, and Central America; several world maps showing areas producing tantalite and maps of Rhodesia and Mozambique, the Belgian Congo, Colombia, Spain, and Brazil showing locations of tantalite deposits; a map of Venezuela showing areas producing cinchona and remigia bark; and a graph showing the total values of imports and exports in Brazil annually from 1921 to 1943.

543. BUREAU OF AREAS. 1944. 1 item.

A photoprocessed map, compiled by the Mining and Engineering Department of the United States Purchasing Commission under the Pan American Branch of the Bureau of Areas, showing inland highway, river, and railroad connections between northern and southern Brazil. Included is a table giving distances along the routes, means of transport, and other pertinent information. The map, originally compiled in 1943, was revised in 1944.

RECORDS OF THE OFFICE OF LABOR (WAR FOOD ADMINISTRATION). RG 224

The Office of Labor, established in 1943 and abolished in 1945, was created by a merger of the Agricultural Labor Administration and the War Food Administration. It had general responsibility in the field of farm labor supply, recruitment, and wage stabilization and supervised the importation of farmworkers from abroad and the transportation and care of foreign and domestic interstate farmworkers.

War Food Administration

544. GENERAL RECORDS. 1944. 2 items.

Two copies of a published preliminary edition of the "Basic Land Resource Areas" map of the United States, one of which is annotated. This map was prepared by the War Food Administration in cooperation with the Soil Conservation Service. A note indicates that it was drawn in connection with "Estimates of the Conservation Needs of the United States." Land resource areas are shown by alpha-numeric symbols and by colors on the annotated copy. Individual areas are listed by name.

RECORDS OF THE PETROLEUM ADMINISTRATION FOR WAR. RG 253

The cartographic records of the Petroleum Administration for War, established in 1942 and abolished in 1946, consist of a general reference file of maps and graphs from various sources and other maps relating to petroleum-producing areas throughout the world. Among these are maps showing pipelines and other conveying facilities, production volumes, export and import volumes, and graphs showing world petroleum resources in relation to those of the United States. Restrictions upon these records prevent further description. Special permission must be obtained to examine the records.

RECORDS OF THE WAR PRODUCTION BOARD. RG 179

The War Production Board, established in 1942 to exercise general direction over war production and procurement, was also given the functions of the Supply Priorities and Allocation Board and the Office of Production Management. The War Production Board was abolished in 1945.

Office of Production Management

545. BUREAU OF RESEARCH AND STATISTICS. 1941. 2 items.

Base maps of the United States overprinted to show the locations of munitions plants, by types of material produced, for June and October 1941. Neither of the maps contains a key to the location symbols.

War Production Board

546. OFFICE OF OPERATIONS. 1942. 1 item.

A base map of the United States overprinted to show the regional boundaries and the regional and subregional offices of the Board.

OTHER SOURCES

RECORDS OF THE AMERICAN BATTLE MONUMENTS COMMISSION.
RG 117

The American Battle Monuments Commission was established in 1923 to commemorate the services of American troops in Europe during World War I by the erection of memorials and the preparation and publication of historical information; to administer and maintain the American national cemeteries and memorials in Europe; and to exercise control over the erection of European memorials by American citizens, States, municipalities, or associations. The Commission published *A Guide to the American Battlefields in Europe in 1927;* this was revised in 1938 and retitled *American Armies and Battlefields in Europe.* In 1944 a series of 28 volumes was published covering the operations of all U.S. divisions that saw combat service during World War I.

The Historical Section of the Army War College aided the Commission in the preparation of much of the data included in the World War I maps; the Engineer Reproduction Plant of the U.S. Army, and its successor, the Army Map Service, assisted in the compilation of the maps and printed the larger ones. The Commission's draftsmen in the field prepared the plans of American Battle Monument grounds and American Military Cemeteries.

In 1946, the Commission's authority was extended to all areas in which U.S. Armed Forces had operated during World War II.

547. GENERAL RECORDS. 1923-44. 381 items.

Manuscript and annotated maps summarizing the operations of the American Expeditionary Forces in Europe during World War I. These show the movements of the opposing forces in various campaigns and the ground gained or lost by each side. Many of the maps are accompanied by instructions for their preparation or notes for corrections. A copy of the publication *American Armies and Battlefields in Europe*, containing numerous maps, and copies of the summaries of operations of the individual American divisions during World War I are included.

548. FIELD SERVICE. 1937-39. 64 items.

The Field Service was in charge of the Commission's construction program, including the erection of chapels and other memorials, and the landscaping and maintenance of American cemeteries and memorials. It also prepared for publication information concerning American military activities, battlefields, memorials, and cemeteries in Europe. Among its records are photoprocessed maps including a map of western Europe showing the itinerary of an unidentified trip to various American cemeteries in 1937; a map showing American cemeteries and monuments in western Europe; ground plans of American cemeteries and monuments, some with attached photographs of the monuments; and city plans locating American monuments.

RECORDS OF THE COMMISSION OF FINE ARTS. RG 66

The Commission of Fine Arts was established in 1910 to advise upon the design and construction of public parks, buildings, and monuments, and the selection of sites for public recreation areas, primarily in the District of Columbia and nearby areas of Maryland and Virginia. The Commission also is consulted on matters of design relating to medals, insignia, and coins produced by any of the executive departments.

549. GENERAL RECORDS. 1797-1952. 7 items.

Photostats of maps of the District of Columbia, including the Dermott ("Tin Case") Map of 1797; the Nicholas King map; an undated map comparing the Ellicott and L'Enfant plans, drawn in the National Capital Park and Planning Commission; a map showing Washington in 1792, drawn in 1952 in the Office of the District Engineer; and an undated map showing the area covered by the Shipstead Act of 1930 and the amendment of 1939, prepared jointly by the National Capital Park and Planning Commission and the Office of the District Engineer. An annotated map of a part of the District of Columbia emphasizing the Federal buildings and grounds, 1941; and an annotated map of the District showing types of land occupancy, the proportions of land area zoned commercial, commercial and industrial, and residential, and the proportions of land "taken by improvements, 1920-28."

RECORDS OF THE FEDERAL INTERAGENCY RIVER BASIN COMMITTEE. RG 315

The Federal Interagency River Basin Committee was created jointly in 1943 by the Chief of Engineers, U.S. Army, the Chairman of the Bureau of Reclamation, the Land Use Coordinator of the Department of Agriculture, and the Chairman of the Federal Power Commission. Its purpose was to offer more complete cooperation in the preparation of reports on the multiple-purpose development of U.S. water resources and to correlate the results of those investigations. The Committee was abolished in 1954.

550. SUBCOMMITTEE ON HYDROLOGY. 1947-49. 2 items.

Atlases relating to river basins in the United States dated 1947 and 1949. Each atlas contains an index map and 79 maps of river basins showing hydrologic stations by type, river and reservoir gages, dams, and reservoirs. The atlases were prepared under the supervision of the Weather Bureau.

551. NEW ENGLAND-NEW YORK INTER-AGENCY COMMITTEE. 1950-54. 25 items.

Maps of the New England States and New York showing forest types, the average size of farms, percentages of land area in farms by counties, percentages of land used for crops, proportion of all farms classified as dairy farms, percentages of farms classified as commercial and noncommercial, average values of farmland and buildings, and the decline in acreage of agricultural land from peak development to 1950. These maps were compiled by the Production Economics Branch of the Agricultural Research Service from the 1950 census statistics and were published by the Soil Conservation Service for the New England-New York Inter-Agency Committee.

Published maps from studies of river basins in the New York-New England area. Included are maps of the Lake Champlain-Lake Memphremagog Basin, the Connecticut River Basin, the Lake Ontario and Black River Basin, and the St. Lawrence River Basin. Among the features shown on the maps are soil types, physiographic areas, land management areas, forest distribution, erosion distribution, open land measures, and forest land measures.

RECORDS OF THE NATIONAL ACADEMY OF SCIENCES. RG 189

The National Academy of Sciences (NAS) was incorporated in 1863 as a quasi-official advisory body of prominent scientists to investigate and report upon any subject of science or art whenever called upon by any department of the Government. In 1916 the Academy organized the National Research Council (NRC) to coordinate the scientific resources of the country in the interests of national defense. In 1919 the Academy decided to perpetuate the Council in order to promote research in the mathematical, physical, and biological sciences and the application of those sciences to engineering, agriculture, medicine, and other useful arts. In performing this function the Council sponsors research organizations and scientific publications and administers funds for research projects. The cartographic records in Record Group 189 relate chiefly to NAS and NRC advisory functions pertaining to cartography. Among these functions was the coordination of work on the *National Atlas of the United States*, which was a responsibility of the Council until 1961 when it was transferred to the Geological Survey.

National Research Council

552. DIVISION OF GEOLOGY AND GEOGRAPHY. 1918-37. 29 items.

A series of maps identified as "Old War Time" maps used by the National Research Council in its studies of mapping during World War I. These records consist of a composite aerial photo of Anacostia, Washington, D.C.; a published topographic map showing woodlands of Mulberry Island, Camp Abraham, Va., with an aerial photograph of the same area; published map-interpretation field exercises prepared for the Harvard ROTC, 1917-18; and directions for making a contour map of a "B-H relief model."

A series of photoprocessed copies of base maps of the United States which had been annotated to show, by means of isopleths, the percentages of land area in subsistence farms; the percentages of lands being farmed, by county; the percentages of land in farms by type of farm; the value of farmlands and buildings; the average farm size in 1930; and the percentage of the total of gainfully employed persons in woodworking industries, in mining and related industries, and in manufacturing industries. These maps appear to have been compiled by Vernor C. Finch in connection with his application for a grant-in-aid from the National Resources Committee in 1934 for technical assistance in drawing isopleths.

A photographic copy, with manuscript additions, of a map showing geological formations in the Caribbean Sea, compiled by the Gravity Expedition of the Navy Geophysical Union, 1936-37.

553. DIVISION OF EARTH SCIENCES. 1954-58. 74 items.

An incomplete set of maps published for inclusion in the *National Atlas of the United States*, a project then sponsored by the Council. Among the records are sheets compiled from the 1954 Census of Agriculture with maps of the United States showing information about farm types and sizes, farm tenure, crop yields, and the amounts and kinds of livestock raised. Maps of the United States compiled by the Weather Bureau showing the standard deviation of temperature by months. Geological Survey maps of the United States and of U.S. possessions showing the status of topographic mapping, 1956 and 1958, and the status of aerial-photo coverage, 1958. A map of the Sacramento River in California, compiled by the Geological Survey. A series of Coast and Geodetic Survey maps of the United States and U.S. territories and possessions showing the coverage by C&GS nautical and aeronautical charts. A sheet prescribing the format for maps to be included in the *National Atlas*.

RECORDS OF THE NATIONAL CAPITAL PLANNING COMMISSION.
RG 328

The National Capital Planning Commission was established in 1952 to succeed the National Capital Park Commission (established 1924) and the

National Capital Planning and Park Commission (established 1926). It is responsible for planning the development of the District of Columbia and for conserving its natural and historical resources.

554. NUMBERED FILES. 1791-1962. 1,500 items.

Two separate series of records from the National Capital Planning Commission, including general maps of the District of Columbia and parts of the District, plans of District school and municipal buildings, plans of Federal buildings and grounds, maps and plans of parks, driveways, and parking facilities, plans and drawings of bridges and monuments, and maps and plans relating to military posts and buildings and proposed highway systems in the Virginia suburbs of Washington. These records are similar and related to the numbered file of cartographic records of the National Capital Parks in Record Group 79 (entry 284).

555. AERIAL PHOTOGRAPHS. 1930-55. 2,390 items.

Aerial photographs from a parked-car survey of the District of Columbia, 1930; aerial photographs of the District and vicinity, 1932; aerial photographs showing flood conditions along the Potomac and Anacostia Rivers, 1936 and 1942; and miscellaneous aerial photographs of the District and adjacent parts of Maryland and Virginia made during the 1950's.

PRIVATE PAPERS GIVEN TO THE NATIONAL ARCHIVES. RG 316

This record group consists of documents (other than photographs or sound recordings) that are appropriate for preservation by the Government as evidence of its organization, functions, policies, decisions, procedures, and transactions, and that have been transferred to the National Archives from private sources.

556. MAPS GIVEN TO THE NATIONAL ARCHIVES BY GEN. W. C. BROWN. 1865-1927. 48 items.

Published and photoprocessed maps of parts of the western territories and military departments in the West; maps showing routes followed by Army units during the Indian campaigns; plans of Indian battlefields, including one showing the plan of the massacre at Fort Kearney, 1868; and plans of forts, especially those in the Department of the Platte. Several of these maps were made from surveys conducted by General Brown when he was a lieutenant. Most of these maps duplicate records in Record Group 77, Records of the Office of the Chief of Engineers, and Record Group 393, Records of United States Army Continental Commands, 1821-1920.

Other records consist of a map showing trails made and routes used by the 4th Cavalry under the command of Gen. R. S. Mackenzie in its operations against hostile Indians in Texas, Indian Territory, New Mexico, and Mexico, compiled from military and other surveys by E. D. Dorchester, 1927; a manuscript copy of part of the 1876 revision of the W. F. Raynolds map of the Yellowstone and Upper Missouri River Basins prepared for Gen. H. L. Scott's *Some Memories of a Soldier;* and a copy of a topographic map of the West Point Military Reservation, N.Y., prepared under the direction of Prof. James Mercur, United States Military Academy, about 1886.

557. MAP RECORDS OF COL. W. H. PAINE. 1861-65. 85 items.

A group of published maps of areas in Virginia compiled by Colonel Paine when he served as an engineer officer with the Army of the Potomac during the Civil War; they are duplicates of items in Record Group 77, Records of the Office of the Chief of Engineers, and Record Group 393, Record of United States Army Continental Commands, 1821-1920.

A group of published maps of parts of Virginia, issued by the Army of the Potomac and the Office of the Chief of Engineers, with manuscript additions, corrections, and changes. Other records consist of several maps annotated to show troop positions and movements, several manuscript location sketches, and some manuscript plans of battlefields.

558. MAP RECORDS OF LT. COL. GEORGE STEWART, JR. 1918.
55 items.

Manuscript, annotated, and published maps relating to the activities of the 29th Division in Europe during World War I. The published maps include general maps of the theater of war and copies of French military maps of parts of France. Most of these are duplicated in the record sets of published maps in Record Group 120, Records of the American Expeditionary Forces (World War I), 1917-23. The manuscript and annotated maps pertain directly to the activities of the 29th Division and show positions of enemy and Allied troops in the sectors in which the Division operated, billeting areas, no man's land, the burial organization of the Division, communications lines, and hospital facilities. There is also a copy of the USGS topographic quadrangle of Anniston, Ala., showing facilities of the military reservation located there.

WORLD WAR II COLLECTION OF SEIZED ENEMY RECORDS. RG 242

During World War II enemy military records that had been captured were sent to the United States for study. In some instances captured records have become integral parts of the documentation of the activities of Government agencies. The records in Record Group 242 are those which were not interfiled with or otherwise made a part of the files of a Government agency but have been separately maintained since their capture.

German Records

559. OBERKOMMANDO DER KRIEGSMARINE. 1934-44. 61 items.

Bound volumes containing descriptive texts, charts, and photographs published under the direction of the Oberkommando der Kriegsmarine containing information about offshore features of countries of strategic importance to Germany and her allies and enemies. Other records consist of published handbooks for the use of submarine commanders operating in the coastal waters of France, Great Britain, North Africa, and the Eastern United States and Canada containing descriptive texts and charts showing aids and dangers to navigation, coastal tides and currents, soundings, bottom contour lines, and bottom sediment; a volume relating to sea ice conditions along the Arctic shores of Siberia and European Russia; several volumes with descriptions of the organization of the French, British, and American navies; and a volume relating to a study of British shipping, particularly in relation to the import of oil into Great Britain, with maps showing tanker routes and facilities in Great Britain for handling oil. Arranged numerically by publication number. The volume relating to Siberian ice conditions is unnumbered.

GIFT STILL PICTURES IN THE NATIONAL ARCHIVES. RG 273

In 1950 the National Archives was authorized to accept for deposit still pictures from private sources that are appropriate for preservation by the Government as evidence of its organization, functions, policies, decisions, procedures, and transactions. The cartographic records in Record Group 273 consist of aerial photographs.

560. BYRD ANTARCTIC EXPEDITION. 1928-30. 1,658 items.

Aerial photographs from the Byrd expedition.

INDEX

This index was prepared with the assistance of SPINDEX II computer programs, which are modifications, developed by the National Archives and Records Service, of standard keyword out-of-context programs. Major headings of the *Guide* and introductory material are referenced by page number, but most of the items are referenced by entry number. Dates given in the text are included. Unless otherwise identified, all subjects and activities cited pertain to the United States.

	ENTRY	PAGE
AACHEN		
Aachen, Germany	36	
ABBE, CLEVELAND		
Cleveland Abbe	398	
Weather Bureau		213-219
ABYSSINIA		
Abyssinia, 1942-43	214	
ACCOTINK CREEK RESERVOIR		
Accotink Creek Reservoir, Virginia	129	
ACID		
Distribution and origin of the use of picric acid, 1921-22	311	
ADAIRSVILLE		
Proposed airway beacon lights at Adairsville, Georgia, 1937	426	
ADJUTANT GENERAL		
Adjutant General's Office		44-47
Adjutant General's Office, World War Division, 1918	65	
Military Information Division, Adjutant General's Office	128	
ADMIRALTY		
British Admiralty charts	46	
British Admiralty charts	44	
AERIAL PHOTOGRAPHY		
Aerial photograph of Camp Bragg, North Carolina	208	
Aerial photograph of Gunpowder Neck, Maryland, 1929	211	
Aerial photograph of the Anacostia section of Washington, D.C.	552	
Aerial photograph of Washington, D.C., 1918	207	
Aerial Photographs		165
Aerial Photographs		115-117
Aerial Photographs		110
Aerial photographs of Antarctica	560	
Aerial photographs of Bermuda, ca. 1940-45	192	
Aerial photographs of Brazil, 1943-44	517	
Aerial photographs of Colombia and Nicaragua, 1932	131	
Aerial photographs of Colombia, 1940	128	
Aerial photographs of Cuba, 1923	192	
Aerial photographs of Fort Leavenworth, Kansas	178	
Aerial photographs of Fort Meade, Maryland	118	
Aerial photographs of France, 1918	131	

☆ U. S. GOVERNMENT PRINTING OFFICE : 1971 O - 427-447

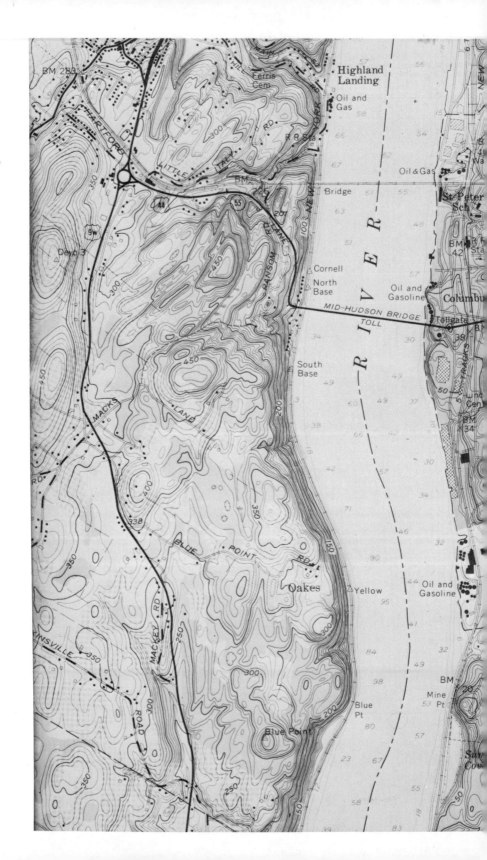